To Ron Baines
Pastor,
Scholar,
Brother-in-Christ,
Friend

After the Second London Confession of Faith, no documents were more important for the early Particular Baptists than the records of the General Assemblies of their English and Welsh churches (1689-94). Until now, these records have been extremely hard to find. James Renihan's new edition demonstrates that the Particular Baptist churches were committed to associational life, that they worked together to confess the same faith and promote the same order, and that they adopted the confession of faith that would provide Reformed Baptists with their most important theological symbol (1689). This new edition of these records is among the most important resources on Baptist history that has ever been published.

Crawford Gribben, Ph.D.
Professor of Early Modern British History
Queen's University, Belfast
Author of *John Owen and English Puritanism*

****

The documents provided in this collection are pivotal and vital for a proper understanding of Baptist self-consciousness at the beginning of the modern Baptist movement. They show that the theological convictions were not simply a mindless parroting of the doctrine of fellow Dissenters, but a deeply conscientious presentation of those things they surely believed to be true. Every Baptist historian, theologian, and serious church member will benefit from paying careful attention to this treasure of primary source material. James Renihan always provides us with carefully conceived matter that will have long term benefits.

Tom J. Nettles, Ph.D.
Senior Professor of Church History/Historical Theology
The Southern Baptist Theological Seminary
Author of *The Baptists*

****

Essential for all of our knowledge and interpretation of the past are primary sources. Failure to use them or even possess them relegates the historian to a position little better than that of an author of historical fiction. By bringing together in one book these valuable documents about English Baptist life from the close of the seventeenth century, James Renihan has given all who are interested in this era a treasure trove that opens up vital perspectives on early English Baptist self-understanding. Nor are these texts of mere antiquarian interest, for the simple fact that being Baptist is a choice that many still make. And these texts can aid immeasurably in making that choice a truly informed one.

Michael A. G. Haykin, Ph.D.
Professor of Church History & Biblical Spirituality
The Southern Baptist Theological Seminary
Author of *Kiffin, Knollys and Keach*

****

Once again Professor James Renihan has put historians and indeed all Confessional Baptists in his debt. He has produced for the first time a collection of documents illustrating the background to the Second London Confession of Faith and the events leading to and surrounding the early General Assemblies of Particular Baptists. Some of this material has only been available in private collections or in works long out of print. Given the growing interest in the Confession around the world and the desire to understand the lives of the Particular Baptist pioneers this book is of great importance. One of the most fascinating pieces is the reprinting of *The Gospel Minister's Maintenance Vindicated*, important not only for its plea for adequate support for the minister, but also for the high view of the Christian ministry advocated. This collection is one to be treasured and consulted.

Robert W. Oliver, Ph.D.
Retired Reformed Baptist Pastor
Lecturer at the London Theological Seminary and John Owen Centre
Author of *History of the English Calvinistic Baptists 1771-1892*

****

Much of modern theological writing is too little-informed by a careful study of the doctrinal history of the Christian church. Similarly, way too little of contemporary Baptist writing is uninformed about the actual doctrinal views of early Particular and Reformed Baptists. We are indebted, then, to James Renihan and RBAP for making these important materials related to the early confessional history of Baptists available to the rest of us. I am hopeful that this volume will further the reformation of Baptists today.

Sam Waldron, Ph.D.
Pastor of Grace Reformed Baptist Church, Owensboro, KY
Author of *The End Times Made Simple*

****

James Renihan has provided a much-needed collection of resources for the continued study of early Baptists. This collection of early documents—some of which have never been published—provides a unique insight into the life of the nascent Particular Baptists as they "came of age" as a proto-denomination at the end of the seventeenth century. Renihan's insightful introductions and notes aid in making the documents accessible to the modern reader while allowing the historical documents to continue to speak for themselves, making this collection an absolute essential for any student of early Baptist theology.

Jonathan W. Arnold, D. Phil.
Assistant Professor of Christian Theology and Church History
Boyce College
Author of *The Reformed Theology of Benjamin Keach (1640-1704)*

****

Faith and Life for Baptists, a collection of early English Baptist documents, is a welcome resource for the Baptist historian. In particular, I appreciate the previously unpublished General Assembly documents that were post Act of Toleration, as well as *The Gospel Ministers Maintenance Vindicated.* This latter treatise, usually attributed to Benjamin Keach, is still relevant for twenty-first-century churches.

Barry Howson, Ph. D.
Academic Dean
Heritage College and Seminary
Cambridge, Ontario, Canada
Author of *Erroneous and Schismatical Opinions:*
The Question of Orthodoxy Regarding the Theology of Hanserd Knollys

****

James Renihan has provided a service to all who desire to learn about the seventeenth-century English Particular Baptist community. By republishing these works that were previously relegated to scholars working in select archives, Renihan has made accessible to all the record of the theological community of fellowship that were these early General Assemblies. Readers will discover the rich theological discussions that were part and parcel of seventeenth-century English Particular Baptist life. Read the enclosed documents and long for such a robust Baptist community in our own day.

G. Stephen Weaver, Jr., Ph.D.
Pastor of Farmdale Baptist Church, Frankfort, KY
Fellow of the Andrew Fuller Center for Baptist Studies
Adjunct Professor of Church History
The Southern Baptist Theological Seminary
Author of *Orthodox, Puritan, Baptist: Hercules Collins (1647-1702)*
and Particular Baptist Identity in Early Modern England

****

Faith and Life for Baptists

The Documents of the London Particular Baptist General Assemblies, 1689-1694

Containing:

1. The Letter Calling for the 1689 General Assembly
2. The Narrative of the 1689 General Assembly
3. The Narrative of the 1690 General Assembly
4. The Narrative of the 1691 General Assembly
5. The Narrative of the 1692 General Assembly & Responses
6. The Narratives of the Bristol & London General Assemblies, 1693 and 1694
7. The Gospel Minister's Maintenance Vindicated
8. A Confession of Faith
9. A Brief Instruction in the Principles of Christian Religion

Edited by James M. Renihan

PALMDALE, CA

Printed by Richard Barcellos for Reformed Baptist Academic Press, MMXVI

Table of Contents

Foreword 13

Preface 15

1. The Letter Calling for the 1689 General Assembly 17

2. The Narrative of the 1689 General Assembly. 23

3. The Narrative of the 1690 General Assembly. 57

4. The Narrative of the 1691 General Assembly. 71

5. The Narrative of the 1692 General Assembly and Responses 85

    The Narrative 87

    The Response from Benjamin Keach 105

    The Response from William Kiffen et. al. 113

6. The Narratives of the Bristol and London General Assemblies,

    1693 and 1694 121

    The Bristol Narrative, 1693 125

    The London Narrative, 1693 131

    A Report of the Bristol Assembly, 1694 135

7. The Gospel Minister's Maintenance Vindicated 139

8. A Confession of Faith 207

    The Letter to the Judicious and Impartial Reader 213

    The Confession 217

    The Appendix 281

9. A Brief Instruction in the Principles of Christian Religion 297

Foreword

The idea of the so-called 'Protestant wind' is now a common feature in historical discussion of the arrival of William III's Dutch fleet to English shores on 5 November 1688, and it has contributed significantly to the mythology surrounding the event. Whatever the meteorological truth may have been it certainly is true to say that the 'Glorious Revolution' heralded the winds of change in the religious climate for Dissenting Protestants in England. In the main the Particular Baptists welcomed the new king openly and quickly took advantage of the religious freedoms he promised. A small group of visionary leaders of the Particular Baptists called for a meeting to take place in London in September of 1689 which established the pattern of an annual General Assembly and helped lay the foundations of a denominational structure with shared beliefs and common commitments. A number of key documents were published by the Particular Baptists between the years 1689 and 1695 and together these testify to this foundational period of denominational history. These documents included accounts of the annual General Assemblies held in London and Bristol, *A Confession of Faith* from 1688 which reissued the so-called Second London Confession of 1677, a very important but often overlooked tract on the *The Gospel Minister's Maintenance Vindicated* which attempted to set the denominational policy of financially supporting the ordained ministry on a proper footing, and a little-known document from 1695 offering *A Brief Instruction in the Principles of Christian Religion*. The reports of the annual General Assemblies are especially significant because they provide us with a listing of which churches were involved, and in the case of the records from 1689 and 1692 the names of the delegates or messengers representing those churches. An invaluable record of the geographical breadth of the denomination and its leadership is thereby set forth. We also get insight into the way that controversy was handled by the churches, as is perhaps best evidenced by the debate over singing within worship services which dominated the proceedings in 1692.

Professor Renihan has here brought together, for the very first time, all of these key texts into a unified discussion under a single title.

Seeing them all presented in this creative way, I found myself asking, 'Why has no one ever thought to do this before?' It is such an obvious and sensible way to present what is in effect a tightly defined, but succinct, collection of documents, that I must admit a certain amount of envy that Professor Renihan came up with the idea before anyone else did. But such simplicity and narrow focus is the genius of this book in a nut-shell. The argument is concentrated in the detail and there is much to ponder and admire here. What Renihan has attempted to do is to present the full text of the relevant documents, together with helpful and informative introductions, all of which is supported by text-critical observations and comments. The result is an invaluable volume which should quickly become the standard introduction to the thought and writing of the Particular Baptists during the latter part of the seventeenth century, a period which has proven to be so influential to what we now recognize as essential to Baptist practice and theology down to the present day.

Congratulations on a very creative volume, Jim. You should consider it a well-deserved feather in your cap. It stands as an excellent companion to your earlier study on Baptist Confessions of Faith and fills a gap in our Baptist denominational history. I am confident it will be as valued as that earlier book was and should become the standard 'first port-of-call' for researchers interested in the subject.

Larry J. Kreitzer
Regent's Park College, Oxford
Author of *William Kiffen and His World*

Preface

The First London Confession of 1644 was issued under the names of leaders from seven London churches. This well-known fact demonstrates that from their earliest appearance, the Particular Baptists recognized and practiced the need for inter-congregational cooperation and mutual action. The 47th article of that Confession expresses the doctrine: "And although the particular congregations be distinct, and several bodies, every one as a compact and knit city within itself; yet are they all to walk by one rule of truth; so also they (by all means convenient) are to have the counsel and help one of another, if necessity require it, as members of one body, in the common faith, under Christ their head." Independency did not imply isolation.

Throughout the next half-century and beyond, this formal connectionalism characterized these churches. In many ways, it was a hallmark of their corporate lives. It provided a means of mutual recognition giving assurance of common conviction, supplying counsel in the face of difficult ecclesiastical and practical matters as well as confidence that the individual church was not alone in its faith and life. At root, they believed it was their duty, based on their understanding of Scripture, to join together for support and assistance; the exigencies of official opposition and persecution only deepened this need. They formed associations of churches throughout England and Wales,[1] and these "communions"[2] of churches served their purpose well.

Until 1689, however, no attempt was made to form a comprehensive national association of churches. There may be benign reasons for this; perhaps the gradual spread of churches did not provide sufficient means for such a body, possibly it simply had not

---

[1] Some transcripts of association meetings have been published: B. R. White, *Association Records of the Particular Baptists of England, Wales and Ireland to 1660*, 3 volumes (London: The Baptist Historical Society, 1971-74); Stephen Copson, *Association Life of the Particular Baptists of Northern England, 1699-1732* (London: The Baptist Historical Society, 1991).

[2] This is the term used for associations in the Second London Confession 26:14 and 15. See James M. Renihan, *Edification and Beauty* (Milton Keynes: Paternoster, 2008), 156 ff.

been considered necessary due to the positive work of the county associations, perhaps there were no leaders with sufficient vision to inaugurate a formative process. A definite and darker cause is the political climate after 1662, since it would have been nearly impossible to form during the days of the enforcement of the Clarendon Code.

When liberty came in the Glorious Revolution, almost immediately the London pastors sought to call and host a meeting to establish just such a body. The rapidity with which they acted may imply that the desire for such a meeting had been present for some time. In any case, the invitation they distributed seems to have been well-received, and the inaugural meeting was held in September 1689. This was followed by others through 1693.[3]

The documents transcribed here record this process. Each General Assembly published a *Narrative* of its acts, and several supporting documents were also released. The 1677 *Confession of Faith* (2LCF) was promoted, a defense of the necessity of financial support for pastors printed, a *Catechism* authorized, and other subordinate but important papers ordered. All of these documents are incorporated here, so far as I know, some of them for the first time in print since the seventeenth century. I have chosen to maintain antiquated orthography as much as possible. Some slight formatting changes have occasionally been made to the texts.

My thanks to Dr. Larry Kreitzer for his kind willingness to write a foreword, to Dr. Richard Barcellos for the careful work he has put into this project, and to Cameron Porter for excellent attention to many details.

James M. Renihan
Escondido, California
January 13, 2016

---

[3] There is evidence to suggest that some London churches held a 1694 meeting. The manuscript church book of the London Maze Pond church indicates that on 20 May 1694 the congregation discussed the propriety of sending messengers to an assembly scheduled for the next week. They declined stating, "A motion being made whether we would send a Messenger or Messengers to the Assembly the next weeke it was agreed in the negative not to send any and further that we did utterly disowne that meeting of the Assembly upon the account of their irregularities," Maze Pond Church Book 1691-1708, The Angus Library, Regent's Park College, Oxford, 98.

1

The Letter Calling for
the 1689 General Assembly

Introduction

Although the 1662 Act of Uniformity and its associated legislation did not directly force the already non-conforming Particular Baptists out of the established church, it nevertheless brought significant consequences to them. The following decades of persecution took their toll on congregations and clergy. In Bristol and London, ministers were imprisoned and worship disrupted.[1] Abraham Cheare of Plymouth was placed in custody and died in his cell—his church spent eighteen years without a pastor.[2] Many more examples might be cited. Suffice to say that it was an era of trouble. Despite periods of relative calm and relief,[3] this quarter-century produced a dark self-evaluation. By 1689, the churches and their ministers needed help.

---

[1] For example, see Hercules Collins, *A Voice from the Prison* (London: Geroge Larkin, 1684). On the title page, Collins is named as a "Prisoner in Newgate", also Roger Hayden, ed., *The Records of a Church of Christ in Bristol, 1640-1687* (Bristol: Bristol Record Society, 1974), 127ff.

[2] Henry M. Nicholson, compiler, *Authentic Records Relating to the Christian Church now meeting in George Street and Mutley Chapels, Plymouth. 1640-1870* (London: Elliot Stock, n.d.), 17-53.

[3] Charles II's Declaration of Indulgence in 1672 provided brief respite, but it was repealed the next year. See R. Tudur Jones with Aruther Long and Rosemary Moore, *Protestant and Nonconformist Texts, Volume 1 1550-1700* (Aldershot: Ashgate, 2007), 259ff.

When William and Mary acceded to the throne in 1688, a new era of toleration dawned, opening opportunities for public meetings, discussion and planning. The London pastors were in some sense, the *de facto* leaders of the cause in England. In light of the difficulties faced, seven of them[4] joined together to issue a call to come together in a national General Assembly of churches. The following letter is that invitation. It opens the window on these documents, hinting at the agenda desired for the meeting.

---

[4] It is noteworthy that none of these men are to be identified with the Petty France church. Messengers from Petty France did attend and actively participate in the Assembly (see page 45 below).

~ The Letter Calling for the 1689 General Assembly (Introduction) ~

𝕿𝖍𝖊 𝕴𝖊𝖙𝖙𝖊𝖗 𝕮𝖆𝖑𝖑𝖎𝖓𝖌 𝖋𝖔𝖗 𝖙𝖍𝖊 1689 𝕰𝖊𝖓𝖊𝖗𝖆𝖑 𝕬𝖘𝖘𝖊𝖒𝖇𝖑𝖞

"The following is a copy of [the letter] sent to the church at Luppitt, in Devonshire, the place where the present church at Upottery then met."[1]

London, July 22, 1689.

"To the Church of Christ in Luppitt, kind Salutations.

"We the elders and [&] ministering brethren of the churches[,] in and [&] about [the city of] London, being several times assembled together to consider of the present state of the [B]aptized [C]ongregations, not only in this city, but also in the country, cannot but first of all, adore the [D]ivine [W]isdom and goodness of Almighty God, in respect of his late most gracious providence, for our deliverance from that dismal dispensation, which threatened us[,] from the continual and [&] unwearied attempts and [&] designs of the enemy of our sacred religion and [&] civil liberties; by which means[,] our sinking and drooping spirits are again revived, and our earnest hopes and long expectations raised, and afresh quickened, in respect of the more full and perfect deliverance of the church of God, and his more glorious appearance, for the accomplishing [accomplishment] of those gracious promises and [&] prophecies contained in the holy [S]cripture relating to the latter days.

"But[2] in the second place, we cannot but bewail the present condition our churches seem to be in; fearing that much of that former

---

[1] This letter is taken from Joseph Ivimey *History of the English Baptists*, (London: Printed for the Author, 1811) 1: 478-480. It has been reprinted in Larry Kreitzer, *William Kiffen and His World (Part 3),* (Oxford: Regent's Park College, 2013), 189-90. Dr. Kreitzer has kindly supplied me with photographs of a 19th century manuscript copy of this letter, held in the collection of the Angus Library, Oxford. It is perhaps the one used by Ivimey. The words in brackets denote the differences between Ivimey's version and the manuscript letter. The manuscript letter has an asterisk next to 'Luppitt' pointing to this note at the bottom of the page: "Luppitt was the former place of worship where the present church at Upottery in Devon met; and this original paper was communicated to Dr. Rippon by his late dear & honoured father, who departed this life December 24, 1800, aged 70 years."

[2] Ivimey includes a paragraph indentation here. The manuscript does not indicate a new paragraph.

strength, life, and vigour, which attended us is much gone; and in many places the interest of [our Lord]³ Jesus Christ seems to be much neglected[,] which is in our hands, and the congregations to languish, and our beauty to fade away (which thing, we have some ground to judge, you cannot but be sensible of as well as we); and from hence we have been put upon most mature and serious considerations of such things that may be the cause thereof, and amongst others are come to this result: That the great neglect of the present ministry is one thing, together with that [general]⁴ unconcernedness there generally seems to be, of giving fit and proper encouragement for the raising up an able and honourable ministry[,] for the time to come; with many other things [(]which[,] we hope, we are not left wholly in the dark about[)][,] which we find we are not in a capacity to prevent and cure (as instruments in the hand of God, and his blessing attending our [C]hristian endeavours) unless we can obtain a general meeting here in London of two principal brethren (of every church of the same faith with us) in every county respectively. We do therefore humbly intreat and beseech you, that you would be pleased to appoint two of your brethren—one of the ministry, and one principal brother of your congregation with him—as your messengers; and send them up to meet with the rest of the elders [&] and and [sic.] brethren of the churches in London, on the 3rd of September next; and then we hope [we shall have that before us, and be also helped] to consider such things that may much tend to the honour of God, and further the peace, well-being, establishment, at [and]⁵ present, as also the future comfort of the churches. We hope you will readily, notwithstanding the charge, comply with our pious and christian desire herein; and in the mean time, to signify your intentions forthwith[,] in a letter; which we would have you direct to our reverend and well beloved brethren, Mr. H. Knowles, or Mr. W. Kiffin [Kiffen]. This is all at present from us, your brethren and labourers in God's vineyard, who greet you well in our Lord Jesus Christ, and subscribe ourselves your servants in the gospel.

---

³ These words are not in the manuscript.

⁴ This word is not in the manuscript.

⁵ Ivimey reads "at;" the manuscript does not include "at" but reads "and."

"WILLIAM KIFFIN [Kiffen],
HANSARD KNOLLYS,
JOHN HARRIS,
GEORGE BARRETT,
BENJAMIN KEACH,
EDWARD MAN,
RICHARD ADAMS."

"Brother Kiffin [Kiffen] lives in White's alley, [in] Little Moorfields [Moorefields]."

~ *The Letter Calling for the 1689 General Assembly* ~

2

The Narrative of
the 1689 General Assembly

Introduction

From all appearances, the Letter of Invitation was well-received, so that by early September 1689 representatives from over 100 churches attended or communicated with the inaugural General Assembly. The list of churches and messengers is impressive, and the enthusiasm palpable. Desiring to provide the churches with an accounting of the events of the week of meetings, it was agreed that a *Narrative* should be printed and distributed.

The document below is a transcription of this *Narrative*. Beginning with an epistle addressing both thankfulness for a new day of toleration and bewailing the deficiencies acknowledged in the churches, it continues to a description of the Assembly itself. It addresses the rules and procedures governing the proceedings, the business proposed and concluded, and the theological matters debated. This is followed by an account of the communicating churches and two supplemental statements. By and large, the portrait given is positive and hopeful.

But not all had been in agreement. A 1688 letter from William Kiffen to Thomas Vauxe[1] indicates that there was some level of difference between the London churches. The matter was political, relating to the rights of James II to grant toleration unilaterally to Dissenters from the Church of England, including Roman Catholics. The Assembly addressed this matter and issued an assertion about it.

---

[1] Kreitzer, *William Kiffen (Part 3)*, 188-89.

Not all of the churches considered this an appropriate action by the Assembly.[2]

The final document directly attached to the *Narrative* is a record of the details related to the development of a fund to assist impoverished ministers. It is a disclosure to the churches of the names of those responsible for collecting and disbursing funds. Based on the Kiffen/Vauxe correspondence, in the previous years this had been somewhat controversial, but this document indicates resolution and agreement.[3]

This *Narrative* and supporting documents open a window into the national associational life of these churches. The Act of Toleration brought a new climate of freedom, and the messengers present seem to have been hopeful of advance in the future.

---

[2] See below.

[3] The presence of the Petty France pastor William Collins's name on the list demonstrates this.

A

NARRATIVE

of the

PROCEEDINGS

of the

General Assembly

Of divers Pastors, Messengers and Ministring Brethren of the *Baptized Churches*, met together in London, from *Septemb.* 3. to 12. 1689, from divers parts of *England* and *Wales*: Owning the Doctrine of Personal Election, and final Perseverance.

Sent from, and concerned for, more than one hundred
Congregations of the same Faith with Themselves.

Acts 15.6. *And the Apostles and Elders came together for to consider of this matter.*
2 Cor. 8.23. *--Or our Brethren be enquired of, they are the Messengers of the Churches, and the Glory of Christ.*

London, Printed in the Year, 1689

The Elders, Messengers, and Ministring Brethren of the Churches met together in their General Assembly in the City of *London*, *Septemb*. from the 3d, to the 11th, 1689.

Unto the Church of God meeting in_____ send Greeting.

Beloved in our Lord Jesus Christ,

It doth not a little affect our Souls to see how ready you were to comply with that Christian and Pious Invitation you had, to send one or two worthy Brethren, as your Messengers, to meet with the rest of us in this great Assembly; for which we return to you our hearty Thanks: hoping, that not only we, and the Churches of the Saints to whom we are related, at this present time will have cause to bless, praise and magnify the Father of Mercies, and God of all Comfort and Consolation upon this account; but that the Ages to come will have some Grounds to rejoice and praise his holy Name, hoping through the riches of his Grace, and divine Blessing upon our holy Endeavours, such great and gracious Effects will attend the result of our Consultations in this Assembly; which were chiefly to consider of the present state and condition of all the Congregations respectively under our Care and Charge; and what might be the causes of that Spiritual Decay and loss of Strength, Beauty and Glory in our Churches; and to see (if we might be helped by the Lord herein), what might be done to attain to a better and more prosperous State and Condition.

And now, Brethren, in the first place, with no little Joy we declare unto you how good and gracious the Lord hath been to us, in uniting our Hearts together in the Spirit of Love, and sweet Concord, in our Debates, Consultations, and Resolves, which are sent unto you, there being scarcely one Brother who dissented from the Assembly in the Sentiments of his Mind, in any one thing we have proposed to your serious Considerations, either in respect of the cause of our Witherings, nor what we have fixt on as a means of Recovery to a better state, if the Lord will.

~ The Narrative of the 1689 General Assembly ~

And therefore, in the second place, be it known unto you that we all see great cause to rejoice and bless God, that after so dismal an Hour of Sorrow and Persecution, in which the Enemy doubtless designed to break our Churches to pieces, not only us, but to make the whole *Sion* of God desolate, even so as she might become as a plowed Field, the Lord was pleased to give such Strength and Power in the time of need to bear up your Souls in your Testimony for Jesus Christ, that your Spirits did not faint under your Burdens in the time of your Adversity; so that we hope we may say in the Word of the Church of old, *Though all this is come upon us, yet we have not forgotten thee, neither have we dealt falsly in thy Covenant. Our heart is not turned back, neither have our Steps declined from thy way. Though thou hast sore broken us in the place of Dragons, and covered us with the shadow of Death*, Psal. 44. 17,18,19. Yet nevertheless we fear Christ may say, *I have somewhat against you, because you have left your first Love*, as he once charged the Church of *Ephesus*, and may possibly most Churches in *England*; it is therefore good *to consider from whence we are fallen, and repent, and do our first works*, Rev. 2.5.

We are persuaded one chief cause of our decay is for want of holy Zeal for God, and the House of God; few amongst us living up we (fear) to what they profess of God, nor answering the terms of the sacred Covenant they have made with him; the Power of Godliness being greatly decayed, and but little more than the Form thereof remaining amongst us. The Thoughts of which are enough to melt our Spirits, and break our Hearts to pieces, considering those most amazing Providences of the ever blessed God under which we have been, and more especially now are exercised, and the many signal and most endearing Obligations he is pleased to lay us under. The Spirit of this World we clearly discern is got too too [*sic*] much into the Hearts of most Christians and Members of our Churches, all seeking their own, and none, or very few, the things of Jesus Christ; if therefore in this there be no Reformation, the whole Interest of the blessed Lord Jesus will still sink in our Hands, and our Churches left to languish, whilst the Hands of poor Ministers becomes as weak as Water, and Sorrow and Grief seize upon their Spirits.

Thirdly, We cannot but bewail that great Evil, and neglect of Duty in many Churches concerning the ministry.

1. In that some though they have Brethren competently qualified for the Office of Pastors and Deacons, yet omit that sacred Ordinance of Ordination, whereby they are rendred uncapable of preaching and administring the Ordinances of the Gospel, so regularly, and with that Authority which otherwise they might do. Those who have failed herein, we desire would in the fear of God lay it to Heart, and reform.

2. In neglecting to make Gospel Provision for their Maintenance, according to their Abilities, by which means many of them are so incumbred with Worldly Affairs, that they are not able to perform the Duties of their holy Calling, in preaching the Gospel, and watching over their respective Flocks.

Fourthly, We find cause to mourn that the Lord's Day is no more religiously and carefully observed, both in a constant attendance on the Word of God in that Church to whom Members do belong, and when the publick Worship is over, by a waiting on the Lord in Family-duties, and private Devotion.

But because we have sent unto you the whole Result of this great Assembly particularly, we shall forbear to enlarge further upon these Causes of our Withering and Decays.

One Thing you will find we have before us, and come to a Resolve about, which we are perswaded will prove an excellent great Blessing and Advantage to the Interest of Jesus Christ in our Hands; and if the Lord enlarge all our Hearts, give a revival to the sinking Spirits of the Mourners in *Sion*, and to languishing Churches too, which is, that of a general or Publick Stock, or Fund of Mony to be raised forthwith. First, By a Free-will Offering to the Lord: And, secondly, by a Subscription, every one declaring what he is willing to give, Weekly, Monthly, or Quarterly, to it.

And now, Brethren, we must say, the Lord is about to try you in another way than ever you have been tried to this Day, because, till now, no such Thing was settled amongst us, and so not propounded to you. It will be known now, whether you do love Jesus Christ, and his Blessed Interest, Gospel, and Church, or no; *i.e.* Whether you love him more than these, or more than Son or Daughter. O that you would at this time shew your Zeal for God, and let Men see the World is not so in your Hearts, but that Jesus Christ hath much room there: 'Tis to be given towards God's Holy Temple, to build up his Spiritual House which hath a long time lain as waste. Remember how willingly the Lord's People offered upon this Account formerly; 'tis some great as well as good Thing the Lord, and we his poor and unworthy Servants and Ministers, do expect from you. God has wrought a great Work for us, O let us make some suitable return of Duty to him, and act like a People called, loved, and saved by him. Shall so much be spent needlesly on your own ceiled Houses, on costly Attire and Dresses, and delicious Diet, when God's House lies almost waste! We are therefore become humble Supplicants for our dear Master, and could entreat you on our bended Knees, with Tears in our Eyes, to pity *Sion*, if it might but move your Hearts to Christian Bounty and Zeal for Her and the Lord of Hosts. We fear God did let in the Enemy upon us to consume us and waste our Substance, because to this Day we have with held it from him, when his Cause, Gospel, and Churches called for more than ever yet you parted with, and that a Blast has been upon our Trades and Estates for our remissness in this Matter. May we not say, *Ye looked for much, and lo it came to little; and when ye brought it home, the Lord did blow upon it?* Why, *because,* saith God, *mine House that is waste, and ye run every one to his own House,* Hag. 1.9. But if now we reform our Doings, and shew our Zeal for Christ and his Gospel, and love to him, and act as becomes a willing People professing his Name, you will see you will be no losers by it: *For I will*, saith the Lord, *open the Windows of Heaven, and pour out a Blessing that there shall not be room enough to receive it,* Mal. 3.10. If the Worth of Souls, the Honour of God, the Good of the Church, the glorious Promulgation of the Gospel in the Nation, the Credit of your Profession, your own Peace, and that weight of Eternal Glory be upon your Spirits, we doubt not but you will give evidence of it at this Time; and so shall you *build the old waste Places, and raise up the Foundations of many Generations; and be the Repairers of the Breaches, and Restorers of Paths to dwell in,* Isa. 58.12.

We to these great and good Ends, have thought upon and appointed a Solemn Day to Fast and Mourn before the Lord, and to humble ourselves, and seek his Face, that a Blessing may attend all that we have done, and you with us may yet further do for his Holy Name sake.

A General Fast appointed in all the Congregations on the 10th *of* October *next,* 1689, *with the Causes and Reasons thereof.*

The main and principal Evils to be bewailed and mourn'd over before the Lord on that Day, are as followeth.

First; Those many grievous Backslidings, Sins, and Provocations, not only of the whole Nation, but also of the Lord's own People, as considered in our publick and private Stations; particularly that great decay of first Love, Faith, and Zeal for the Ways and Worship of God; which hath been apparent, not only in our Churches, but also in private Families.

Secondly; That this Declension and Backsliding hath been, we fear, for a long series of time, and many sore Judgments God has brought upon the Nation; and a strange Death of late come upon the Lord's faithful Witnesses, besides divers painful Labourers in Christ's Vineyard called Home, and but few raised up in their stead; little success in the Ministry; storms of Persecution having been raised upon us, a new war commenced by the Beast, (through the Divine Permission of God, and Hand of his Justice) to a total overcoming to appearance the Witnesses of Christ in these Isles; besides his more immediate Strokes of Plague and Fire *etc.* God blasting all Essays used for deliverance, so that we were almost without hope, therefore our Sins that provoked the Righteous and Just God to bring all these Evils upon us, we ought to bewail and mourn for before him. But withal not to forget his Infinite Goodness, who when he saw that our Power was gone, and that there was none shut up or left, that he should thus appear for our Help and Deliverance, in a way unexpected and unthought of by us.

Thirdly; The Things we should therefore in the next place pray and cry to the Lord for, is, that he would give us true, unbroken, and penitent Hearts, for all our iniquities, and the Sins of his People, and wash and cleanse away those great Pollutions with which we have been defiled; and also pour forth more of his Spirit upon us, and open the Mysteries of his Word, that we may understand whereabouts we are, in respect of the latter Time, and what he is doing, and know our Work, and that a blessing may attend all the Churches of his Saints in these Nations, and that greater Light may break forth, and the Glory of the Lord rise upon us, and that the Word may not any more be a miscarrying Womb and dry Breasts, but that in every place Multitudes may be turned to the Lord, and that Love and sweet Concord may be found among all the Lord's People in these Nations, that the great work begun therein so unexpectedly, may go on and be perfected, to the praise of his own Glory.

Likewise to put up earnest Cries and Supplications to the Lord for the lineal Seed of *Abraham*, the poor Jews, that they may be called, and both Jews and Gentiles made one Sheepfold, under that one Shepherd Jesus Christ.

These are some of those Things we have thought good to lay before you, and which we hope we shall be helped with you to spread before the Lord on that Day, with whatsoever else you or we may be help'd to consider of: hoping you will not forget your Pastors and Ministers in your Prayers, and what we have been enabled to come to a Resolve about, so that all may be succeeded with a glorious Blessing from the Almighty, that the present Churches, and those Saints who shall come after us, may have cause to praise his Holy Name. Which is the unfeigned Prayer and Desire of us, who subscribe our selves your Servants for Jesus sake.

Hanserd Knowllys,	*John Carter,*	*Richard Sutton,*
William Kiffin,	*Samuel Buttall,*	*Robert Knight,*
AndrewGifford,	*Isaac Lamb,*	*Leonard Harrison,*
Robert Steed,	*Christopher Price,*	*Edward Price,*
Thomas Vauxe,	*Robert Keate,*	*William Phips,*
William Collins,	*Richard Tidmarsh,*	*William Facey,*
John Tomkins,	*James Webb,*	*John Ball,*
Toby Willes,	*John Harris,*	*William Hankins,*
George Barrette,	*Thomas Winnell,*	*Samuel Ewer,*
Benjamin Keach,	*James Hitt,*	*Paul Fruin.*
Daniel Finch,	*Hercules Collins,*	*Richard Sutton,*

In the Name and behalf of the whole Assembly.

[Memorand. 'Tis agreed to by us, that the next General Assembly be held at London, on that Day which is called Whitson-Monday, 1690.]

The ***NARRATIVE*** *Of the Proceedings of the Elders and Messengers of the Baptized Congregations, in their* General Assembly, *met* in London *on* Septemb. 3, to 12, 1689.

Whereas we Pastors and Elders of the several Churches in and about *London*, did meet together, and seriously take into our consideration the particular States *of the Baptized Churches* among our selves; and after a long Persecution, finding the Churches generally under great Decays in the power of Godliness, and Defects of Gifts for the Ministry; Also, fearing the same Decays and Defects might be among the Churches of the same Faith and Profession throughout England and Wales, many of their Ministers being deceased, many having ended their Days in Prison, many scattered by Persecution to other Parts, far distant from the Churches to which they did belong. From a due sense of these Things, did by their Letter, dated *July* 28. 1689[1], write to all the aforesaid Churches throughout *England* and *Wales*, to send their Messengers to a General Meeting at London, the 3*d* of the 7*th* Month, 1689. And being met together, the first Day was spent in humbling ourselves before the Lord, and to seek of him a right way to direct into the best Means and Method to repair our Breaches, and to recover our selves into our former Order, Beauty, and Glory. In prosecution thereof, upon the 4*th* day of the same Month, We, the Elders, ministring Brethren & Messengers of the Churches in and about *London*, and Elders, Ministring Brethren & Messengers of the several Churches from several parts of *England* and *Wales* hereafter mentioned, being again come together, after first solemn seeking the Lord by Prayer, did conclude upon these following Preliminaries, and lay them down as the Foundation of this our Assembly, and Rules for our Proceedings; Wherein, all the Messengers of the Churches aforesaid in City and Country (as well for the Satisfaction of every particular Church, as also to prevent all Mistakes, Misapprehensions and Inconveniencies that might arise in time to come concerning this General Assembly) do solemnly, unanimously, profess and declare:

---

[1] According to Ivimey, the letter calling for the Assembly was dated July 22, 1689. See above.

~ The Narrative of the 1689 General Assembly ~

1. That we disclaim all manner of *Superiority*, *Superintendency* over the Churches; and that we have no *Authority* or *Power*, to prescribe or impose any thing upon the Faith or Practice of any of the Churches of Christ. Our whole Intendment, is to be helpers together of one another, by way of Counsel and Advice, in the right understanding of that Perfect Rule which our Lord Jesus, the only Bishop of our Souls, hath prescribed, and given to his Churches in his Word, and therefore do severally and jointly agree,

2. That in those things wherein one Church differs from another Church in their Principles or Practices, in point of Communion, that we cannot, shall not, impose upon any particular Church therein, but leave every Church to their own liberty, to walk together as they have received from the Lord.

3. That if any particular Offence doth arise betwixt one Church and another, or betwixt one particular Person and another, no Offence shall be admitted to be debated among us, till the Rule Christ hath given (in that Matter) be first Answered, and the Consent of both Parties had, or sufficiently endeavoured.

4. That whatever is determined by us in any Case, shall not be binding to any one Church, till the Consent of that Church be first had, and they conclude the same among themselves.

5. That all things we offer by way of Counsel and Advice, be proved out of the Word of God, and the Scriptures annexed.

6. That the Breviats of this Meeting be transcribed, and sent to every particular Church with a Letter.

7. That the Messengers that come to this Meeting, be recommended by a Letter from the Church, and that none be admitted to speak in this Assembly, unless by general Consent.

The Letters from several Churches being read, the Meeting was dismissed till next day, and concluded in Prayer.

Septemb. 5. 1689

After solemn seeking the Lord, all the Elders, Ministring Brethren, and Messengers aforesaid, considered, debated and concluded, That a publick Fund, or Stock was necessary: And came to a Resolve in these three Questions;

~ The Narrative of the 1689 General Assembly ~

1. How to Raise it. 2. To what Uses it should be disposed. 3. How to Secure it.

Quest. 1. *How or by what Means this Publick Fund, or Stock, should be raised?* Resolved,

1. That it should be raised by a *Free-Will Offering.* That every Person should communicate (for the Uses hereafter mentioned) according to his Ability, and as the Lord shall make him willing, and enlarge his Heart, and that the Churches severally among themselves do order the Collection of it with all convenient speed, that the Ends proposed may be put into present practice.

2. That for the constant carrying it on, there be an annual Collection made in the several Churches, of a Half-penny, Penny, 2*d*, 3*d*, 4*d*, 6*d*, *per* Week, more or less, as every Person shall be made willing, and that every Congregation do agree among themselves to collect it, either Weekly, Monthly, or Quarterly, according to their own convenience, and that Ministers be desired to shew a good Example herein. *Exod.* 35.4,5. 1 *Chron.* 29.14. *Mal.* 3.10. *Hag.* 1.9. 2 *Cor.* 8.11,12.

3. That every particular Church do appoint their Deacons, or any other faithful Brothers to collect, and to acquaint the Church with the Sum collected, and remit it Quarterly into the Hands of such Persons as are hereafter nominated and appointed to receive it at *London*; the first quarterly Paiment to be made the 5*th* of *December* next.

4. That the Persons appointed to receive all the aforesaid Collections be our Honoured and well-beloved Brethren, whose Names we have sent you in a printed Paper by it self, all living in and about *London*; and when any of these aforesaid Brethren die, then the major part of the Survivors of them, shall nominate and appoint another Brother in his stead, to be confirmed, or refused, at the next General Meeting of this Assembly. And that the said nine Brethren shall disburse it, from time to time, for the uses hereafter mentioned, according to the satisfaction they, or the major part of them, shall have from the Information and Testimony of any two Churches in this Assembly, or from the Testimony of any particular Association of Churches in the Country, or from the Satisfaction they shall have by any other means whatsoever.

~ *The Narrative of the 1689 General Assembly* ~

Quest. 2. *To what Uses this Fund, or Publick Stock, shall be disposed?* Resolved,

1. To communicate thereof to those Churches that are not able to maintain their own Ministry; and that their Ministers may be encouraged wholly to devote themselves to the great Work of preaching the Gospel.

2. To send Ministers that are ordained (or at least solemnly called) to preach, both in City and Country, where the Gospel hath, or hath not yet been preached, and to visit the Churches; and these to be chosen out of the Churches in *London*, or in the Country; which Ministers are to be approved of, and sent forth by two Churches at the least, but more if it may be.

3. To assist those Members that shall be found in any of the aforesaid Churches, that are disposed for Study, have an inviting Gift, and are sound in Fundamentals, in attaining to the knowledg and understanding of the Languages, Latin, Greek, and Hebrew. These Members to be represented to the Nine Brethren in *London*, by any two of the Churches that belong to this Assembly.

Resolved, The Mony collected, be returned, as is expressed in a printed Paper before mentioned, to one of the Nine Brethren mentioned in the said paper.

Resolved and Concluded, That every quarter of a Year, an Account shall be taken by those Nine Brethren in *London*, nominated in the printed Paper aforesaid; of all the Receipts and Disbursments belonging to this aforesaid Fund, or Stock: With an Account signed by them, or the major part of them, shall be sent and transmitted to one Church in every County, with all convenient speed. The first Account to be made and sent the 5*th* of *January* next.

Resolved, That what Charges soever the said Nine Brethren are at in the Service of this Assembly, shall be discharged out of the aforesaid stock.

The Questions Proposed from the several Churches, Debated, and Resolved.

Quest. *Whether it be not expedient for Churches that live near together, and consist of small numbers, and are not able to maintain their own Ministry, to join together for the better and more comfortable support of their Ministry, and better Edification one of another?*

Answ. Concluded in the Affirmative.

Q. *Whether it is not the Duty of every Church of Christ to maintain such Ministers as are set apart by them, by allowing them comfortable Maintenance according to their Ability?*

A. Concluded in the Affirmative, 1 *Cor.* 9.9,10,11,12,13,14. *Gal.* 6.6.

Q. *Whether every Church ought not to endeavour not only to provide themselves of an able Ministry for the preaching of the Word, but also to set apart to Office, and in a solemn manner ordain such as are duly qualified for the same?*

A. Concluded in the Affirmative. *Act.* 14.23. *Tit.* 1.5.

Q. *Whether it is not the liberty of Baptized Believers to hear any sober and pious Men of the Independent and Presbyterian Persuasion, when they have no opportunity to attend upon the preaching of the Word in their own Assembly, or have no other to preach unto them?*

A. Concluded in the Affirmative, *Act.* 18.24,25,26.

Q. *Whether the continuing of Gifted Brethren many Years upon trial for Eldership, or any Person for the Office of a Deacon, without ordaining them, altho qualified for the same, be not omission of an Ordinance of God?*

A. Concluded in the Affirmative.

Q. *What is the duty of Church Members when they are disposed to marry, with respect to their Choice?*

A. To observe the Apostle's Rule, to marry only in the Lord, 1 *Cor.* 7.39.

Q. *Whether, when the Church have agreed upon the keeping of one day weekly, or monthly, (besides the first day of the Week) to worship God, and perform the necessary Services of the Church, they may not charge such Persons with evil that neglect such Meetings, and lay them under Reproof, unless such Members can shew good cause for such their absence?*

A. Concluded in the Affirmative, *Heb.* 10.25.

Q. What is to be done with those Persons that will not communicate to the necessary Expences of the Church whereof they are Members, according to their Ability?

A. Resolved, That upon clear Proof, the Persons so offending, as aforesaid, be duly admonished; and if no Reformation, the Church to withdraw from them, *Eph.* 5.3. *Mat.* 25.42. 1 *Joh.* 3.17.

Q. What is to be done with those Persons that withdraw themselves from the Fellowship of that Particular Church whereof they are Members, and join themselves to the Communion of the National Church?

A. To use all due means to reclaim them by Instruction and Admonition; and if not thereby reclaimed, to reject them. *Mat.* 18.17. *Luk.* 9.63. *Heb.* 10.38. *Jude* 19.

Resolved, That the like method be taken with those that wholly forsake the Fellowship of that Congregation to which they have solemnly given up themselves.

Q. Whether Believers were not actually reconciled to God, actually justified and adopted when Christ died?

A. That the Reconciliation, Justification, and Adoption of Believers are infallibly secured by the gracious purpose of God, and merit of Jesus Christ. Yet none can be said to be actually reconciled, justified, or adopted, until they are really implanted into Jesus Christ by Faith; and so by virtue of this their Union with him, have these Fundamental Benefits actually conveyed unto them. And this we conceive is fully evidenced, because the Scripture attributes all these Benefits to Faith, as the instrumental cause of them. *Rom.* 3.25. *Chap.* 5.11. *Chap.* 5.1. *Gal.* 3.26. And gives such Representation of the state of the Elect before Faith as is altogether inconsistent with an actual Right in them, *Eph.* 2.1,2,3,—12.

Q. Whether it be not necessary for the Elders, Ministring Brethren, and Messengers of the Churches, to take into their serious consideration those Excesses that are found among their Members, Men and Women, with respect to their Apparel?

A. In the Affirmative. That it is a shame for Men to wear long Hair, or long Periwigs, and especially Ministers, 1 *Cor.* 11.14. or strange Apparel, *Zeph.* 1.8. That the Lord reproves the Daughters of *Sion*, for the Bravery, Haughtiness, and Pride of their Attire, walking with stretched-out Necks, wanton Eyes, mincing as they go, *Isa.* 3.16. As if they affected Tallness, as one observes upon their stretched-out Necks, tho some in these Times seem, by their high Dresses, to out do them in that respect. The Apostle *Paul* exhorts, in 1 Tim. 2.9,10. *Women adorn themselves in modest Apparel, with Shamefac'dness and Sobriety: not with Broidered Hair or Gold, or Pearls, or costly Array; but with good Works as becomes Women professing Godliness.* And 1 Pet. 3.3,4,5. *Whose adorning let it not be the outward adorning of plaiting the Hair, of wearing of Gold, or of putting on of Apparel: but the Ornament of a meek and quiet Spirit, which is in the sight of God of great price. For after this* (fashion) *manner, the holy Women who trusted in God adorned themselves.* And therefore we cannot but bewail it with much Sorrow and Grief of Spirit, That those Brethren and Sisters who have solemnly professed to deny themselves, *Mat.* 16.24. And who are by Profession obliged in Duty not to conform to this World, *Rom.* 12.2. should so much conform to the Fashions of this World, and not reform themselves in those Inclinations that their natures addicted them to in days of ignorance, 1 *Pet.* 1.14. From these Considerations we earnestly desire, That Men and Women, whose Souls are committed to our Charge, may be watched over in this matter, and that care be taken, and all just and due means used for a Reformation heretaken, and that such who are guilty of this crying Sin of Pride, that abounds in the Churches as well as in the Nation, may be reproved; especially considering what Time and Treasure is foolishly wasted in adorning the Body, which would be better spent in a careful endeavour to adorn the Soul; and the charge laid out upon Superfluities, to relieve the necessities of the poor Saints, and to promote the Interest of Jesus Christ. And though we deny not but in some cases Ornaments may be allowed, yet whatever Ornaments in Men or Women which are inconsistent with Modesty, Gravity, Sobriety, and a Scandal to Religion, opening the Mouths of the Ungodly, ought to be cast off, being truly no Ornaments to Believers, but rather a Defilement; and that those Ministers and Churches who do not endeavour after a Reformation herein, are justly to be blamed.

~ The Narrative of the 1689 General Assembly ~

Q. *Whether it be not the Duty of all Christians, and Churches of Christ, religiously to observe the Lord's Day, or first Day of the Week, in the Worship and Service of God both in publick and private?*

A. It is concluded in the Affirmative. Because we find that Day was set apart for solemn Worship of God by our Lord Jesus, and his Holy Apostles, though the infallible Inspiration of the Holy Spirit.

1st. Because it appears that the Son of God, who was manifested in the Flesh, had Authority to make a change of the Solemn Day of Worship, being Lord of the Sabbath. *Mat.* 12.8. *Mark* 2.28. *Luke* 6.5.

2*dly*. It is manifest that our Blessed Lord and Saviour arose on that Day, as having completed and confirmed the work of our Redemption. *Mat.* 28.1. *Mark* 16.2. *Luke* 24.1. *Joh.* 20.1. whereby he laid the Foundation of the Observance of that Day.

3*dly*. Our Lord Jesus did then on that Day most plainly and solemnly appear to his Disciples, teaching and instructing them, and giving them their Commission, breathing on them the Holy Ghost. *Luke* 24.13,31,36. *Joh.* 20.19,20,21,22.

Moreover, on the first day of the Week, he appeared to them again, giving them a further infallible proof of his glorious Resurrection. And then convinced the Apostle *Thomas*, who being absent the first Day before, was now with them, *Joh.* 20.26. Whereby it appears he sanctified and confirmed the religious Observation of that Day by his own Example.

4*thly*. Our Lord and Saviour remained with his Disciples forty days after his Resurrection, and spoke to them of the things pertaining to the Kingdom of God, *Act.* 1.3. And we question not but he then gave command about the Observation of this Day.

5*thly*. Which appears, in that for a further confirmation thereof, after his Ascension, when his Disciples or Apostles were assembled together, solemnly with one accord, on the Day of *Pentecost*, which (by all computation) was the first Day of the Week; and recorded, *Act.* 2.1,2. He then poured out his Holy Spirit in a marvellous and an abundant Measure upon them.

6*thly*. Accordingly, afterwards, we find this Day was solemnly observed by the Churches, as appears. *Acts* 20.7. where we have the Churches assembling on that day plainly asserted, with the solemn Duties then performed, which were Preaching, and breaking of Bread;

and all this recorded as their usual Custom, which could be no other cause but Divine and Apostolical Institution. And it is most remarkable and worthy the serious Observation of all the Lord's People, that although the Holy Apostles, and others that were Preachers of the Gospel, took their opportunities to preach the Word on the Jewish Sabbath-day, and on other days of the Week as they had convenient seasons afforded; yet we have no Example of the Churches then assembling together to celebrate all the Ordinances of our Lord Jesus peculiar to them, but on the first Day of the Week. Which manifest practice of theirs is evidently as plain a Demonstration of its being a Day set apart for religious Worship, by the Will and Command of our Lord Jesus, as if it had been exprest in the plainest Words. Forasmuch as they did nothing in those purest Primitive Times in the sacred Worship of God, either as to time or form, but by a Divine Warrant from the Holy Apostles, who were instructed by our Lord Jesus, and were guided in all those Affairs by his faithful and infallible Holy Spirit.

7thly. In like manner the solemn Ordinance of Collection for the necessities of the poor Saints, was commanded by the Lord to be performed on that Day, 1 *Cor.* 16.1,2. By an Apostolical Ordination; which without question, by reason of their observing that Day for their holy assembling and worship, was then required.

8thly, and *lastly.* It is asserted by all the considerate and able Expositors of the Holy Scriptures, that the denomination or Title of the Lord's Day, mentioned *Rev.* 1.10. was attributed to the First Day of the Week, as the usual distinguishing Name given to that solemn Day by the Christians, or Churches, in the Primitive Times, as being a Day to be spent wholly in the Service and Worship of the Lord, and not in our own worldly and secular Affairs, which are lawful to be attended unto on others Days of the Week.

From all which, laid together and considered, we are convinced, that it is our Duty religiously to observe that Holy Day in the Celebration of the Worship of God.

Q. *Whether the Graces and Gifts of the Holy Spirit be not sufficient to the making and continuing of an Honourable Ministry in the Churches?*

A. Resolved in the Affirmative, *Eph.* 4.8,9. 1 *Cor.* 12.7.

Q. *Whether it be not advantageous for our Brethren now in the*

Ministry, or that may be in the Ministry, to attain to a competent knowledg of the Hebrew, Greek, and Latin Tongues, that they may be the better capable to defend the Truth against Opposers?

A. Resolved in the Affirmative.

Q. *Whether an Elder of one Church may administer the Ordinance in other Churches of the same Faith?*

A. That an Elder of one Church, may administer the Ordinance of the Lord's Supper to another of the same Faith, being called so to do by the said Church; tho not as Pastor, but as a Minister, necessity being only considered in this Case.

We the Ministers and Messengers of, and concerned for, upwards of one hundred Baptized Congregations in *England* and *Wales* (denying *Arminianism*) being met together in *London* from the 3d of the 7th Month to the 11th of the same, 1689, to consider of some things that might be for the Glory of God, and the good of these Congregations; have thought meet (for the satisfaction of all other Christians that differ from us in the point of Baptism) to recommend to their perusal the Confession of our Faith, Printed for, and sold by, Mr. *John Harris* at the *Harrow* in the *Poultrey*; Which Confession we own, as containing the Doctrine of our Faith and Practice; and do desire that the Members of our Churches respectively do furnish themselves therewith.[2]

Moreover, this Assembly do declare their Approbation of a certain little Book, lately recommended by divers Elders dwelling in and about the City of *London*, Intituled, *The Minister's Maintenance Vindicated.* And it is their Request that the said Treatise be dispersed amongst all our respective Congregations; and it is desired that some Brethren of each Church take care to dispose of the same accordingly.

---

[2] The *Third Edition* of the Confession of Faith, published in 1699, is prefaced by this statement along with the following thirty-seven names: *Hanserd Knollys, William Kiffin, John Harris, William Collins, Hercules Collins, Robert Steed, Leonard Harrison, George Barret, Isaac Lamb, Richard Adams, Benj. Keach, Andrew Gifford, Tho. Vaux, Tho. Winnel. James Hitt, Richard Tidmarsh. William Facey, Samuel Buttall, Christopher Price, Daniel Finch, John Ball, Edmond White, William Pritchard, Paul Fruin, Richard Ring, John Tomkins, Toby Willes, John Carter, James Web, Richard Sutton, Robert Knight, Edward Price, William Phips, William Hawkins, Samueal Ewer, Edward Man, Charles Archer.* It is then stated "In the Name and behalf of the whole Assembly."

An Account of the several Baptized Churches in England *and* Wales (*owning the Doctrine of Personal Election and Final Perseverance*) *that sent either their Ministers, or Messengers, or otherwise communicated their State in our General Assembly at* London, *on the 3d, 4*[th]*, and so on to the 11*[th]*, Day of the 7*[th] *Month, called September, 1689.*

Barkshire.

1	Reading	*William Facy*, Pastor.
		Reyamire Griffin, Messenger.
2	Farringdon	*Richard Steed,* Minister.
		William Mills, Minister.
3	Abbington	*Henry Forty*, Pastor.
		John Tomkins.
		Philip Hockton.
4	Newberry	
5	Wantage	*Robert Keate*, Minister.
6	Longworth	*John Man*, Preacher.

Bedfordshire.

7	Steventon	*Stephen Howtherne*, Pastor.
		John Carver.
8	Evershall	*Edward White*, Pastor.

Bristol.

| 9 | Broad-Meade | *Thomas Vaux*, Pastor. |
| 10 | Fryers | *Andrew Gifford*, Pastor. |

~ The Narrative of the 1689 General Assembly ~

𝔅𝔲𝔠𝔨𝔦𝔫𝔤𝔥𝔞𝔪𝔰𝔥𝔦𝔯𝔢.

11 Haddington   *Peter Tyler.*
12 Stukley   *Robert Knight*, Pastor.

ℭ𝔞𝔪𝔟𝔯𝔦𝔡𝔤.

13 Cambridg   *Thomas Cowlinge.*
14 Wisbich   *William Ricks*, Preacher.

ℭ𝔬𝔯𝔫𝔴𝔞𝔩𝔩.

15 Looe   *Thomas Cowling,*[3] Minister.

𝔇𝔢𝔟𝔬𝔫𝔰𝔥𝔦𝔯𝔢.

16 Boly-Tracy   *Clement Jackson*, Minister.
17 Dartmouth   *Philip Cary*, Minister.
18 Ladswell   *Samuel Hart*, Minister.
19 Luppit   *Thomas Halwell.*
20 Plimouth   *_____ Holdenby*, Pastor.[4]
                          Samuel Buttall, Minister.
21 South-Molton   *Thomas Stoneman*, Messenger.
22 Tiverton   *John Ball.*
                          Tristram Truvin, Minister.

𝔇𝔬𝔯𝔰𝔢𝔱𝔰𝔥𝔦𝔯𝔢.

23 Dorchester   *Thomas Cox*, Minister.
24 Dalwood   *James Hitt*, Preacher.
                          Thomas Payne, Preacher.
25 Lime   *Simon Orchard*, Minister.

---

[3] This name, very similar to the messenger from 'Cambridg' is in the original, so also in the 1692 *Narrative*.

[4] Name is absent in the original. Holdenby's first name was Robert.

Durham.

26	Muggleswick	*John Ward.*
		Henry Blackhead.
27	Newcastle *on* Tine	*Richard Pitts*, Pastor.
		John Turner.

Essex.

28	Hadfield-Braddock	*William Collins*, Pastor.
29	Harlow	*William Woodward*, Pastor.
		James Newton.

Exon County.

30	Exon	*William Phipps*, Pastor.
		Richard Adams.

Gloucestershire.

31	Burton *on the Hill, and*	*John Goring*, Pastor.
	Morton Hinmarsh	*Anthony Freeman.*
32	Cirencester	*Giles Watkins*, Minister.
33	Dimmock	*William Hankins*, Pastor.
34	Marring-Hampton[5]	
35	Nimpsfield	*Robert Williams.*
36	Sudbury[6]	
37	Tewksbury	*Eleazer Herringe*, Pastor.
		Edward Canter.

---

[5] No names are given in the original.
[6] No names are given in the original.

~ The Narrative of the 1689 General Assembly ~

Glamorganshire.

38 Swanzey   *Lewis Thomas*, Pastor.
                              Francis Giles.

Hartfordshire.

39 Hempstead   *Samuel Ewer*, Pastor.
                              William Aldwin.
40 Kingsworth   *James Hardinge*, Minister.
                              Daniel Finch, Minister.
41 Perton[7]
42 Theobalds   *Joseph Masters*, Pastor.
                              Joseph Steward.
43 Tringe   *Richard Sutton*, Pastor.
                              John Bishop.

Hampshire.

44 Christ-Church   *Joseph Brown.*
                              John Lillington.

45 Ringwood[8]

46 South Hampton   *Richard Ring*, Pastor.
                              John Greenwood.
47 White-Church   *Richard Kent,*
                              Stephen Kent, } Messengers.

Herefordshire.

48 Hereford City   *Edward Price*, Pastor.
49 Weston *and* Pinnard   *Richard Perkins*, Preacher.

---

[7] No names are given in the original.
[8] No names are given in the original.

~ The Narrative of the 1689 General Assembly ~

Kent.

50 Sandwich   *Thomas Fecknam*, Pastor.
                             Edward Taylor.

Lancashire.

51 Warrington   _____ *Loe*, Pastor.[9]

Leicestershire.

52 Kilbey   *Henry Coleman*, Pastor.
                             Benjamin Winckles.

London.

53 Broken-Wharf   *Hanserd Knowllys*
                             Robert Steed, } Pastors.
                             John Skinner.
                             Thomas Lampet.
54 Devonshire-Square   *William Kiffin*, Pastor.
                             Morris King.
                             William Clarke.
55 Joyners-Hall   *Samuel Boneal.*
                             William Dicks.
                             John Merriot.
56 Houndsditch   *Edward Man*, Pastor.
                             John Burkes.
                             Richard Hollowell.
57 Petty-France   *William Collings*, Pastor.
                             John Collet.
                             Thomas Harrison.

---

[9] Name is missing in the original. In the 1692 *Narrative*, Loe's first name is given as Thomas.

~ The Narrative of the 1689 General Assembly ~

𝕸𝖎𝖉𝖉𝖑𝖊𝖘𝖊𝖝.

58	Lime-House	*Leonard Harrison*, Pastor.
		Samuel Booth.
		John Hunt.
59	Mile-end Green	*George Barret*, Pastor.
		Isaac Marloe.
		John Putipher.
		Daniel Hawes.
60	Culman-Green[10]	
61	Pennington-Street	*Isaac Lambe,* Pastor.
		Humphrey Burroughs.
		John Gillet.
62	Wapping	*Hercules Collins*, Pastor.
		Humphrey Hutchings.
		John Overinge.

𝕸𝖔𝖓𝖒𝖔𝖚𝖙𝖍𝖘𝖍𝖎𝖗𝖊.

63	Abergaviny	*Christopher Price*, Minister.
64	Blainegumt	*William Prichard*, Pastor.
65	Galeon	
66	Lanwamouth	
67	Glanmenock[11]	

𝕹𝖔𝖗𝖋𝖔𝖑𝖐.

68	Pulham-Market	*Henry Bradshaw.*
69	Norwich	_____ *Austin*, Pastor.[12]
		Thomas Flatnam, Minister.

---

[10] No names are given in the original.

[11] No names are given in the original for these three churches.

[12] No name is given in the original. Austin's first name was Henry.

~ The Narrative of the 1689 General Assembly ~

Oxfordshire.

70	Finstock	*John Carpenter*, Minister.
		Joshua Brooks.
71	Hook-Norton	*Charles Archer*, Pastor.
72	Oxford *City*	*Richard Tidmarsh*, Minister.

Pembrookshire.

73	Neare	*Griffith Howel.*
		William Jones, Pastor.

Somersetshire.

74	Bath-Haycomb	*Richard Gay*, Minister.
75	Bridgwater	*Tobias Wells*, Pastor
		William Coleman.
76	Chard	*William Wilkins*, Minister.
77	Charton	*William Woodman.*
78	Dunster *and* Stockgomer[13]	
79	Froome	*William Randalfe.*
80	Hallistraw	*John Andrews.*
81	Hatch	*Jeremiah Day.*
82	Kilmington	*Robert Cole*, Minister.
83	Taunton	*Thomas Winnell*, Pastor.
84	Wedmore	*George Stant*, Minister.
85	Wells	*Timothy Brooke*, Minister.
86	Yeovel *and* Perriot	*Thomas Miller*, Pastor.

Suffolk.

87	Framingsham	*Thomas Mills*, Minister.

---

[13] No names are given in the original.

~ The Narrative of the 1689 General Assembly ~

𝔖urry.

Southwark

88	Horse-lie-down	*Benjamin Keach*, Pastor. *John Leader.* *Thomas Dawson.* *Edward Sandford.*
89	Mayes Pond[14]	
90	Shad-Thames	*Richard Adams*, Minister. *Nathaniel Crabb.* *John Bernard.*
91	Gilford	*John Ward.*
92	Richmond	*Hezekiah Brent*, Minister. *John Scot*, Minister.

𝔚arwickshire.

93	Alestree	*John Wills.* *John Higgins.*
94	Warwick	*Paul Fruine*, Minister. *Robert Paule.*

𝔚iltshire.

95	Bradford	*John Flouret.*
96	Calne	
97	Cley-Chase[15]	
98	Devises	*James Webb.*
99	Ecclestocke	*William Aldridge.* *Edward Froud.*
100	Knolles	*John Williams*, Pastor.

---

[14] No names are given in the original.
[15] No names are given in the original for these two churches.

~ The Narrative of the 1689 General Assembly ~

101 Malmsbury	_____ *Arch*, Pastor.[16]
102 Milsham[17]	
103 Porton	*Walter Pen.*
	John Andrews.
104 Southweeke	*Joseph Holton.*
	John Layes.
105 Warminster	*John Werell*, Pastor.
106 Westbury	*Roger Cator.*

𝔚orcestershire.

107 Bromsgrove	*John Eccles*, Pastor.

[Hearty Thanks are returned to you for your great Love and Charity towards our poor Brother *Richard Dorwood,* upon the account of his Loss by Fire.]

---

[16] No first name is given in the original.

[17] No names are given in the original.

The Assembly of the Elders, Messengers, and Ministring-
   Brethren, sent by and concerned for, more than one
   hundred Baptized Congregations of the same Faith with
   themselves, for many parts of England *and* Wales *(met*
   together in London Sept. 3 *to 12, 1689, to consider of*
   several things relating to the well-being of the same
   Churches.) And having that opportunity, judged it their
   Duty to clear themselves from the Reproaches cast on
   them, occasioned by the weakness of some few of their
   Perswasion, who in the late King's Reign, were imployed
   as Regulators for the Support of his Dispensing Power.

There having been many Reflections cast upon us, under the Name
of *Anabaptists*, as such, as having in the late Times, for our
Liberties-sake, complied with the Popish Party, to the hazard of
the Protestant Religion, and the Civil Liberties of the Nation: We
being met together, some from most parts of this Kingdom, judg it our
Duty to clear our selves from the said Reflections cast upon us. And
we do first declare, that to the utmost of our Knowledg, there was not
one Congregation that had a hand, or gave consent to any thing of that
Nature, nor did ever countenance any of their Members to own an
Absolute Power in the late King, to dispense with the Penal Laws and
Tests; being well satisfied, that the doing thereof by his sole
Prerogative, would lay the Foundation of Destruction of the Protestant
Religion, and Slavery to this Kingdom.

But yet we must confess, that some few Persons (from their own
Sentiments) which were of our Societies, used their endeavours for the
taking off the Penal Laws and Tests; and were employed by the late
King *James* to go into divers Counties, and to several Corporations, to
improve their Interest therein but met with little, or no Encouragement
by any of our Members; though considering the Temptations some
were under (their Lives being in their Enemies Hands) the great
Sufferings, by Imprisonments, Excommunications, &c. that did attend
the Ecclesiastical Courts, as also by the frequent Molestations of

Informers against our Meetings, by means whereof many Families were ruined in their Estates, as also deprived of all our Liberties. And denied the common Justice of the Nation, by the Oaths and Perjury of the Vilest of Mankind, might be some abatement to the severe Censures that have attended us, tho if some amongst us, in the hopes of a Deliverance from the heavy Bondage they then lay under, might miscarry, by falling in with the late King's Design. It being also well known that some Congregations have not only reproved those among them that were so employed, but in a regular way have further proceeded against them. From whence it seems unreasonable, that for the miscarriage of a few Persons, the whole Party should be laid under Reproach and Infamy.

It being our professed Judgment, and we on all Occasions shall manifest the same, to venture our *All* for the Protestant Religion, and the Liberties of our Native Countrey.

And we do with great Thankfulness to God acknowledg his special Goodness to these Nations, in raising up our present King *William*, to be a blessed Instrument, in his Hand, to deliver us from Popery and Arbitrary Power, and shall always (as in duty bound) pray that the Lord may continue Him and His Royal Consort long to be a Blessing to these Kingdoms, and shall always be ready to the utmost of our ability, in our Places, to join our Hearts and hands with the rest of our Protestant Brethren, for the Preservation of the Protestant Religion and the Liberties of the Nation.[18]

---

[18] Though unnamed in this statement, two or perhaps three of the regulators (Nehemiah Cox and William Collins; perhaps Edward Roberts) were from the Petty France church. In response to this action, the Petty France Church Book entry for October 8, 1689 states "…the following question was put viz. whether it bee the opinion of the Brethren that the substance of the paper at ye end of our late Assemblies narrative referring to regulators & regulations was a proper subject for their consideration, and the publication of that paper expedient, this was carried in the negative." See Scott Sowerby, "Forgetting the Repealers: Religious Toleration and Historical Amnesia in Later Stuart England" in *Past and Present*, no. 215 (2012): 85-123.

William Kiffin
Hanserd Knollys
Andrew Gifford
Robert Steed
Thomas Vaux
John Tomkins
Toby Wells
George Barret

Benjamin Keach,
Samuel Buttall,
Isaac Lamb,
Christopher Price,
Robert Keate
Richard Tidmarsh
James Webb
John Harris

Thomas Winnel,
James Hitt
Edward Price,
William Phips,
William Facey,
John Ball,
William Hankins,
Paul Fruin.

Finis.

The Names of the Receivers of all Money to be raised for the General Fund, or Publick Stock.[1]

The Persons appointed to receive all the Collections made in the respective Congregations, are our honoured and well-beloved Brethren Mr. *William Kiffin*, Mr. *Robert Bristow*, Mr. *Morice King*, Mr. *John Leader* Sen. Mr. *Isaac Marlo*, Mr. *John Skinner*, Mr. *Richard Hallowell*, Mr. *John Collet*, and Mr. *Edward Harrison*.

Resolved, That the Money be remitted from the Countrey, to our beloved Brother Mr. *Edward Harrison*, (one of the nine Brethren before mentioned) living at the Sign of the *Hen* and *Chickens* in *Cheapside, London*; with another Letter signifying the same; to our beloved Brother Mr. *Morice King*, living at the sign of the *Mermaid* in *Lawrence-lane*, Silk-Man, another of the nine Brethren aforesaid.[2]

We whose names are subscribed,
testify, that the Persons afore-
named were unanimously chosen by the whole Assembly.
Septemb. 12. 1689.

---

[1] This is the "printed Paper" referred to in the minutes for September 5, 1689. See above.

[2] The Petty France Church Book entry for October 15, 1689 states, "The question was put to ye congregation whether the money collected amongst them towards the general fund should have a distinct accot kept of it and bee disposed of with their knowledge & consent & it was carried in the affirmative."

~ The Narrative of the 1689 General Assembly ~

Hanserd Knowllys,
Robert Steed,
William Collins,
Andrew Gifford,
Thomas Vauxe,
John Harris,
Benjamin Keach,
George Barrette,
Samuel Buttall,
Christopher Price,
William Pritchard,

William Hankins,
Edmond White,
Daniel Finch,
John Tomkins,
Edward Man,
James Webb,
Thomas Winnell,
Richard Adams,
William Phips,
John Ball,
Richard Ring,

Charles Archer,
James Hitt,
Hercules Collins,
Leonard Harrison,
Edward Price,
William Facey,
Paul Fruin,
Richard Sutton,
Robert Keate,
John Carter,
Robert Knight.

3

The Narrative of

the 1690 General Assembly

Introduction

The General Assembly of 1689 determined that messengers from the churches would meet again in less than a year—"Whitsun Monday, 1690."[1] The *Narrative* published for 1690 is much briefer than the previous year's, but it nevertheless provides interesting insights into their attempts at organization. It commences with a "General Epistle" which is devotional in style, rehearsing some of the actions already taken in the months following the previous Assembly, rejoicing at the good start made in church planting. The Epistle mentions a "method" for further growth to be commended to the churches, and asserting unanimity in the conclusions drawn. The *Narrative* addresses matters of interest to all the churches, and hints at the distribution of more particular concerns for specific and unnamed churches or perhaps individuals.

The *Narrative* follows, enumerating six resolutions focused on outreach and details of the administration of the Fund. More space is devoted to the method recommended for "settling" the churches, administering the Fund, and encouraging associationalism. It is suggested that county associations be formed, with formal annual visitations made to the constituent churches by ministers appointed from among the congregations.

---

[1] According to the Julian calendar still in use in England, Easter was observed on 20 April, making Whit Monday 9 June. This is the date recorded in the 1690 *Narrative*.

Finally, an "Account" is given of the proposed local associations. Unlike the 1689 *Narrative*, this is not a report of the participants in the 1690 Assembly. The only notation of individuals or churches present is in the list of twenty names attached to the Epistle.

~ The Narrative of the 1690 General Assembly (Introduction) ~

A

Narrative

of the

Proceedings

of the

𝕲eneral 𝖠ssembly

Of the Elders and Messengers of the Baptized Churches sent from divers parts of *England* and *Wales*, which began in *London* the 9th of *June*, and ended the 16th of the same, 1690.

[Owning the Doctrine of Personal Election and Final Perseverance]

Hag. 1.4
Is it time for you, O ye, to dwell in your ceiled Houses, and this House lie waste?

London, Printed in the Year, 1690

The
GENERAL EPISTLE

To all the Churches of Christ walking in the same Faith and Order.

Dearly Beloved;

Grace, Mercy and Peace be multiplied upon you from God the Father, through Jesus Christ, by the Holy Spirit, to the transforming and changing you into the Divine Image and Likeness, in order to the glorifying him here, and you having Glory with him hereafter. To which ends, as God is pleased by his wonder working Providences to give us the greatest advantages, it is our greatest Concern, Prudence and Interest to use our utmost Diligence in the due Improvement of them; And now to prefer the good of Souls, and the Glory of God, the furtherance of the Gospel as subservient thereto, above our private Concerns. If we will build his House, he will build ours. O that the complaint of old may not be found amongst us, *All Seek their own things, none the things of Christ*, but rather follow the Apostle Paul's Example, who sought not his own Profit, but the Profit of many, that they might be saved. As it is our Priviledg to be in a capacity to do good in our Generation; so it is our Duty, and will be our Crown and Glory to lay out our Selves and our Talents, not only Spiritual, but also Temporal, speedily, while the Power is in our Hands, and faithfully, to the utmost we can. *To whom much is given, of them much is required.* O that God would give us great souls disposed to great things for him, and help us to do it humbly, sincerely and chearfully, that like David, we may serve our Generation by the Will of God before we fall asleep. Amongst all the rest of his great Acts, his great Preparation for the House of God (a Work that was much on his Heart) was not the least, at whose desire the People was stirred up to

~ The Narrative of the 1690 General Assembly ~

offer willingly and abundantly, for which he blessed God, and said, *Of thine own have we given thee.* Beloved, we began the last year to lay a Foundation for carrying on of Temple-work, and upon the view of what is done in it, as they of old in the rebuilding of the Temple, when the Foundation was laid, some wept, because it was no greater; others rejoyced that it was begun; so may we. It is matter of Joy that any have had their Hearts and Hands in so good a Work, and the more because of the great Good that hath been effected by it, especially in *Essex* and *Suffolk*, where were no Baptized Churches. Some at the cost of the Fund were sent out to preach the Gospel, with which the People were so affected, that they were forced to ride from place to place, and preach every day till they were even spent; and divers were baptized, and two Churches are like to be gathered; and the People have sent again for their help; their Meetings were very great, and a great Door is open in those Eastern Parts, the Lord make it effectual. This Work seems worth all our Cost, it is too large here to insert Particulars: Besides, many poor painful faithful Servants that labour in the Lord's Vineyard, bless God for your Bounty, of which they have received. But to be lamented it is, that so little hath been done amongst the Churches, and too many that can, have done nothing. Now to the end that a lasting Structure may be raised on this Foundation, a Method is now concluded on, which with this will be commended to you, which we pray and beseech for our dear Lord's sake, may be speedily followed; and that if any are slack and backward, others will encourage them. We ought to provoke to Love and Good-Works. We hope we can say we have been (notwithstanding our many Infirmities) in Peace, and unanimous in all our Conclusions. Those that are of general Concern, will come with this to you: but those that are particular, to those whom it concerns. So with our earnest Desires to you, and Prayers to God for you, that your Hearts may be affected with, and engaged in this so good and great a Work, with all others we are called to, we remain your Servants for Jesus sake.

Signed, by the Appointment of the Whole Assembly, by us,

~ The Narrative of the 1690 General Assembly ~

Han. Knollyes,
Will. Kiffin,
John Tomkins,
Will. Collins,
Rich. Adams,
John Ward,
Benj. Keach,
Isaac Lamb,
Sam. Shere,
Tho. Harrison,

William Dix,
James Hitt,
Hercules Collins,
George Barret,
Thomas Whinnell,
Andrew Gifford,
Henry Austin,
Will. Pritchard,
Hen. Brett,
John Skinner.

The Narrative of the Proceedings of the Elders and Messengers of the Baptized Churches in their General Assembly in London, June 9th, 1690.

1. Resolved, that neither in our former Assembly, or in this, or any other (according to our former Preliminaries) that we do not in any thing impose our Conclusions on any Churches, or particular Persons; but advise according to the best of our Understanding, as not being Lords over their Faith, but Helpers of their Joy.

2. That this Assembly do desire the Elders and Brethren in *London*, to send down one Elder or two to assist our Brother *Henry Austin*, in the Ordination of Brother *Henry Brett* of *Pulham*.

3. That we do desire our Brother *Benj. Keach*, and one Brother more, to visit our Friends at *Colchester, Suffolk,* and *Norfolk, &c.* to preach the Gospel, and to assist them in all those things they need, for the settlement in the Faith and Order of the Gospel, as the Lord shall open a Door of opportunity to them.

4. That Brother *Gregory Page*, Brother *R. Carter*, and Brother *Humphrey Burroughs* be added to the nine Treasurers appointed for the Fund. Resolved also, that any five of the said twelve Brethren may act and do any business.

5. That every particular Congregation contributing towards the Fund, do signify to the Trustees when they send any Sum of Money to them, what particular use they design it for, or how much for one use, and how much for another of the said Sum, and keep a distinct Account of it.[1]

6. That the particular Cases of those poor Ministers that have not been concluded on by this Assembly, are left to the Trustees of the Fund to act concerning them as in the direction given in the Narrative of the last Assembly.

---

[1] Perhaps this stipulation reflects the concerns expressed in the Petty France Church Book noted above.

~ The Narrative of the 1690 General Assembly ~

For the better settling of the Churches, and maintaining the Fund, and amicable Communion one with another;

Resolved,

I. That all the Churches that can, should have their Associations of several Counties together once or more a Year, according as they shall in respect of their Distance agree.

II. That of each Association, two Persons should be chosen to visit all the Churches of that Association once in the Year, for the Ends following.

1. Besides preaching to them, to enquire what orderly Officers are amongst them, and press them that are short therein to come up to the Rule, and that Care be taken in each Association to lend all needful Assistance.

2. To enquire what Provision they make for their Minister, whether it be according to their Minister's Necessity and the Churches Ability, that their Ministers may give themselves more to the Work of the Lord.

3. That where any Members lie short of their Duty, they endeavour to stir them up to it.

4. Where Churches are that have Ministers that have no need, and will not receive, that they be stirred up to do what they can to the Fund.

5. Those Churches who are able to maintain their own Minister, and can do something to the Fund, be stirred up thereto.

6. That when a Church hath done all they can do to their utmost, and all will not be sufficient, then those Messengers do acquaint their respective Association, and they together do consider what may be needful to be had out of the Fund: and also what Gifted Brethren in each Division are desirous to learn the Tongues, shall be presented to the Association, and if approved, then by them to the Trustees.

7. That no Minister that receives of the Fund should be any of those Messengers, if others can be had.

~ *The Narrative of the 1690 General Assembly* ~

And in order to the effecting these things:

1. That a Division be made of all the Churches into Associations, and commended to all the Churches good liking.

2. That a Catalogue of all the Ministers that need Supplies out of the Fund, be made by the Trustees against the next General Meeting.

3. That an Account be given what is like to be the Yearly Income of the Fund.

4. That no Messengers be sent to visit Churches out of the Fund's Cost, except in extraordinary Cases.

5. That Seeing the Churches in the Country are at so much Charge in their Associations, and sending of their Messengers to *London*, that the Churches in *London* would send Messengers into the Country to preach the Gospel, or to plant Churches at their own particular Charge, except in extraordinary cases.

6. That the Churches would speedily associate in their respective Divisions in order to the executing of the aforesaid things.

An Account of the Several Associations of the Churches in England and Wales

The Association of the Churches in *London, Middlesex, Kent,* and *Essex.*	The Association of the Churches *in* *Wiltshire, &c.*
	Porton,
George-Yard,	*Warminster,*
Devonshire-Square,	*Seghill,*
Morefields,	*Westbery,*
Joyners Hall,	*Stoak,*
Houndsditch,	*Devizes,*
Virginia-Street,	*Calne,*
Wapping,	*Milsom,*
Lyme-house,	*Bradford,*
Horsly-down,	*Southwitck,*
Winchester-house,	*Malmsbery.*
Mile-end,	
Richmond,	The Association of the Churches in
Turnum-green,	*Gloucestershire.*
Mays-pond,	
Sandwitch,	*Ninisfield,*
Hatfield-Heath.	*Sudbury.*
The Association of the Churches in *Somerset* and *Dorsetshire.*	The Association of the Churches in *Bristol.*
Tanuton,[2]	*Broadmead,*
Bridgwater,	*Fryers.*
Croscome,	
Stedmore,	The Association of the Churches in
Hallowtrow,	*Abbington, &c.*
Haycomb,	
Killminton,	*Abbington,*
Hatch	*Wantage,*
Periton-evil.	*Longworth,*

[2] *Sic.* Should read "*Taunton.*"

~ The Narrative of the 1690 General Assembly ~

Oxford,
Farington,
Flinstock,[3]
Mazittampton,[4]
Cizensister,[5]
Reading.

The Association of the Churches in *Norfolk* and *Suffolk, &c.*

Norwich,
Pulham,
Sudbury,
Wisbich,
Debbitch.

The Western Association of the Churches

Looe,
Plymouth,
Southams,
Bouye,
Southmoltowne,
Tyverton,
Exon,
Lyppet,
Dolwood,
Lyme,
Chard and *Taunton,* and *Dunster* are desired to be added if they think fit.

The Association of the Churches in *Newcastle, Yorkshire, Northumberland, and Cumberland.*

Newcastle,
 Bichbarn,

Pontefract,
Broton,
Eggermont.

Woolverston infurnis in *Lancashire* to be invited.

The Association of the Churches in *Hartfordshire, Buckingham* and *Bedfordshire.*

Kensworth,
Evershall,
Perton,
Hempsteed,
Stutly,
Harlow,
Tring.

The Association of the Churches in *Stepton* and *Hadnam*

Stepton, alias *Steventon,* and *Hadnam.*

The Association of the Churches in South *Wales*

Monmouthshire	*Langon,* *Bergavenny,* *Lanwenarth,* *Blainegwent,* *Golchon,* part of *Herefordshire.*
Glamorganshire	*Craig yr Allt,* and *Lanvahon.*
Carmarthen, Pembroke & Cardiganshire	*Ynys vach,* *Rushacre,* *Lanydwr.*

---

[3] *Sic.* Should read "*Finstock*"?
[4] *Sic.* Should read "*Marring-Hampton.*"
[5] *Sic.* Should read "*Cirencester.*"

~ The Narrative of the 1690 General Assembly ~

The Association of the Churches in *Worcestershire, Warwick, Oxford, Leicestershire.*[6]

Bromsgrove,	Tewxbury,
Warwick,	Mortonhinmash,[7]
Dimmuck,	Hookorton,[8]
Hereford,	Alcester,
	Kilby.

The next General Meeting is to be at *London* in the Week commonly called *Whitson-week,* 1691, to begin on the third day of the Week (called Tuesday) in Prayer, and then on the fourth day to proceed on business.

FINIS.

---

[6] Original is formatted in this fashion.
[7] *Sic.* Should read "*Mortonhinmarsh.*"
[8] *Sic.* Should read "*Hooknorton.*"

4

The Narrative of
the 1691 General Assembly

Introduction

According to the decision of the previous Assembly, messengers from the churches met again in General Assembly in June 1691. This time, however, they convened on Tuesday and remained in session until the following Monday.[1] The brief *Narrative* proceeds along familiar lines, beginning with an Epistle, followed by an account of the meeting and finally a list of participating churches.

The Epistle speaks of two matters—the encouraging nature of the deliberations at the Assembly, and the importance placed on the Fund. It expresses thankfulness for the good things done, and urges the churches to do more. The country churches are exhorted to greater involvement in both the Assembly and the Fund, while they are also the largest recipients of its resources.

The formal *Narrative* largely dwells on the Fund. Clearly this cooperative endeavor was at the forefront of concern among the churches. They believed that the best means to provide relief and encourage church-planting was such combined action. As in their previous meetings, they also addressed some practical questions, in this case matters related to the proper method to be used by an aggrieved individual who claims to have been abused in church

---

[1] All of the General Assemblies met for a week or more, apparently including Sunday. One wonders how this was practiced. Did the messengers attend worship services at the London churches? Did they transact any business on these Lord's Days?

discipline procedures. The method approved is interesting. One wonders, however, if there are hints of the growing schism in London present here. The language "the preserving of Peace and Concord amongst the Churches of our Association," may point in this direction. Certainly, dissension was growing within some of the London churches, and perhaps this was an attempt to head things off. Sadly, as will be seen in the 1692 *Narrative*, discord would only increase. The concluding list of churches once more groups them into local Associations.

A

NARRATIVE

OF THE

PROCEEDINGS

OF THE

General Assembly

Of the Elders and Messengers of the Baptized Churches sent from divers parts of *England* and *Wales*, which began in *London* the 2*d* of *June*, and ended the 8*th* of the same, 1691.

[Owning the Doctrine of Personal Election and Final Perseverance.]

Hag. 1. 4.

Is it time for you, O ye, to dwell in your cieled Houses; and this House lie waste?

London, Printed in the Year, 1691.

A

General Epistle

To all the

CHURCHES

Dearly beloved Brethren,

The God of all Grace hath brought us into a near and spiritual Relation to you, and you have such a rooted Interest in our hearts, that through Grace we shall always be ready to lay out our selves to the utmost of our Capacity, to promote the eternal Well-being and Happiness of your Souls: Our Sighs, Groans and Prayers in secret, and our Labours in Publick, in all the Holy Administrations of the House of God, are sincerely directed to this End; God is our Witness, who hath called us out (though very unworthy) to this Service, in pursuance of his own Glory, and his gracious Design towards you. And whereas you have freely chosen us as your Messengers, and entrusted us with Power to consider, discourse about, and conclude upon these Things proposed to us, in order to the general Good of those Churches to which we respectively belong, we have addressed our selves to this Work, with earnest supplication to the father of Lights, for his special Assistance and Direction therein: And we are not without some good Assurance, that he bowed his Ear unto us, in regard of that Harmony and good Agreement which was observable in most our Debates and Conclusions. And though we can impose nothing upon you, yet hereby is derived a greater Authority unto what was concluded, and it deserves to be so much the more regarded by you. We do heartily wish that you would look back to those Things which you were formerly pressed and exhorted to, in the two last Assemblies of your Messengers, for the promoting of the

~ The Narrative of the 1691 General Assembly ~

Glory of God, and your own Good; and although we may not have found the full End of our Endeavours in all Things answered, yet we bless God in many Things we have; which gives us encouragement to hope, that we may have some Success in this, who unfeignedly desire the thorow Reformation, the happy Settlement, and firm Peace and Well-being of all those Christian Churches we are immediately concerned with.

One thing formerly pressed upon you, was a liberal Contribution, by a Free-will Offering, and quarterly Subscriptions or Collections towards the raising of a Publick Stock, for Ends and Uses fully known to you. And we return you our hearty Thanks for what you have already done, and doubt not but that thereby Fruit will abound to your Account in the Day of Christ: And we hope you will not grow weary in well-doing, having the Promise of God that you shall then reap. Many Things might be urged to quicken you in this good Work, whereby several Labourers in the Lord's Vineyard have been already relieved; several pious, studious, and hopeful young Men have been assisted in the aquirement of Learning; and some have been sent forth to visit the Churches, and to give their helping Hand in order to their Settlement, according to the Rule of the Gospel. But we hope that this disposure of your Money, according to your Intention, may render motives of that kind very much unnecessary: However, that we may not be wanting in a Matter of this Nature, wherein the Honour of God, the keeping up his Publick Worship in the World, the Edification of Churches, and the Conversion of the Residue of God's Chosen is so much concerned, we shall humbly take the boldness to press you to a farther progress therein; and the rather, because several of our Fellow-Christians, who after us fell into this Method, have far exceeded us: And why should not the Glory of Christ, and the Advancement of his Kingdom, be as dear to us as to them? We hope it is, and therefore will not despair of prevailing with you.

If any Churches, or Members, upon a review of what is past, shall be sensible of their own Defect, we desire it may be made up, lest others should be discouraged, and the Work in a little time cease. Things of this Nature never prosper well without a free and cheerful concurrence of all jointly concerned therein, according to their Ability; and should we find such a concurrence generally, it would be matter of great rejoicing to us, and be esteemed by us as a remarkable Effect of the Spirit of Love, which is diffused through all the Members of Christ's Mystical Body.

To further such a Concurrence, let us consider,

First, From whom we have received all that we enjoy, and what Promises of Future Supplies we have through Grace and Interest in.

Secondly, That we are but Stewards of what we have; and that God can, by his secret and just Providence, soon take away our Stewardship, if we are not found faithful therein.

Thirdly, That the End of what we have, is the Honour of God; *Prov. 3. 9. Honour the Lord with thy Substance, and with the first Fruits of all thine Increase.*

Fourthly, That the keeping up God's Publick Worship, which is inclusive of all the Ends proposed in this Publick Stock, is a principal way of honouring God; and all other ways of expending what we possess, are inferior to this.

Fifthly, That Giving in this way, will be a great evidence of the sincerity of our Possession, and will be a great comfort in the latter End.

Other Things of this Nature might be added, but we hope that God's Grace will carry you beyond all that our Arguments can amount to, as was of old exemplified in the Churches of *Macedonia*, 2 Cor. 8. 1, 2.

In the next place, We would desire you that live in the Country, to send up your particular Messengers to this General Meeting, that we may have the more abundant evidence of your Approbation of that good Work intended and carried on therein; and let not the incident Charges you are thereby exposed unto, be a discouragement to you, we being perswaded that our Friends here in the City, who are not liable to such Charges, will make a Compensation by a more liberal Contribution unto the Publick Stock.

To conclude;

Dear Brethren, We commend you to God, and to the Word of his Grace, which is able to build you up, and to give you an Inheritance among them who are sanctified, amongst whom we desire to be found, who subscribe our selves,

Your Brethren in the Faith, and Fellowship of the Gospel,

Han. Knollyes,	Rich. Adams,
John Tomkins,	John Eccles,
Chr. Price,	William Collins,
Andrew Gifford,	James Jones,
Benjamin Keach,	Hercules Collins,
Sam. Buttall,	Thomas Whinnell,
George Barrett,	Tho. Harrison,
John Ward,	John Butt.
Nath. Crabb,	

Signed in the Name, and by the Appointment of the whole Assembly, *June* the 8*th*, 1691.

A NARRATIVE *of the Proceedings of the Elders and Messengers of the Baptized Congregations, in their General Assembly in* London, *begun the second Day of* June, 1691, *and ended the eighth of the same Month.*

W e the said Elders and Messengers of the Churches of Jesus Christ assembled together, having it under our consideration how much the Name of God, the Honour of the Gospel, and the Good of all the Churches to whom we belong, is concerned in our Perseverance in those good Things resolved upon in our former General Assemblies, Do agree and resolve unanimously, for the better increase and continuance of the Fund, to propound it to, and exhort all our Churches, and each Member thereof, with all our Christian Friends and Well-wishers thereto, to a liberal and cheerful Contribution, as God hath blessed them in the good things of this Life.

1. By their bringing in their Free-will-Offering, that have not yet paid it in (propounded at first as the foundation of this Fund) with all readiness of Mind, as a Sacrifice with which God is well pleased.

2. By the continuance of their Quarterly-Subscriptions, according as God shall bless them.

3. By a liberal Contribution in a Quarterly-Collection, which we unanimously agree to promote in all our Churches and Assemblies, to this end that all whom God hath blessed with Ability and a ready Mind, may have opportunity to shew their good Will for the promoting those great and good Things for which this Fund is raised, (*viz.*) For the support of such Ministers which the Churches to which they belong, through Poverty are not able to supply with what is necessary to their comfortable Subsistence; that so they may be encouraged to take the better care of their own Charge, and to preach the Gospel where there is need, and a door open; and also Godly young men, Members of the Churches, whom God hath gifted, and are approved of, may be instructed in the Knowledge of the Tongues in which the holy Scriptures were written.

And we judge it not reasonable that they who contribute nothing to the Fund, should desire any thing out of it. Therefore it is expected, that those Churches which are poor, should make their Collections for the Uses aforesaid, and raise what they can, be it more or less. Moreover, We judge that those that have subscribed either to the Free-will-Offering, or other Contribution for the Uses aforesaid, ought in conscience to perform what they have thereby engaged to do: For although before it was their own, yet after their subscribing, it remains so no longer; see *Acts* 5. 4.

It's further agreed, that what is or shall be gathered by the Free-will-Offerings, not yet paid in, and what is collected and to be collected, by Subscription; as also what shall be gathered by the first publick quarterly Collection, by and from all the Churches both in the City of *London* and the Countrey, shall be paid in, by the Twenty ninth Day of *September* next, with a Signification of what use or uses they design the Money so paid in for.

And for the better Encouragement of this good Work, it is agreed as followeth.

1. That the Trustees do put down the particular Uses assigned to every particular Sum, as in the last Narrative is expressed.

2. That the particular Sums that are given to one and the same use, be put together, and kept in a distinct Account by itself, by Brother *King* and Brother *Harrison*.

3. That the Money given to one use, be not disposed of to another.

It is also Agreed and Resolved, That no Money shall be paid or disbursed out of the Fund, but what is agreed upon by this present Assembly, until this Assembly shall by the good Providence of God meet again here in *London*, in 1692.

For the preserving of Peace and Concord amongst the Churches of our Association; in a due Tenderness to all the Members in communion with us, the following Questions were proposed, and Answers concluded thereupon as followeth;

Query 1. *Whether a Person Excommunicated, or withdrawn from by the Church he is in Fellowship with, and judgeth himself wronged therein, may not have Relief in that Case?*
Carried in the Affirmative.
Query 2. *What then is the Regular way such a Person ought to take for Relief?*

1. Such a Person ought (after all due endeavours in Humility and Love to satisfy the Church so dealing with him, of the wrong done him therein, and if not relieved thereby) to address himself to some other Church for Communion.

2. That Church to whom the Person so dealt with, shall propound himself, ought by their Messengers to enquire into the Grounds and Reasons of the Church's dealing with the said Person, with the manner or way of their proceeding against him to such a Sentence, that they may as fully as possible inform themselves of the ground of the Church's so dealing with him, of the Crime or Crimes alledged against him, with the Circumstances therefore for their own Information, how to carry it both to the Church and the Person so dealt with by them.

3. That the Church so dealing with a Member, ought to give a full and true Account accordingly in all Brotherly Love and Meekness, from the Mutual Obligation that one Church stands in to another, to keep their Communion pure, being all Members of that Body whereof Christ is Head.

4. And if upon due Inquiry and Information had of the Case, the Church to whom the aggrieved Person shall propound for Fellowship, shall see cause to judg that he has received wrong therein; then they ought in all Brotherly Love to endeavour to restore the Person dealt with to his former Communion, if he shall desire it, or else to receive him into Communion with themselves.

~ The Narrative of the 1691 General Assembly ~

An Account of the several Associations of the Churches in England *and* Wales

The Association of the Churches in
    London, Middlesex, Kent,
    and *Essex.*

    Theobald[s],
    George Yard,
    Devonshire Square,
    Morefields,
    Joyners-Hall,
    Hounsditch,
    Virginia-Street,
    Wapping,
    Lymehouse,
    Horsly-down,
    Winchester-house,
    Mile-end,
    Richmond,
    Turnum-green,
    Mays-pond,
    Sandwich,
    Hatfield-Heath.

The Association of the Churches in
    Somerset, Dorset, Wilts,
    Glocestershire, and *Bristol.*

    Taunton,
    Bridgwater,
    Croscome,
    Hallotrow,
    Haycomb,
    Killminton,
    Hatch,
    Periton-evil,
    Dunster,
    Froome,
    Sarum,
    Warmister,
    Seghill,
    Westbery,
    Devizes,

    Calno,
    Milsom,
    Bradford,
    Southwick,
    Malmesbery,
    Ninisfield,
    Sudbury,
    Broadmead,
    Fryers.

The Association of the Churches in
    Abbington, &c.

    Abbington,
    Wantage,
    Longworth,
    Oxford,
    Faringdon,
    Flinstock,
    Mazithamton,
    Cirencester,
    Reading.

The Association of Churches in
    Norfolk and *Suffolk,* &c.

    Norwich,
    Pulham,
    Sudbury,
    Wisbich,
    Debbitch,
    Colchester.

The Western Association of the
Churches.

    Looe,
    Plymouth,
    Southams,
    Bouye,
    Southmoltowne,

Tyverton,
Exon,
Lyppet,
Dolwood,
Lyme,
Chard.

The Association of the Churches in
Newcastle, Yorkshire,
Northumber-land and
Cumberland.

Newcastle,
Bichbarn,
Pontefract,
Broughton,
Eggermont,
Woolverstone.

Hampshire Association.

Christ church,
Ringwood,
Southampton,
Whit church.

The Association of the Churches in
Hartfordshire,
Buckinghamshire and
Bedfordshire.

Kensworth,
Evershall,
Perton,
Hempsteed,
Stutly,
Harlow,
Tring.

The Association of the Churches in
Stepton and *Hadnam.*

Stepton, alias *Steventon,*
and *Hadnam.*

The Association of the Churches in
South-*Wales*, *Monmouthshire*, and
part of *Herefordshire.*

Langone,
Bergavenny,
Lanwenarth,
Blainegwent,
Golchon,
Craig yr Allt, and
Lanvabon.

Carmarthenshire, &c. Association

Ynys vach,
Rushacre,
Lanydwr.

The Association of the Churches in
Worcestershire,
Warwickshire, Oxfordshire,
Leicestershire, and part of
Herefordshire.

Bromsgrove,
Warwick,
Dimmuck,
Hereford,
Tewxbury,
Mortonhinmash,
Hooknorton,
Alcester
Kilby.

~ *The Narrative of the 1691 General Assembly* ~

The next General Meeting is to be at *London* in the Week commonly called *Whitsun-week*, 1692, to begin on the third day of the Week (called *Tuesda*y) in Prayer and then on the fourth day to proceed on business.

FINIS.

Advertisements.

Those who desire to have the Confession of Faith of all these Churches, may have them of Mr. *John Harris*, at the Sign of the Harrow in the Poultry. Price bound 1 *s.*

The Ministers Maintenance Vindicated, published by the Elders in London. Price 6 *s.*

Where also you may have that excellent treatise of Baptism, wrote by Mr. *Philip Carey.* Price bound 2 *s.*

As also that very useful and profitable Book for children, and young People, called *Instructions for Children*; wrote by *Benj. Keach.* Price bound 6 *s.*

Distressed *Sion* relieved, a Poem. By *B. K.*

Antichrist stormed, and the time of the End. By *B. K.*

Both sold by *Nath. Crouch*, at the Bell in the *Poultry.*

An Exposition containing 2 Sermons on that Parabolical Speech of our Saviour, *Matt.* 12. 43, 44, 45. By *B. Keach.* Sold by *John Pike*, at the upper end of *Breadstreet.* Price stitch'd 6 *d.*

5

The Narrative of

the 1692 General Assembly

and Responses

Introduction

1692 was an important year for the young General Assembly, for it was necessary to address a difficult and divisive controversy which had erupted (largely) among the pastors of the London churches. Four years previously, Benjamin Keach had introduced hymn singing into the worship of the Horse-ly-down church he led. While the majority of the church seems to have approved and participated, a very vocal minority protested loudly and in print. A pamphlet war ensued,[1] a church split erupted birthing the Maze Pond church, and previously close relationships among the London ministers were shattered.

Many considered this hullabaloo a deep stain on the reputation of the ministers and their churches, and realized it was essential to seek an end to the ongoing battle. The potential consequences of division were significant, thus the matter must be addressed directly. The *Narrative* describes the matter as concluded by the Assembly. Following this, the letters requested by the Assembly are incorporated here.

The *Narrative* indicates that other matters were likewise discussed by the messengers. They were forward looking men, and perhaps understood that the present controversy carried serious implications for

---

[1] More than twenty books and tracts appeared in print.

their joint actions. The nascent Fund supporting poor ministers must continue, churches must be strengthened, and young men cultivated for pastoral ministry.

An innocent enough note indicates an important decision— beginning in the next year, the Assembly would be broken into two— one continuing in London, and the other meeting in Bristol. Each new Assembly was to send observers to the other in order to maintain mutual love and support. But this innocent note does not forebode the fact that while the Western Association meeting in Bristol would continue for a century, the London Assembly would not recover from the singing controversy, and would only gather once more—in 1693.

A

NARRATIVE

OF THE

PROCEEDINGS

OF THE

General Assembly

CONSISTING

Of Elders, Ministers, and Messengers, met together in *London*, from several Parts of *England* and *Wales*, on the 17*th* Day of the 3*d* Month, 1692, and continued unto the 24*th* of the same.

Asserting the Doctrine of Personal Election and Final Perseverance.

London, Printed in the Year, 1692

A General Epistle unto the churches of Christ, Baptized upon Profession of Faith; From the Elders, Ministers and Messengers in the General Assembly meeting at *London*, May the 17*th*, 1692.

Dearly beloved in our Lord Jesus Christ;

Considering *the near Relation we stand in one to another, as Children of one Father, Members of one Body, Heirs of one Kingdom, our Souls are engaged to pray for you as for our selves, that you may increase in Number, and in all Grace in the Church Militant, as a Preparative for the Church Triumphant.*

Beloved, we think it necessary to acquaint you, that your sending Messengers, and an Epistle, which informed us of your State, was very grateful to us; and where-ever it hath been neglected, it hath caused some concernedness of Spirit among us: but we hope that will be rectified for the future, and every other Neglect which hath a tendency to the weakening and withering the Interest of Christ in our Hands, which he hath intrusted us withal. We can say, through Grace, your Persons, and the most glorious Cause you have espoused, lie very near our Hearts; for which we can say, without vain Glory, we are willing to spend and to be spent, and should rejoice in your out-doing any of us, in seeking the Things of Christ more than your own. Since our coming together, we have done according to our Ability, that which we hope will tend to the lengthening of Sion's Cords, and strenthning her Stakes, and be of Advantage to the Saints of the next Generation. To this end we humbly conceive a chearful Perseverance in the Work you have well begun, may be necessary to effect these great Things, namely, the maintaining, upholding, and inlarging that Fund, or Stock, which is appointed for the continuing of an honourable Ministry in the Churches of Christ. And forasmuch as God hath given us a little reviving from our Bondage, let us act as Persons that have a mind to work, in laying out our Gifts, Graces, and earthly Blessings, in the building, strengthening, enlarging and continuing the Lord's Spiritual Temple. You know it is upon Divine Record, to the everlasting Honour of David, Solomon, *and the Old Testament Church, for their giving freely and largely to the building of the Temple and Tabernacle, bringing Gold, Silver, and precious Stones, &c. to that degree as forbidden to bring any more. If the Egyptians were so much concerned for the preservation of a natural Life, that for Bread in the Famine, they first parted with their Monies, then their Cattel, after that their Lands, and lastly offer'd their Persons to* Pharaoh*: O how much more should we be willing to part with our earthly Substance for the upholding of an honourable Gospel-Ministry, that may break the Bread of Everlasting Life to poor Sinners! Let us look upon it as part of our Generation-Work, to do something in order to the Comfort of the Churches of the Saints in succeeding Ages. It will be to your Honour, (as it was to* David *and* Solomon*, before mentioned) to erect convenient Places to worship God in; and give your Children the best Learning you can bring them up in the Nurture and Admonition of the Lord, not knowing but that they may be blessed Instruments for Christ when our Work is ended. Moreover, our desire is, that you would look among your selves for some Godly young Men inclined to the Ministry, the Fund being partly intended to afford them what Helps may be proper to that Work, and let them be presented at the next Association. We also earnestly desire that you would appoint Meetings among yourselves, for the Discovery, Exercise, and Improvement of Gifts; the neglect whereof, we humbly conceive, is one Reason of the withering of some Churches; and this we hope, by God's Blessing, will prove a means of our Reviving and Flourishing. But above all, our desire is, That the Churches may not forget to cry mightily to the Lord for the Spirit of Prayer and Supplication, and that degree of Divine Anointings which is absolutely necessary for the making of a Gospel-Ministry. Beloved, we need not use Arguments to press you to these Duties, seeing it is your own Interest: Yet this we have experience of, to be ready to every good Work, is the way to prosper in all things we put our Hands to, whether they are Spiritual or temporal. God told the Jews, when he commanded them to build his material Temple, that the Silver was his, and the Gold was his, yet promises to bless them from that very day that it was laid out in his Service. To cast our Bread upon the Waters, may bring in a Blessing many Years after upon our Persons or Posterity: And seeing it is all your Delight to honour the Lord, one of the wisest of men hath told us, we do it when we dedicate our substance to his Service.*

~ The Narrative of the 1692 General Assembly and Responses ~

To conclude; As we desire all your Prayers for us; so our Prayers shall be for you, That the God of Peace, that brought again from the Dead our lord Jesus, the great Shepherd of the Sheep, through the Blood of the Everlasting Covenant, may make you perfect in every good Work[:] to do his Will, working in you that which is well-pleasing in his sight, through Jesus Christ; To whom be Glory for ever, and ever. Amen.

Your Brethren in the Faith, and Fellowship of the Gospel,

Andrew Gifford.	William Kiffin.
Robert Keate.	Samuel Buttall.
Henry Austin.	Benjamin Keach.
Leonard Harrison.	Hercules Collins.
George Westbury.	John Scott.
John Hunt.	Benjamin Dennis.
Edmund White.	Robert Cabbel.
John Willis.	Richard Adams.
	William Collins.

Signed in the Name, and by the Appointment of the Assembly, *May* 24, 1692.

In order to the more comfortable Communion of those Churches that
are in a Union, it hath been thought expedient,

I. That whereas, for some Years last past, the Churches have had,
in several Counties, particular Associate Meetings, and one General at
London, annually:

It is now proposed, to divide this one General into Two, and to
keep one in the West, and one here for the East: That in the West to be
at *Bristol*, and the other in *London*; desiring, That all Churches will
send Messengers to one or the Other, once a Year, as may be most for
their Conveniency; and that either from their particular Churches or
they that live remote from such Associations as they think meet to
keep.

II. That the meeting at *Bristol* be kept Annually at the Time called
Easter, and that at *London* at the Time called *Whitsontide.*

III. That two Messengers be sent down from *London* every time to
that at *Bristol*, and also two sent up from that at *Bristol* to that at
London, for the maintaining of General Communion.

IV. For the better keeping up of the Fund, that this Method be
observed;

1. That all Churches make Quarterly Collections in what
Method they think best, for the Encouragement of the Ministry,
(though it be never so little) by helping those Ministers that are Poor;
and to educate Brethren, that may be approved, to learn the Knowledg
of those Tongues wherein the Scriptures are written.

2. That each Church bring to that Annual Assembly to which
they send, what they collected for the Year, and signify there for what
Uses.

3. That each of those Assemblies shall dispose of such Monies,
that so all the Churches may have a hand in disposing their Money to
their satisfaction.

4. That what Money may not be disposed in either Assembly,
they may instruct whom they please therewith till their next Meeting.

~ *The Narrative of the 1692 General Assembly and Responses* ~

V. That those Assemblies are not to be accountable to one another, any more than Churches are.

VI. That no Churches make Appeals to them, to determine Matters of Faith, or Fact, but propose or query for Advice.

VII. That after both the Meetings in *West* and *East* have been held, that a General Narrative be printed and sent to all the Churches, of such Matters as may be of general Use.

There being a Controversy manag'd and maintain'd in Print, by several Persons of the Baptized Churches. Upon the 23d of the 3d Month 1692, it was agreed by both Parties, to refer the Matter to the Examination and Determination of the Persons subscribed: And for that end, this Question was proposed to both Parties in the General Meeting, (viz.)

Quest. Whether you are willing to be determined by the said Brethren, and resolve to do what they shall determine, in order to the removing all those Reflections that are writ in all the Books that are printed on both sides, about the Controversy of *Singing?* &c. The Matters to be debated and determined, are only respecting Reflections and Matters of Fact.

Answ. Those Persons being enquired of, and that agreed to it fully, were, Brother *Kiffin,* Br. *Man*, Br. *Barret*, Br. W. *Collins*, Br. *Keach*, Br. *Steed*, Br. *Hollowell.*

The Persons nominated to examine and determine the Matters abovesaid, were, Brother *Andr. Gifford, Edm. White, Hen. Austin, Rob. Keate, John Willis, Sa. Buttal, John Scot.*

The Reflections and Offenses presented, were as followeth, (*viz.*)

The Examination of the Offenses of the Author or Authors of the Book called A Sober Reply,[1] *&c.*

The abovesaid Brethren do conclude these things as unbrotherly Censures. *Pag. 3. line 15, to 20. P. 11. l. 6, to 10.*
These as unsavoury Expressions, *P. 4. l. 2, 3, 4. (P. 5. l. 13 to 16, on both sides.)*
A great wrong to the first Baptized Churches, *P. 9. l. 9, to 25.* And that our Brother *Keach* should acknowledg his Error in Print, or otherwise.
Needless Recitals of Names, *P. 11. l. 14, 15. P. 32. l. 10, 11.*

---

[1] *A Sober Reply to Mr. Robert Steeds Epistle Concerning Singing* (London: n.p. 1691). No author is given on the title page.

Recitals without Injury, *P. 12*. The two last lines, and *P. 14. l. 1, to 7.*

An unfair Representation, and if intended to be upon the Afternoon of the same Morning (as appears by Information) false, *P. 14. l. 31, 32, 33.*

A Weakness and Oversight; and if they intended to call themselves Renowned, savouring of Vain-glory, *P. 42. l. 9, 10.*

The Offences out of B. W's Epistle.[2]

An uncharitable Insinuation, when applied on either side, *line 2. 3.*

Uncharitable Expressions on both Sides, not thinking well of their Brethren differing from them, *Line 25, to 38.*

Out of the Book call'd A 𝕾erious 𝕬nswer,[3] &c. concluded.

An uncharitable Censure, *P. 5. l.* last.

That the Charge of Forgery, and things inconsistent with Christian Sobriety, or Common Honesty, exibited against Br. *Keach*, in *P. 6.* Upon examination into all the Particulars of it, appears to us to be false and ungrounded; and that our Brethren were unwarily lead into that Charge, for want of plain and full Information, and therefore do conclude our Brethren should acknowledg their Error therein, in Print, or otherwise.

That in Pag. 9. we find great Reflections on both sides, but especially in the Answer.

Unchristian Reflections, *P. 11. l. 27, to 31. P. 12. l. 12, to the end, P. 13. l. 2, to the end.*

Andr. Gifford.	Ed,. White.
Hen. Austine.	Rob. Keate.
John Scot.	John Willis.

Samuel Buttall.

---

[2] It is difficult to identify this document. *A Sober Reply* includes an epistle by Thomas Whinnel—*T.W.* The "offences" noted seem to fit Whinnel's epistle. If that is the case, "B.W." is a printer's error.

[3] *A Serious Answer to a late Book, stiled, A Reply to Mr. Robert Steeds Epsistle Concerning Singing* (London: n.p, 1692). No author is given on the title page.

The Determination of the seven Brethren followeth; which was read to both Parties in the Assembly, the 24th of the 3d Month, 1692, and signed by them.

Beloved and Honoured in the Lord for your Work-Sake;

We your unworthy Brethren, whom you have chosen to Examine and Determine the Matters aforesaid, (so far as we know in our own Hearts) have singly, without respect of Persons, judged as for the Lord, and unanimously concluded, That those Persons who have been concern'd in this Controversy, have on both sides err'd in most of the Particulars that were laid before us. If we have been partial in anything, it is only, (for which we beg your pardon) That we lay your Evils before you in easy Terms, from this Confidence, That the Grace of God will help you much more to aggravate them in your own Souls, especially when you compare how unlike to Jesus Christ, and the Holy Commands he hath given for Brotherly Love; your Treatment hath been one towards another; *who when he was reviled, reviled not again, I Pet.2.22,23.* And how far short, in this Controversy, you have come, in answering that Character which the Spirit of God gives of true Charity, *I Cor. 13.4, &c.* Had the things wherewith you charge one another, been true, we humbly conceive you should have taken those Rules Christ hath prescrib'd, in a more private Debate, Way, and Method, that would not have reflected upon your Holy Profession, and the Name of God, to convince one another of your Errors; and that the Ways you have taken to discover the Nakedness of your Brethren, have been irregular, and tended rather to beget greater Offences and Stumblings, than Convincing, Healing, and Recovering. *Ham* for discovering the Nakedness of *Noah,* was accursed of God, *Gen. 9. 29.* To proclaim one another's Errors to Reproach, is from the Evil One; and to give our Enemies occasion to rejoice over our Failings, forbidden to be told in *Gath and Gilgal,* 2 Sam. I.20. You know who hath said, That the issue of Biting, will be to devour one another, (if God prevent not). We grieve to think what Dishonors your Methods will bring to the Name of God, Reproach to your Holy Profession, Stumbling to Sinners, and Divisions among the Churches of Christ: and therefore as Brethren, partakers of the same Grace, we humbly exhort you, and pray, God would make you all sensible of your Errors, humble you for them; and as God for Christ's sake hath forgiven you, you would for his Name's-Sake forgive one another. And as he is pleased to make you sensible of your Errors, acknowledg them one to another; and give us cause of great Rejoicing, that have greiv'd us whilst we have been searching into your uncharitable unsavory Censures, Reflections and Reproaches, which you have in your Books loaded one another with, and through Temptation have been prevail'd upon to take wrong Measures and Misrepresentations of one another within yourselves: And therefore, in the Name of the Lord, and for his sake, we entreat and determine, That you proceed no longer in such Methods.

We have also considered and determined, (that for the prevention of any further Reproach and Dishonour that may come upon the Name of the Lord, and your Holy Profession, that nothing will prove more effectual for this End, than) That all Persons that are concern'd on both Sides in this Controversy, be desired, and we do desire and determine, That they should call in, and bring all their Books hereafter mentioned into this Assembly, or to whom they shall appoint, and leave them to their dispose. And that if any do persist in this reproachful Method, we do seriously deliver it as our Sense, [That that Person or Persons, do those things that sow Offences, Discord, and Divisions among the Churches of Christ, and should be so remarked.] We could entreat you, upon our Knees, might we prevail with you in this Matter, that you would join together to keep the Unity of the Spirit, and of our Holy Profession, in the Bond of Peace.

Moreover, we entreat and determine, that it be inserted in the *Narrative*, That none of the Members of the Churches do buy, give, or disperse any of these Books aforesaid underwrit, nor any other that have those uncharitable Reflections in them against their Brethren; and that no Person do sell them, or give them to others.

The Names of the Books, some of which we have seen, and all others that have such Reflections, though not seen, are,

1.   *A sober Reply to* Robert Steed's *Epistle.*
2.   *Truth soberly defended.*[4]
3.   *A serious Answer,* &c.
4.   *Truth cleared, or a brief Narrative of the Rise,*[5] &c.

Your Brethren, mourning for your Divisions,

Andr. Gifford.	Ed. White.
Hen. Austine.	Rob. Keate
John Scott.	John Willis.
Samuel Buttal.	

The Person appointed by the Assembly to receive the above said Books, is Br. *Rich. Adams.*

---

[4] Isaac Marlow, *Truth Soberly Defended, In a Serious Reply to Mr. Benjamin Keach's Book, intituled, The Breach Repaired in God's Worship* (London: n.p., 1692).

[5] *Truth Cleared: Or a brief Narrative of the Rise, Occasion, and Management of the present Controversy concerning Singing in the Worship of God.* This seems to have been printed as a tract, without publishing information. Internal evidence places it within the sphere of Isaac Marlow.

An Account of the Several Baptized Churches concerned in the aforesaid General-Assembly at London

[*We want the Names of several Pastors and Ministers.*}

𝕭arkshire.

1. Reading   *Jo. Ward*, Minister.

2. Farrington   *Richard Steed*, Minister.
       William Mills, Minister.
3. Abbington   *John Tomkins*, Minister.
4. Newberry
5. Wantage   *Robert Keate*, Minister.
6. Longworth   *John Man*, Preacher.

𝕭edfordshire.

7. Steventon   *Stephen Howtherne*, Pastor.
8. Evershall   *Edmond White*, Pastor.

𝕭ristol.

9 Broad-Meade   *Thomas Vaux*, Pastor.
10. Fryers   *Andrew Gifford,* Pastor.

𝕭uckinhamshire.[6]

11 Haddington   *Peter Tyler.*
12 Stukeley   *Robert Knight*, Pastor.

ℭambridg.

13 Cambridg   *Thomas Cowlinge.*
14 Wisbich   *William Rix*, Preacher.

ℭornwal.

15 Looe   *Thomas Cowling*, Minister.

---

[6] *Sic.* So also the following unusually spelled county names.

~ *The Narrative of the 1692 General Assembly and Responses* ~

Devonshire.

16 Exon	Mr. *Sampson*, Minister.
17 Boly Tracy	*Clement Jackson*, Minister.
18 Dartmouth	*Philip Cary*, Minister.
19 Ladswell	*Samuel Hart*, Minister.
20 Luppit	*Thomas Halwell.*
21 Plimouth	*James Hitt*, Minister.
	Samuel Buttal, Minister.
22 South-Molton	
23 Tiverton	*Richard Tidmarsh*, Minister.

Dorsetshire.

24 Dorchester	*Thomas Cox*, Minister.
25 Dalwood	*Thomas Payne*, Minister.
26 Lime	*Simon Orchard*, Minister.

Durham.

27 Muggleswick	*John Ward*, Minister.
	Henry Blackett, Minister.
28 Newcastle *upon* Tine	*Richard Pitts*, Pastor.

Essex.

29 Hadfield-Braddock	*William Collins*, Pastor.
30 Harlow	*William Woodward*, Pastor.
31 Colchester	*John Hammond*, Pastor.

Gloucestershire.

32 Burton *on the Hill, and* Morton-Hinmast[7]	*John Greening*, Pastor.
33 Cirencester	*Giles Watkins*, Minister.
34 Dimmock	*William Hankins*, Pastor.

---

[7] *Sic.* for Morton-Hinmarsh.

~ *The Narrative of the 1692 General Assembly and Responses* ~

35 Marring-Hampton
36 Nimpsfield　　　　　　　　*Robert Williams.*
37 Sodbury
38 Tewksbury　　　　　　　　*Eleazer Herringe*, Pastor.

Glamorganshire.

39 Swanzey　　　　　　　　*Lewis Thomas*, Pastor.

Hartfordshire.

40 Hempstead　　　　　　　　*Samuel Ewer*, Pastor.
41 Kingsworth　　　　　　　　*James Hardinge*, Minister.
　　　　　　　　　　　　　　Daniel Finch, Minister.
42 Perton
43 Theobalds　　　　　　　　*Joseph Masters*, Pastor.
44 Tringe　　　　　　　　　　*Richard Sutton*, Pastor.

Hampshire.

45 Christ-Church　　　　　　　*Joseph Brown.*
46 Ringwood
47 South-Hampton　　　　　　*Richard Ring*, Pastor.
48 White-Church　　　　　　　*Richard Kent*, Minister.

Herefordshire.

49 Hereford　　　　　　　　*Edward Price*, Pastor.
50 Weston *and* Pinerell　　　　*Richard Perkins*, Preacher.

Kent.

51 Sandwich　　　　　　　　*Thomas Fecknam,* Pastor.

Lancashire.

52 Warrington　　　　　　　*Thomas Loe*, Pastor.

Leicestershire.

53 Kilbey　　　　　　　　　*Henry Coleman*, Minister.

London.

54 Newgatestreet	*Robert Steed*, Pastor.
55 Devonshire-Square	*William Kiffin*, Pastor.
	Richard Adams.
56 Joyners-Hall	*Tobias Russel*, Minister.
	Thomas Mariot, Minister.
57 Hounsditch	*Edward Man*, Pastor.
58 Petty-France	*William Collins*, Pastor.
	Thomas Harrison, Minister.

Middlesex.

59 Lime-House	*Leonard Harrison*, Pastor.
60 Mile-end Green	*George Barret*, Pastor.
61 Pennington-Street	*Humphrey Burroughs*, Messenger.
62 Wapping	*Hercules Collins*, Pastor.

Monmouthshire.

63 Abergaviny	*Christopher Price*, Minister.
64 Blainegumt	*William Prichard*, Pastor.
65 Galoen	
66 Lanwamouth	
67 Glanmenock	

Norfolk.

68 Pulham-Market	*Henry Brett*, Pastor.
69 Norwich	*Edward Austin*,[8] Pastor.
	Edward Williams, Pastor.

Oxfordshire.

70 Finstock	*John Carpenter*, Minister.

---

[8] The first name is probably an error, and should be *Henry*.

~ The Narrative of the 1692 General Assembly and Responses ~

71 Hook-Norton   *Charles Archer*, Pastor.
72 Oxford *City*

Pembrookshire.

73 Neare   *Griffith Howel.*
                                   William Jones, Pastor.

Somersetshire.

74 Bath-Haycomb   *Richard Gay*, Minister
75 Bridgewater   *Tobias Wells*, Pastor.
76 Chard   *William Wilkins*, Minister.
77 Charton   *William Woodman.*
78 Dunster *and* Stockgomer
79 Froome
80 Hallitraw
81 Hatch   *Jerimiah Day.*
82 Kilmington   *Robert Cox*, Minister.
83 Taunton   *Thomas Winnell*, Pastor.
84 Wedmore   *George Stant*, Minister.
85 Wells   *Timothy Brooke*, Minister.
86 Yeovel *and* Perriot   *Thomas Miller*, Pastor.

Suffolk.

87 Framingham   *Thomas Mills*, Minister.

Surry.

88 Southwark
89 Horse-lie-down   *Benjamin Keach*, Pastor.
90 Mayes Pond   *Samuel Mee*, Minister.
91 Winchester House   *Richard Baxter,* Minister.
                                   David Towler, Minister.
92 Richmond   *John Scot*, Pastor.

Warwickshire.

93 Alcester   *John Wills*, Minister.
94 Warwick   *Benjamin Boyer*, Minister.

~ The Narrative of the 1692 General Assembly and Responses ~

𝔚iltshire.

95 Bradford	*John Flouret.*
96 Calne	
97 Cley-Chase	
98 Devises	
99 Ecclestock	
100 Knolles	*John Williams*, Pastor.
101 Malmbury	____ *Arch*,[9] Pastor.
102 Milsham	
103 Porton	
104 Southweeke	
105 Warminster	
106 Westbury	

𝔚orcestershire.

107 Bromsgrove	*John Eccles*, Pastor.

Ordered, That this *Narrative* be read in all the Churches.

Ordered, That as many Messengers as can, come in on *Whitson-Munday*; and its appointed that *Tuesday* be spent in Prayer, and to begin Business on *Wednesday*.

---

[9] First name is missing in original.

~ The Narrative of the 1692 General Assembly and Responses ~

Published remarks

in response to the

Controversy about Singing

From

Benjamin Keach,

William Kiffin et. al.

To all the Baptized Churches and faithful Brethren in England and Wales, Christian Salutations.[1]

[Benjamin Keach]

Behold how good and how pleasant it is (saith the Psalmist) *for Brethren to dwell together in Unity*, Psal. 133.1. But O how grievous a thing is the contrary, viz. to see Brethren live in Discord, in Strife and Contention. Our Saviour saith, *By this shall all Men know ye are my Disciples, if ye love one another*, John 13.35. Nay 'tis an Evidence we are passed from Death to Life, when we love the Brethren: and as this Grace is from hence to be coveted and laboured after, so the Nature thereof is by the Apostle plainly described, I Cor. 13. "*Charity suffereth long*, and is kind; *Charity envieth not*. A Soul possessed of Love will suffer long, i.e. not be too quick and touchy with Brethren that offend or displease us. The charitable Man will with-hold and refrain his Wrath, not be rash in the Expressions of it, and hasty in Revenge," say our late *Annotators*.[2] I fear that great Precept has been forgot, *Love thy Neighbour as they self; Charity beareth all things, believeth all things, hopeth all things, endureth all things*, I Cor. 13.7. "The charitable Man beareth real Injuries with Patience, he believeth all things that are good of his Brother, will make the favourablest Constructions of his Words and Expressions; so far is he from being credulous to his Prejudice, rejoiceth not in Iniquity, will not rejoice in the real and sinful Falls of others; nor dare he spread or proclaim his Brother's Weakness to the Dishonour of God, and Prejudice to the Truth of the Gospel."[3] *Charity will cover a Multitude of Faults*. My Soul mourneth to see how this Grace is and hath been wanting. What saith the Apostle *James; But if ye have bitter Envying and Strife in your Hearts, glory not, and lie not against the Truth.* You may pretend (as if he should say) you do it out of Zeal, and may glory in it, but if

---

[1] Benjamin Keach, *To all the Baptized Churches and faithful Brethren in England and Wales, Christian Salutations* (London: n.p., 1692).

[2] The quotation is from Matthew Poole, *Annotations upon the Holy Bible* (London: John Richardson, 1683) on 1 Cor. 13:4. It is not an exact quotation.

[3] Cf. Poole on 1 Cor. 13:6 and 7. The quotation is significantly altered, though the sense is the same as in Poole.

you have *bitter Envy* and Strife in your Hearts, *glory not*, and *lie not against the Truth*; glory not of your Zeal, for your glorying is a real and just cause of Shame. *This Wisdom descendeth not from above,* Jam. 3.15. This Wisdom which you pretend so much to, "[who (say our Annotators) criticize on other Mens Actions, and inveigh against them, accompanied with Strife and Envy]"[4] is not from above, but is *earthly, sensual, devilish: for where Envy and Strife is, there is Contention, and every evil Work,* ver. 16.

The Spirit of Christ is compared to the harmless, meek and innocent Dove; 'tis easy to discern who are acted and influenced by that Spirit, and who are not. But *the Wisdom that is from above is first pure, then peaceable, gentle, easy to be intreated, full of Mercy and good Fruits, &c. And the Fruit of Righteousness is sown in Peace of them that make Peace.* If we were acted by this Wisdom, by this Spirit, we should not bite and wound, and reproach one another, because we in some things see not alike, but may differ in our Sentiments. I have, dear Brethren, passed under the hardest Dispensation of late, that ever I met withal since I have been in the World; but I hope I can say my Sorrow or Grief is chiefly because the Name of God hereby suffers, and his People are exposed to Reproach. I desire to live no longer than to promote Peace and Union to my Power in all the Churches of the Saints; though I am represented as one that hath not indeavoured after it, because of my Writing in the Defence of Singing the Praises of God. But I would have you all know and bear me Witness, I am grieved in my very Soul that this Ordinance should be deemed to have such a Tendency, for I for my own part can as freely have Communion with my Brethren who do not own Singing, I mean proper Singing of God's Praises, as with such who are of my Judgment in that matter: every Truth is not an Essential of Communion, some Precepts are appointed for the Being of a visible Church, and others for the more comfortable Being thereof.

Satan be sure has got in his Feet among us, there has been a giving way or place I fear to him, our poor Brethren bewail it, and mourned over us in the late Assembly, and not without Cause: methinks I see how the Tears ran down their Cheeks. Does not the Apostle say, Hatred, Variance, Emulations, Wrath, Strife, Sedition, Heresies, are

---

[4] Cf. Poole on James 3:15.

~ The Narrative of the 1692 General Assembly and Responses ~

the Works of the Flesh? O that we would consider what Spirit we have been led by, or some of us, and repent in Dust and Ashes: Is not the Evil of making Discord among Brethren, one of the six things that God hates, yea that thing which is Abomination to him? *Prov.* 6.

Brethren, You will find in the Narrative of the Proceedings of the late Assembly, a Relation of those sad and grievous Reflections that are contained in some Books lately printed and dispersed amongst the Churches, wrote about the Controversy of Singing the Praises of God.

And that we by joint Agreement referred all Matters of Fact or Reflection to the Hearing and final Determination of seven worthy Brethren, chosen in the said Assembly: The Persons who agreed as aforesaid, were, Brother *Kiffin*, Brother *Steed*, Brother *Man*, Brother *Barret*, Brother *W. Collins*, Brother *Hollowell*, and my self.

Now that which the said seven Brethren took notice of in respect of me, as it is written in that Book, called, *A Sober Reply to Mr.* Robert Steed's *Epistle concerning Singing*; I shall give an impartial Relation of, and according to their Determination make my Acknowledgments as publickly as the Offences were given.

The seven Brethren were these following, *viz.* Brother *Andrew Gifford*, Brother *Samuel Buttal*, Brother *Hen. Austin*, Brother *Edmond White*, Brother *Willis*, Brother *Keat*, Brother *Scot.*

The Matter exhibited against me was chiefly my misrepresenting the first baptized Churches about the Ministers Maintenance. I have in *pag.* 9. of the said Book, wrote thus, *viz.* "We ask you whether or no generally the same baptized Churches did not as unanimously conclude and declare it too, that for a Gospel-Minister to have a yearly Allowance or a competent Maintenance, was not an humane Invention, and Antichristian. We speak in part upon our own Knowledg, and by good Information we have had from others, that both those Gospel-Duties (that is, Singing of Psalms, and the Ministers Maintenance) were equally decried, and we suppose you are not ignorant of it: Nay, and we hear some Churches, or Members of those Churches, are of the same Opinion still."

This the seven Brethren say is a great Wrong to the first baptized Churches, and their Request and Determination hereupon was, that I should acknowledg my Error in Print, or otherwise. Now because I have declared this Mistake and Wrong to the said Churches in Print, I cannot to the Satisfaction of all clear them, unless I print my

Acknowledgment; and I am ready also to acknowledg it otherwise, as indeed I have done particularly to the offended Brethren.

Nor do I think it grievous to me to retract any Fault or Error this way; but contrariwise; since I have seen a Confession of Faith, put forth by several Brethren in Behalf of themselves and seven of the first baptized Churches in *London*, published in the Year 1644, I am glad I have this to say for the clearing of the said baptized Churches in this great Case; though I declare to you I knew nothing of that Confession till I was informed of it by the offended Brethren, which was about a Fortnight before the last Assembly met together, which was not till after their Books were printed and dispersed into the Country, and I told them then, I was willing forthwith to acknowledg my Error in Print; but afterwards, notwithstanding, they published their Books in and about this City.

And, Brethren, such is my Love to the Baptized Churches (if I know my own Heart) and for the Truth of Christ as 'tis professed by them, that I would suffer any thing in my Name or otherwise to promote their Honour and Reputation in the World.

Therefore with hearty Sorrow, according to the Determination of the seven Brethren, I do now acknowledg my Error in this matter (though it was through Ignorance done) yet I ought to have inquired further about that Business before I published any such thing about it. As to what I speak of my own Knowledg, all impartial Men must believe could not refer to those first baptized Churches in London, I being but about four Years old when that Confession of Faith was first printed, and but about eleven (as it appears) when it was the last time reprinted, but of some Churches in the Countrey of a later Date, and since it hath been received by the baptized Churches from their first being planted, viz. that they who preach the Gospel, should live of the Gospel. I hope all the Churches will accordingly to their utmost Abilities discharge their Duties to their Ministers herein, with all Faithfulness, and not expose them to the Cares and Incumbrances of the Affairs or the World, to get their own Bread.

Secondly, our Brethren also were offended with me for some hard Expressions which they alledged against me in the Assembly, as they are written in the said Answer to Mr. *Steed*'s Epistle.

The first Offence is in *pag.* 3. *l.* 15, to 20. in these Words, *viz.* "And it seems as if the Sermon you formerly preached against this

Truth of Christ was *that muddy Fountain* from whence his Lines (*viz.* Mr. *Marlow*) proceeded."

Thirdly, In *pag.* 11. *l.* 6, to 10. in these Words, "Brother, 'tis a hard Case Prejudice against an Ordinance should so blind your Eyes, that with all your Learning you should not know what Singing is, but conclude simple praising of God in Prayer is Singing." These words the seven Brethren call unbrotherly Censures: to which Determination I submit.

4th Offence is in *pag.* 4. *l.* 1, 2, 3. *viz.* "But 'tis like you foresaw some great Advantage by your Essay, in that you find some of your People so hardened and prejudiced against Singing the Praises of God."

5th Offence is in *pag.* 5. *l.* 13 to 16. *viz.* "To suggest that Satan may beguile them by their adhering to this Ordinance of singing Psalms in God's Worship, shews you are of a bitter and very censorious Spirit—."

The seven Brethren say both these are unsavory Expressions on both sides; that it is as well in Mr. *Steed* as in me: to this Determination I yield also.

6th Offence is in *pag.* 11. *l.* 14, 15. in these Words, *viz.* "As Mr. *Gosnold* once told Mr. *Kiffin*."

This the seven Brethren say is a needless Recital of Names.

I say so too, yet am also sorry I mentioned Mr. *Kiffin's* Name at all on that occasion.

7th Offence is in *pag.* 13. two last Lines: "But what do you mention Mr. *Harrison* for as one on your side, may not we cite Reverend Mr. *Tombs*, Mr. *Gosnold*, Mr. *Jesse*? &c."

The seven Brethren say this was a Recital without Injury.

8th Offence is in *pag.* 14. *l.* 31, 32, 33. *viz.* "We shall examine what you lay down in *pag.* 4. of your Epistle, which seems is the Heads of a Sermon you preached against Singing, after Reverend Mr. *Knowlles* had in the Morning preach'd it up as a Gospel-Duty."

This the seven Brethren say, is an unfair Representation; and, if intended to be the Afternoon of the same Day, as appears by Information, false: to which Determination I consent also. Though I said not in the said Book it was the Afternoon of the same Day; yet I was informed (to the best of my Remembrance) it was the Afternoon of the same Day: but it appears it was on another Day, and not on that Day: Therefore I am very sorry I did so write.

The ninth and last Offence is in pag. 42. where are these Words, viz. "Why do you not answer what the Renowned Mr. *Cotton*, Dr. *Roberts*, Mr. *Sidenham*, Mr. *Caryl*, Mr. *Wells*, Mr. *Jesse*, Mr. *Knowlles*, Mr. *Keach*, Dr. *Wright*, Mr. *Whinnel*, and Mr. *Ford* have said."

The seven Brethren call this a Weakness and Over-sight; and if we intend our selves, viz. to call our selves Renowned, savours of Vain-glory.

To this I yield and consent also, *viz.* That it was a great Weakness and Oversight to place *Renowned* upon the Head of Mr. *Cotton*, if the Reader must necessarily conclude all the other Persons mentioned next after are intended in that word Renowned also; but I declare and testify (who ought to be allowed to give the true Sense of our meaning) that we intended it only of Mr. *Cotton* of *New-England*.—And though some others there mentioned were eminent Persons, and might deserve that Epithet as well as he; yet some others there named we could not look upon to be Men that might be called Renowned; and if we should intend our selves, we were not guilty only of Vain-glory, but of the greatest Folly imaginable: But on this Occasion Reverend and Renowned *Cotton* was only meant, who hath wrote so excellently and learnedly on the Duty of Singing Psalms, &c. whose Works we never yet saw answered. These were all the hard Expressions brought against me, which those seven Brethren saw any Ground or Reason to take notice of; and I have answered their Result and Determination, and as publickly acknowledg my Errors as the Offence was given, and may be more fully than they intended. I am heartily sorry any thing like a Reflection should pass from me in Print; but if no worse had fallen from the Pen of my Brethren, I cannot see how the Name of God and the Truth should suffer by it, save only that Mistake concerning the first baptized Churches, about the Ministers Maintenance.—Yet if all knew and did consider what I have from my Youth suffered, as a Testimony for the Truth, (as 'tis professed by us called Baptists) sure none of them could once suppose (if they have the least Charity) I wrote it out of Design to reproach any of the Churches, but looking upon it, had that been true, the Neglect also of Singing of the Praises of God, I mean proper Singing of Psalms, Hymns, &c. was of like Nature, arguing like Imperfection in them, as I conceived.

And since I have been fully cleared by the seven Brethren in the late Assembly of all those hard Words and Reproaches cast upon me by the Brethren in their Writings, (save what is here mentioned) and have been freed and fully acquitted (as 'tis expressed in the printed Narrative) of *gross Forgery, and of things inconsistent with Christian Sobriety and common Honesty*; and they (that is to say, Mr. *Kiffin*, Mr. *Steed*, Mr. *Barret*, and Mr. *Man*) are desired, as the Result and Determination of those seven Brethren, to acknowledg their Faults and Abuse of me in Print, (they agreeing to do and stand by what those Brethren should determine) I hope and expect they will do it; nor have I any just Cause to doubt it of one of them, since he has signified to me in the hearing of one or two Brethren, how much he has been troubled, and that he was willing to contribute towards the Charge of the printing those Books wherein those sad Reproaches are contained, and to call them all in, and to have them obliterated.

Lastly, I desire all who have that Answer to Mr. *Steed*'s Epistle concerning Singing, that they would be pleased to send them to Mr. *Richard Adams*, as 'tis ordered by the late Assembly.

But I would not have any suppose I am changed in my Judgment about singing the Praises of God; nay, but by this late kind of Opposition I am the more confirmed in it, with many others; and in a short time you may see the said Answer with some Additions reprinted, though all those things that have offended shall be wholly left out. The Lord cause Love and Tenderness to be exercised, and deliver all from such Temptations as tend to make Divisions in the Churches upon that Account.

From my House by Horslydown, *June* 27. 1692   *Benjamin Keach.*

Reader, Observe that all the three late Books, written on the Controversy of Singing, &c. are condemned by the Brethren in the Assembly, and ordered not to be sold, nor given away, but are all to be sent in to Brother *Richard Adams*, because of those base Reproaches and unchristian Reflections contained in them.

FINIS.

~ *The Narrative of the 1692 General Assembly and Responses* ~

TO THE

𝔅aptized Churches,

THEIR

Elders, Ministers, and Members.[1]

[William Kiffin, George Barrette, Robert Steed and Edward Man]

The Truth of the Gospel is greatly to be prized, (whether it be concerning the Doctrine or the Institutions of our Lord and Saviour) it is more worth than all the Gold of *Ophir*: And therefore deserves our serious endeavour to obtain it, and our earnest striving to keep it. But while we would appear to be Zealous in pleading for the Truth, we should also follow after Peace with all that contradict the Principles of Religion that we profess, or that would introduce into the Churches a Humane Invention for an Ordinance of Christ. That is, we ought to be careful that we be not provoked by the False Accusations, or undue and causless Reflections of others, in their opposing the Truth that we own, to aggravate any thing more than is meet, lest it stir up Passion more than promote Conviction.

Now for as much as the Seven Brethren to whom in the last general Assembly we submitted to be determined (concerning what we have published in Answer to the Reflections, and the Representation we thereby made of the Actions of those Persons with whom we had to do, in that Controversie about Common set Form Singing) have agreed and declared that we (as well as our Brethren) should in Print, or otherwise, acknowledge that wherein they judge we have exceeded the Bounds of Moderation or Verity in that matter; which we are ready to comply withall as far as we can with a good Conscience. And therefore had made it evident before this time in Print to the view of others, had we not hoped, and in that expectation waited for a private

---

[1] Kiffin, William, George Barrette, Robert Steed and Edward Man. *To the Baptized Churches, THEIR Elders, Ministers, and Members* (London: n.p., (presumably) 1692).

~ The Narrative of the 1692 General Assembly and Responses ~

Friendly Conference with Mr. *Benjamin Keach* (with whom we are principally concern'd in this matter) wherein we might mutually have examined in a Spirit of Love and Meekness, where any weakness or miscarriage had lain on both sides, and in a Christian way made our Acknowledgments to each other. And then to have considered what Course might have been used to prevent any offence that therein might be taken by others; which was several times propounded by one of us to Him, and several others of the Brethren. But instead of accepting thereof, we find a printed Paper published (by *Benjamin Keach* aforesaid,) wherein are more Reflections on us, (with a misrepresentation of our Judgment about Singing in the Church,) than Acknowledgments of his many Mistakes (not at present to give them any other Title) in the said Book.

Moreover, we were many Weeks prevented by a Summons sent us from the Church whereof Mr. *Benjamin Keach* is Elder, delivered to us by two Messengers, with a Letter wherein we were expresly *required* to appear before them, to make good our Reflections against Mr. Keach, Printed in our Reply to his Book.

"In answer to which we by a Letter sent them, readily offered to give them a Meeting with any Four Persons that might be nominated by them, (provided they were none of those that subscribed the Epistle to Mr. *Keach* his Book:) And we would chuse Four more; which might meet with them at a convenient Season agreed on by each Party. And then mutually to examine all the Paragraphs in both Books that contain matter of Fact or Reflection, we then declaring that by the Grace of God we should be ready to acknowledge any weakness or failing that might be made manifest in what we had written; hoping their Elder (Mr. *Benjamin Keach*) would do the like in those things that might be justly Charg'd on Him."

We did not question but they would readily have comply'd with so fair and reasonable a Proposition, whereby our Differences might have been composed, and the Controversie as to the heat of it might have been asswaged, if there should be any occasion to revive it again: But they were silent to us, and returned us no Answer. Therefore not knowing the Reason of that silence; after long waiting we sent again to them the Copy of the Letter aforesaid, with our Names Subscribed to it, and then we had an Answer sent which was Signed by Four

Persons, who call themselves Helps in Government; who therein did not only declare therewith that Churches absolute rejecting of our Proposal aforesaid, but also did therein reflect upon us, (without any provocation given them in that Letter) with that Rancour and Bitterness that is more fit to be lamented over than to be repeated. The Lord forgive them, and grant they may have Wisdom and Grace to shew themselves more like Men and Christians in all such Cases for time to come.

We shall not now Repeat or Answer his renewed Reflections or Misrepresentation, but only give this brief account of our selves as follows.

That it was about Six Months after Mr. *Keach* and Mr. *Whinnel's* Book was Printed, before some of us took any notice of those severe Reflections and false Accusations therein published. Wherein we were unduely and not rightly represented by Mr. *Whinnel* in his Epistle to the Baptized Churches, their Elders, Ministers and Members, though no provocation was given by that Epistle they undertook to answer, there being no reflecting on any of them, or any Answer thereby returned to any of their Books formerly Printed. But that which most of all grieved our Souls, was the exposing (in that Treatise or Book) those that were first in the Truth concerning Believers Baptism to great Reproach and Scandal, contrary to their Publick Declaration in their Confession of Faith so often Printed and Signed by them; and was accordingly practised by them even beyond their Ability; and yet to have it publisht in Print to the contrary as a publick Testimony against them, and the Truth they professed, by such popular Persons as Mr. *Keach* and Mr. *Whinnel*, &c. which was greatly aggravated (as that whereby that bitter, false Calumny might have the greater Credit) by the Subscription of seventeen Names (in the Epistle recommending his Book) of Persons being well known in City and Countrey, who without any exception do upon their declared perusal of that Book recommend it as a Sober piece; we say again without any restriction or limitation. All which was the more grievous, for as much as the Publishers of that great Charge might have had full satisfaction from us to the contrary, would they but have made any Enquiry of us about it; had it not been for this and the Challenge therein made, we might have forborn to return any answer. But the sence of our Duty to God, and the respect we have to the Truth we profess, and to the Memory of those precious Churches wherein so much of the Gracious presence of Christ appeared, did engage us that we could not forbear: And it is our grief that there is not a Remedy yet made use of that is large enough to cover or cure that Malady. For as to what He (that is Mr. *Keach*) hath published to the contrary; we fear that retractation, such as it is, or rather excuse, is not sent abroad so far as the Books are wherein that Accusation is inserted. We are apt to think by the scarcity of them, that there are hardly enough to inform the Churches in this City. Besides, we find he is still publishing and dispersing those Books wherein that false Calumny or Charge is inserted: Some of them with a slight Cross on the Page wherein those Reflections are contained, and some of them with none; though it be directly contrary to the determination of the Seven Brethren; to which He did so solemnly consent and submit in the General Assembly. And how it comports with his Advertisement added in the Postscript of his Printed Paper, whereby He intimates, that his Book aforesaid, (which He hath been since selling or dispersing) by the determination of the Seven Brethren in the Assembly, is not to be sold or given away, but is to be sent in to Brother *Richard Adams*, as well as the rest, we shall leave to others to judge. Finally, it still grieves us to behold that He would fasten that Reproach on some of the Baptized Churches, of which we believe He cannot give one true instance; they having all (who are sound[2] in the Faith and in Communion together) declared the contrary to be their Judgment, (even that the Ministers in the Churches ought to be maintained by the free Contribution of the Members) by their fully owning the Confession of Faith, wherein that Duty is professed and owned.

But as for what we have Charged on Mr. *Keach* in our Book, we are not as yet conscious to our selves that any thing of it is untrue, as to the substance of it; although in our Answer there might be too much severity in Reflecting on Him, which we desire to own.

Therefore as to what the Brethren to whom the Examination and Determination of the Matter was referr'd, have judged concerning those passages they except against in our Book, which they have

---

[2] The original may read "found." The expression "sound in the faith" is a common one.

presented to us; we shall candidly and sincerely own them, as far as we can arrive to any sence of our Miscarriages or Mistake therein; which are as followeth.

First, In our Book, *page* 5. *line* the last, we say, "That it's probable that Mr. *Keach* expects to have the greatest Honour, &c."

We do now say it had been more suitable for us to have said the greatest share in Writing that Book, rather than to have used the word Honour.

Secondly, They except against our Charging Mr. *Keach* with Forgery, and things inconsistent with common Honesty; we shall therefore declare that which occasioeed[3] that Expression concerning Him, and leave it to every one's Censure that shall hear of it, or read it.

That we blame him for, is, putting in the Names of several Persons as Approvers of his Book, who never did subscribe the same. And for satisfaction to all, we shall declare their own words as near as we can.

First, There is the name of *Richard Adams*, who being asked about his Name to the said Book, made this Answer, "That indeed he saw his Name in it, but knew not how it came there."

Secondly, Another Person whose Name is subscribed to the Book is *J. Warner*, who saith, *1st*, "That when the said Book was read to Him, he made Objections against some part of it, as that which they could not prove."

2dly, "That in the Title it's declared to be by several Elders and Members of the Baptized Churches, but He (as he told then) was not under any of those Capacities, being neither Elder nor Member of any."

3dly, "That being urged notwithstanding to Subscribe, He granted that only two Letters of his Name might be Subscribed, but (told them) that by no means he would have any more of his Name written in words at length."

4thly, "He affirms that He never saw the Epistle to which his Name is subscribed: He desiring to see it, Answer was made to Him, *That it was not yet drawn up.*"

5thly, "That He was very much troubled when He saw his Name at large to the Epistle of the said Book, which Epistle (He saith) if He

---

[3] *Sic.*

had seen it, He would by no means have had so much as one Letter of his Name to it."

A Third Person whose Name is subscribed to the Epistle is *Thomas*[4] *Marriot*, who saith, That He told Mr. *Keach* when He importuned Him to have his Name set to it, "That He should not consent to have his Name subscribed to it, because of the Reflections that were in it."

These being Three of the Persons whose Names are set down in the Epistle, and these being their own Affirmations concerning it, as is before rehearsed: What to call such practices we shall not at present determine. We do acknowledge the calling it by the Name of Forgery, &c. might have been forborn; we should have left it to others to give it what Title they please.

As for the other Offence, in that we say in our Book, *page* 6. mentioning Mr. *Keach's* taking Gold out of another Man's Mine, made ready to his Hand, and present it as His to the great prejudice of the Author:

We say the Truth of it is well known to most of the Elders who had the hearing of it. But we do acknowledge it was not so well done of us to revive the fame, seeing the Author was willing to put it up, without any further contest about it.

And as for any other harsh Expressions in our Book, either against Mr. *Keach* or Mr. *Whinnel*, we are sorry for them; and we judge we ought to have been careful with milder words to have returned an Answer, whatever their Provocations or Reflections were; imitating therein that Holy pattern of Meekness and Patience which our Lord Jesus hath set before us.

Lastly, Whereas Mr. *Keach* in the Conclusion of his Printed Paper, doth intimate as if He would Reprint his Book which we have Answered, without Reflections, and with additions to the Argument: We shall only remember Him and others, That He in the last General Assembly of the Messengers, did of his own accord, without any one's perswading Him to it, (that we know of) openly declare and solemnly

---

[4] In the available copy, 'Thomas' has been crossed out and replaced in the margin by 'Richard.' The name is 'Richard' in the book Kiffin *et. al.* criticized. See *A Sober Reply to Mr. Robert Steeds Epistle Concerning Singing* (London: n.p., 1691), unnumbered page 2 of the prefatory epistle.

promise more than once, That he would write or meddle no more about the Argument concerning Singing; which Speech of his (hoping He would be as good as his word) was the very reason that some of us submitted to be determined by the Seven Brethren; reckoning thereby there might be a stop put to that troublesome Contest about that Question; whereby we might with the more Amity, Peace and Love maintain our mutual Converse together as in former Times, in those Holy Doctrines and Blessed Ordinances of our Lord and Saviour, wherein through Grace we do agree. But if notwithstanding He shall persist in his Writing and Printing about that Controversie, we shall seriously Examine it: And if need require, return an Answer to it as the Lord shall enable us. But the Lord grant that he and we may study the things that make for Peace, and wherein we may Edifie one another.

William Kiffin,
George Barrette,
Robert Steed,
Edward Man.

FINIS.

6

The Narrative of the Bristol and London General Assemblies, 1693 and 1694

Introduction

The first Bristol Assembly of 1693 seems to have followed the pattern established by the earlier London meetings, though in much briefer compass. After a day of prayer, reports were heard from the churches and queries discussed and resolved.

The Epistle to the churches expresses thankfulness for blessings received, followed by exhortations to unity and peace. One wonders if undertones of the recent singing controversy continued their deleterious effects on the churches, and the Bristol ministers found it necessary to address them obliquely.

The most interesting element in the report is the lengthy discussion of spiritual gifts and human learning in the choice of ministerial candidates. A *prima facie* reading of this material might lead one to conclude that the Baptists opposed formal training and advocated a more pneumatic approach. Apparently there were some advocating such a view. But this would be a mistaken conclusion if attached to the Assembly churches, for at least three reasons. In the first place, it must be remembered that after the enforcement of the Act of Uniformity in 1662, no dissenters were allowed to matriculate at Cambridge or Oxford. The Established Church controlled the Universities, and some of its leaders taunted the Baptist ministers' lack of education.[1] This embittered many Dissenters. Secondly, during the periods of persecution two decades earlier, the two Bristol Particular Baptist congregations (Pithay and Broadmead), the Congregational church there, and the Presbyterian congregation attempted to hold joint worship services when their ministers were imprisoned or driven away. But this arrangement proved difficult since the Presbyterians hesitated to recognize the credentials of anyone not trained at a University and classically ordained.[2] Once again, the Baptists had cause to suspect the advocacy of human learning. But in the third place, it was the Broadmead Church in Bristol and its elder Edward Terrill who provided the funds necessary for the establishment of the first Baptist training college in England—Bristol Baptist College. The messengers could hardly have opposed formal training while meeting (figuratively speaking) on the doorstep of the young college. Their concern is simply to say that formal education must not be elevated above spiritual gifts when evaluating the qualifications of a ministerial candidate. The London *Narrative* also mentions this matter.

The 1693 London *Narrative* subtext is ominous. The authors complain of reduced interest on the part of churches, acknowledge the divisions present, and express fear that the Fund will fail to produce its wonted fruit. But one very important decision was reached and soon implemented—the adaptaion of the *Westminster Shorter Catechism* for better use in Baptist households. We have included that revised catechism below.

The brief 1694 Bristol letter describes the meeting held there. It includes a letter addressed to William Kiffen and William Collins, lamenting the decline of the London Assembly, and urges the completion of the proposed revised Catechism.

---

[1] The stigma attached to the relative lack of education among Baptist ministers persisted from the 1640s onward. The Presbyterian Thomas Edwards famously referred to some of them as "illiterate mechanick preachers." Thomas Edwards, *The first and Second Part of Gangraena* (London: Ralph Smith, 1646), *sig. B*.

[2] Hayden, ed. *Records of a Church of Christ in Bristol*, 149. The records were originally penned by Edward Terrill.

~ *...Bristol and London General Assemblies, 1693 and 1694 (Intro.)* ~

The Narratives

of the

General Assemblies

held in

Bristol

and

London

In

1693

A narrative of the proceedings of the Elders, Messengers, and Ministering Brethren of divers baptized churches in England and Wales, holding the doctrines of particular election and final perseverance, in their general assembly at Bristol on the 19th of the second month, called April, 1693, and continued to the 21st of the same. Also, containing the proceedings of the general assembly held in London the sixth day of the fourth month, called June, and continued till the 12th of the same. [1]

The elders and messengers of the several churches of Christ met together at Bristol, from the 19th of the second month to the 22nd of the same, to the respective churches of the same association.

Dearly beloved and longed after in the Lord,

The Comfortable account we have given and received from most of the churches, their increase and peace among themselves; as also the comfortable union and sweet and amicable communion we have had together in this present assembly, give great cause of rejoicing in the Lord: and we desire that you also may be made partakers of the same joy. But we are greatly grieved that upon any pretence whatever, any one of the churches of Jesus Christ, should withhold its help in the work of the Lord, in such a working day and dispensation, wherein our Lord hath given us an opportunity to promote his interest. Were our hearts enlarged, fitted for his service, and suitable to our opportunity, how glorious and inviting might the house of the Lord be in our Day! But oh! we mourn that we can do no more, and that there should be any found among ourselves to weaken our hands. The security, jealousies, divisions, and worldliness of some in pursuing their own things, and building their own houses, say the time is not come, the time that the Lord's house should be built, as they did Hag. 1.2. Yet certainly it is a time, if not the time, for building: And as we doubt not

---

[1] This material is taken from Joseph Ivimey, *A History of the English Baptists*, 1:524-33.

~ The Bristol Narrative, 1693 ~

but God will take pleasure and delight in them that bring the least stick from the mountain to the building of his house, ver. 8. in like manner (to bear with our plainness) we fear a blast from the Lord will be upon those that bring not their offering to the house of the Lord, ver. 6,9,10,11. And therefore as fellow-servants and labourers in the Lord's vineyard, we humbly exhort you with the same prophet in the 5th verse, to consider your ways. We think there is great need of awakening and stirring up our own spirits as well as yours. God's judgments are abroad, though his salvation is at home; peace in the gates of Sion, and peace within our borders. The Lord grant that through a cold, lukewarm, careless, divided, uncharitable, indifferent frame of spirit, we may not provoke him to take away peace, and the gospel of peace from our nation, and cause us to feel those judgments which we do not fear (that have fallen terribly upon other parts) because of the house of the Lord that lies waste. If God doth enlarge your hearts to give to the fund, declare your use, and send by your next messenger, and it shall be disposed accordingly. Herewith we have sent you our breviates. Your messengers can give you a further account of our proceedings. The God of all grace give peace, rule amongst you, dwell with you, and richly supply all your wants. This is the earnest desire of

Your brethren waiting for the consolation of Israel.
Signed by us in the name of the whole.

WILLIAM GOUGH,	RICHARD ADAMS,
GEORGE FOWNES,	BENJAMIN DENNIS,[2]
WILLIAM TANNER,	DANIEL GUILLIM,
GEORGE JOHN,	EDWARD MORTIMER,
JAMES JAMES,	WILLIAM HANKINS,
EDWARD ELLIOTT,	THOMAS WHINNELL,
JOHN SINGER,	THOMAS WARBURTON,
ANDREW GIFFORD,	JOHN FORD,
SAMUEL BUTTALL,	JAMES MURCH.

---

[2] Richard Adams (of the Devonshire Square Church) and Benjamin Dennis (of the Petty France Church) were apparently the representatives sent from London to the Bristol assembly.

~ The Bristol Narrative, 1693 ~

The Breviate of the proceedings of the Elders and Messengers of several churches met together at Bristol the 19th of the second month, 1693, and continued to the 22nd of the same.

The first day was improved in solemnly seeking the face of God in prayer, for counsel, advice, and guidance in our whole work.

The second day—After seeking the Lord, the letters from the several churches were read, and a particular relation of the state of all the churches was given in by their several messengers. Some questions were proposed, and the meeting was dismissed with the blessing of God.

Q. Whether a gifted brother may administer in all ordinances?[3]

A. That no private brother (however gifted) if not solemnly called to ministerial office, and separated thereto, ought to administer the ordinances of baptism and the Lord's supper.

Q. Whether a brother called to the office of elder by the suffrage of the church, may not administer all ordinances, though he be not immediately ordained by the laying on of the hands of the elders?

A. In the affirmative.

Whereas we have heard of some persons, who being vainly puffed up by their fleshly minds, do presume to preach publicly without being solemnly called and appointed by the church thereto, and some administer all ordinances,

We advise and desire, that every particular church would do what in them lies to discountenance this practice, and to prevent all such from exercising their pretended gift, it being contrary to Rom. x. 15. And also that they would not send forth any person among themselves, to preach publicly, of whose qualifications they have not had sufficient trial, and whom they have not called thereto; that the name of God may not be dishonoured, the peace of the churches disturbed, nor the reputation of the ministry blemished.[4]

That we may remove all jealousies, and give satisfaction to all our brethren, that there is no intention or design in this assembly, in

---

[3] A *gifted brother* was a man who had been formally tried, recognized, called and approved by a church for the purpose of exercising a public preaching or teaching ministry, but who was not an elder in any of the churches. Cf. 2LCF 26.11.

[4] This reflects the teaching of 2LCF 26.11, see below. For a full discussion of the matter of Gifted Brethren, see Renihan, *Edification and Beauty*, 107ff.

~ *The Bristol Narrative, 1693* ~

relation to the education of youth, to promote human learning or acquired parts above, or to make them equal with the gifts of the Spirit, and the teachings thereof in and by his word, we do unanimously declare:—

1. That we abhor such a principle and practice, being satisfied and assured, that the gift for edification is a distinct thing from acquired parts; and that men may attain the greatest degrees in human learning, and yet notwithstanding be ignorant of Christ, and his glorious gospel.

2. That God does sometimes bestow greater gifts, for the edification of his church, on some who have not attained the knowledge of tongues,[5] than he doth on some others who have; and that the churches of Jesus Christ should improve what gifts they have, and pray for more.

3. That it is a great snare and very dangerous for any persons to think they can comprehend the great mysteries of the gospel, called *the hidden wisdom of God*, 1 Cor. 2,7,8. which he reveals unto by his Spirit, ver. 10. with their human learning, or worldly wisdom. 1 Cor. i. 19, 20,21.

4. That they greatly abuse their knowledge of the tongues who are puffed up thereby to lean upon it, and to despise their brethren, who have the gift for edification, though they have not the same acquired abilities.

5. That the knowledge of the tongues is not itself essential, or absolutely necessary to constitute a minister of the gospel; nor the greatest degree thereof, without the gift for edification, a sufficient qualification for the ministry; neither,

6. Dare we to limit the Holy One, who bestows the gift for edification upon the learned, as well as the unlearned, and who chooseth some of the wise, prudent, learned, though not many, 1 Cor. i. 26. And that when the knowledge of the tongues and the gifts of the Spirit meet together, and the knowledge of the tongues is made use of in subserviency to the gifts of the Spirit, they ought so much the more be esteemed as they are made useful, being beneficial for the conviction of gainsayers, by supplying apt words to convey the truths

---

[5] I.e., Greek, Hebrew and Latin.

~ The Bristol Narrative, 1693 ~

of the gospel into the understanding of their hearers. Yet when learned Paul plants, and eloquent Apollos waters, it is God only who can give the increase, 1 Cor. iii.6. It is not the gifts of either the learned or the unlearned, but the blessing of God upon the gift of both, that makes successful; that no flesh should glory in his presence, but that he that glorieth may glory in the Lord.

Concluded, that brother Gifford, and brother Fownes, be appointed messengers from this assembly to the general assembly meeting at London upon the time called Whitsuntide.

That the time called Easter next, be the time for this assembly to meet at Bristol: and that the third day of that week be appointed as a day of prayer, and that one of our London brethren do preach at the close of it.

~ *The Bristol Narrative, 1693* ~

A Narrative of the General Assembly holden in London the sixth day of the fourth Month, called June, and continued until the twelfth day of the same, 1693.

The General Epistle to the Churches.

Dearly beloved in our Lord Jesus,

THE great God who hath given us a being in this world, and through our blessed Lord Jesus delivered us when fallen into a miserable state by sin calls for all both of nature and grace to be employed for his glory; and our continual study should be, how we should give up both soul and body a living sacrifice to him: his service is both our duty and reward, the highest honour and happiness of our nature both here and to eternity. It exceedingly becomes us who are the redeemed of the Lord to say so, and to render the glory of it to him, both in purity of doctrine concerning the grace of redemption, and in holiness of life.

The former your confession of faith has published to the world, which will be a standing monument to your honour in ages to come, as in this age it hath much taken away your reproach amongst all sorts of Protestants. That which remains is a life thoroughly suited to your doctrine, and in this you and we have need to be continually put in mind, that our conversation be as becomes the gospel. Satan endeavours, if he cannot corrupt our heads with false doctrine, to defile our conversation either with a worldly and sensual frame, or to fill us with a spirit of contention and bitterness among ourselves; or towards other saints that differ from us. The holy apostle hath counselled us against his toils, and warned us to look to ourselves, lest any root of bitterness spring up in us. Brethren, ye carry about the relics of the old man, a body of sin and death, against which as against the evil angels you must maintain a continual war. We have reason, we humbly think, thus to caution you, because we fear, nay too much experience, that this day of liberty, though it hath eased us of the yoke of persecution, hath set the devil upon other methods, and given a lure to our corruptions through our want of watchfulness, which too evidently appears in the decay of piety and charity among us, and a general minding of our own things, not the things of Christ; together with fears and jealousies one of another on account of our assembling these two or three years last past together, and the methods that have been taken for the promotion of the truths of God professed by us, and the assisting of the churches of God with our humble advice and counsel, things so excellent in their own nature: and although in our acting in the first assembly security was given, whereby the power of the churches was fully preserved, yet a great declining appears, both with respect to your sending messengers to this assembly, and to that which met at Bristol, and also with respect to that which was one end of it, the fund for the maintenance of necessitous ministers and brethren gifted to preach the gospel, and also for the educating of young men of inviting gifts for the ministry in learning; a thing of that use and advantage, that time will fully shew the benefit of it, and confirm the arguments that have been used for it. Against this a mighty wind hath been raised, both in this city and all the churches of our way in the nation, as if from hence would follow a neglect of gifts already in the churches, where there is not the advantage of learning: and although this objection was obviated in the beginning, yet in what follows in this narrative you will see it again removed, if possible, out of the way.[1]

Dear Brethren, we must say, if this day of liberty be lost with trifling and quarelling amongst ourselves, or from a covetous spirit in us this work of the Lord be hindered, the account will be dreadful, and the next generation may reflect back with grief upon us, that we did not what we could for the service of God and of truth in our generation.

We have cause to bless God that we are on the side of truth; but if we do not labour to clothe and nourish it by the blessings God hath given us, it may suffer exceedingly. There are human ways and means wherein we may be serviceable to truth, and God will require is at our hands if we fail in the performance of them. David blessed God that he and his people had a heart to offer willingly to the service of the temple.

Many worthy ministers have been assisted hitherto by the Fund, and some young men brought up who are likely to be exceedingly

---

[1] Based on this statement, one wonders if Ivimey abbreviated the *Narrative* in his book.

useful in their generation, and may in a few years standing shew that the methods designed were not only religious, but very prudent.

Brethren, let not this work die in your hands; send cheerfully your messengers the next year either to Bristol or London, and there at least they will behold the good fruit of their fund: and if God please, we purpose here to follow their steps, hoping you will countenance and encourage what you can.

JOHN TOMKINS,	JOHN WARD,
RICHARD ADAMS,	WILLIAM KIFFIN,
ANDREW GIFFORD,	JOSEPH HARDING,
LEONARD HARRISON,	BENJAMIN GUNDIN,
BENJAMIN DENNIS,	GEORGE RICHARDSON,
GEORGE FOWNES,	JOHN SCOT.

The elders and messengers met at London the 6th day of the month called June, and continued to the 12th of the same.

The first day was spent in prayer to God for counsel and direction in matters that should lie before them, and for a blessing on the churches.

The second day was spent in reading the letters, and making an account of the state of the churches from their messengers, to whom, in answer to divers questions which they propounded, the advice and resolution of the elders and messengers were given. And with respect to the orderly management of matters, it was resolved:

1st. That every one have his liberty to speak without interruption.

2nd. That if any be of a different opinion from what is proposed, he may have liberty to speak his opinion, and argue with Christian charity.

The proceedings of the assembly at Bristol were read by their messengers, and assented to.

3d. Concluded, that the fund be continued and upheld, according to a former agreement Anno. Dom. 1691, and that the money given for the poor ministers of Christ shall be continued, and the money given for educating of young men of inviting gifts for the ministry in the knowledge of the tongues be appropriated to them.

~ *The London Narrative, 1693* ~

4th. That a Catechism be drawn up, containing the substance of the Christian religion, for the instruction of children and servants, and that brother William Collins be desired to draw it up.

5th. That the confession of faith of the baptized churches, of the last impression, be translated into Latin with all convenient speed.[2]

6th. That the next meeting of elders and messengers be at London, beginning at the time called Whitsuntide, the 2nd day of the week, and that the next day be kept in prayer.

---

[2] If this was done, there is no extant evidence that it was actually printed.

~ *The London Narrative, 1693* ~

Joseph Ivimey's report of the 1694 Bristol Assembly, including a Letter sent from the Bristol Assembly which met on the 16th day of the second month 1694 to the Brethren in London.[1]

"The next year the Bristol assembly met according to appointment. We have before us an account of their proceedings in manuscript; but we presume it was never printed. It is as follows:

'The messengers of the several churches hereafter named, viz. of the churches of Sudbury, Plymouth, Looe, Southwick, Calne, Haycombe, Westbury, Melksham, Bridgewater, Taunton, Bristol, Bradford, Lanow, and in the counties of Carmarthen, Cardigan, Pembroke, Brecknock, Monmouth, and Glamorgan, met together at Bristol the 16th of the second month, 1694.

The first day was spent in solemnly seeking the face of God for Wisdom, counsel, and direction, and concluded with a sermon suitable to the occasion.

On the 2nd day, (being the 11th[2] of the 2nd month, 1694,) after seeking the Lord, the letters from the several churches were read, and an account was taken from the messengers of the state of the churches, and several cases were considered, and questions answered, &c.'[3] These proceedings, with a letter to the churches, were sent to London, addressed as follows:

To our Honoured and beloved Brethren William Kiffin, and William Collins, to be communicated to the assembly of messengers held in London at the time called Whitsuntide.

BELOVED,

THE assembly held in Bristol at the time called Easter desired us to acquaint you, that they were grieved because you, who some years ago did zealously promote such associations for the general good of the churches and the glory of Christ, have declined it. They willingly joined with you, and would still, were you willing. You know how often the country sent to London, whilst you have sent but once to the country, and are weary. Nevertheless to shew their desire of

---

[1] All of the following has been taken from Ivimey, *HEB*, 1:534-36.

[2] Is this a printer's error for the 17th?

[3] Perhaps the quotation ends here and the next sentence is Ivimey's? The punctuation in the original is unclear.

communion with you, they ordered us to send you a copy of their epistle, and of the account of the meeting, both which they sent to the churches that sent them. Moreover they desire you will remember your agreement at your last assembling, and minuted in the narrative that brother Collins should draw up a catechism, and that it should be printed, a thing so needful and useful that the country have been longing to have it, and are troubled at the delay of it, and earnestly desire that you will hasten the printing of it. They suppose that the greatness of the number that will be sold will pay the cost. There had need be thousands of them printed, pray let it be done, and sent abroad to the churches. They think you cannot do any thing that will be of more general use.

With the tender of our hearty respects to you, and our earnest desires for the revival of that good work which has been began by you, we remain,

Your unworthy brethren, &c.'

From this it appears that the zeal of the London churches had greatly declined: It is with pleasure we copy the following extract, because it is honourable to the churches in the West. "We greatly rejoice to find the several churches to which we stand related, manifesting so much hearty and cordial love and good will to our associations, and that our last narrative from this assembly hath been so useful in removing the jealousies and misapprehensions that divers persons, and some churches, had concerning our designs in bringing up several young men, who were gifted brethren, to the knowledge of the tongues in which the holy scriptures were written; a work for God in our generation, which we hope not only the churches in this day will have cause to bless God for, but also the generations to come.

This letter was signed by

RICHARD GAY,	EDWARD ELLIOTT,
WILLIAM GOUGH,	ROBERT MORGAN,
THOMAS WHINNELL,	GEORGE JOHN,

~ *A Report of the Bristol Assembly, 1694* ~

JOSEPH HOLTON,   SAMUEL BUTTALL,
JOHN BELTON,   ROBERT BODENHAN,
ANDREW GIFFORD,   JEREMIAH REED,
SAMUEL HEMMEN,   JOSHUA JAMES, &c.
GEORGE FOWNES,

The next meeting to be at Bristol, and to begin on Tuesday in the week called Easter 1695.

7

The Gospel Minister's
Maintenance Vindicated

Introduction

For some, the *Gospel Minister's Maintenance Vindicated* will be the
most interesting document in this book, since it has not been reprinted
before. It is a brief anonymous work (attributed to Benjamin Keach)
urging churches to the duty of financially supporting their pastors. A.
J. Klaiber speaks of it as "an old book handling one of our practical
religious problems for us in an altogether admirable way" for it "deals
with a perpetually recurring question with such sanity of judgment,
breadth of outlook, and intelligent conviction"[1] that it is still of great
practical usefulness.

Published in 1689, this book length treatment of the obligation and
duty of churches to provide adequate financial support for its ministers
serves as something of the theological basis for the establishment of
the Particular Baptist Fund. It is no surprise that it saw the light of day
just as the London pastors were contemplating calling for a General
Assembly.

In a fascinating note prefixed to the body of the book, these
ministers felt it necessary once again to distance themselves from the
term 'Anabaptist.' In this case, it had been used in the *Thirty-Nine
Articles* of the Church of England referring to the communalism
sometimes practiced among earlier Continental Anabaptists. The

---

[1] A. J. Klaiber, "The Gospel Minister's Maintenance Vindicated" in *The Baptist
Quarterly* 2.5 (January 1925): 224-31.

English Particular Baptists did not emerge from these groups, and consistently sought to disabuse any notion of connection.

This is followed by a brief assertion of a "regular ministry," i.e., a ministry ordained, recognized and supported by the churches. Apparently some argued that proper order called for something of a lay-ministry, and it was necessary to refute this idea. The bulk of the work then seeks to lay out the scriptural and theological principles for ministerial support, and applications to press the duty home to the consciences of believers. The book concludes with a presentation of the importance of the duties of pastors.[2]

---

[2] The document contains much unusual orthography. Some have been noted by "*Sic.*" But there are too many occurrences to do this constantly.

~ The Gospel Minister's Maintenance Vindicated (Introduction) ~

THE

Gospel Minister's

𝕸𝖆𝖎𝖓𝖙𝖊𝖓𝖆𝖓𝖈𝖊

VINDICATED.

Wherein,

A Regular Ministry in the Churches, is first Asserted, and the Objections against a Gospel Maintenance for Ministers, Answered.

ALSO,

The Dignity, Necessity, Difficulty, Use and Excellency of the Ministry of Christ is opened.

LIKEWISE,

The Nature and Weightiness of that Sacred Work and Office clearly evinc'd.

Recommended to the Baptized Congregations by several Elders in and about the City of London.

1 Cor. 9.14. *Even so hath the Lord Ordained that they who Preach the Gospel shall live of the Gospel.*
2 Cor. 2:16. *And who is sufficient for these things.*

London. *Printed and are to be sold by John Harris, 1689.*

To[1] the Congregations of Baptized Believers in *England* and *Wales*, Grace, Mercy and Peace be multiplied through the saving Knowledge of our Lord Jesus Christ,

Beloved Brethren,

We *have* read *and* considered *of* this ensuing Treatise *and do conclude it may be of great profit to the Churches of Jesus Christ; we fearing some* Congregations *have not duly* weighed *and* considered, *of their indispensible Duty to the Ministry; in respect of providing such a* Maintenance, *for those who Labour amongst them, and are over them in the Lord, as they ought to do, by which means (it may be feared that) many of them may be hindered or obstructed in attending on their Work, in serving of Christ and his People, as the Nature of their* sacred Imployment *and* Office *requires, and the* present Day especially calls for, *and as* the Lord himself hath also Ordained: *Therefore, our earnest Desires are, that our Brethren, both* Ministers *and* Members, *would be pleased to get this little Book, and both Read and well Weigh what is said therein, without Prejudice,* both *in Respect of a* Regular Ministry, *the* Ministers Maintenance, *and the* Greatness and Difficulty *of* their Work; *and now, that it may be blessed by JEHOVAH, to the Great and Good Ends it is designed, is and shall be, the Hearty Prayers of us, your Brethren, in the Faith and Fellowship of the Gospel of our Lord Jesus Christ.*

Hanserd Knollys,
William Kiffin,
William Collins,
John Harris,
George Barret,

---

[1] The *Errata* page precedes this page in the original. The corrections noted on that page have been made in the present text. Minor corrections not included in the original *Errata*, such as placing "and" for the printer's error "aud," have not been noted.

Richard Adams,
Benjamin Keach,
Isaac Lamb,
Edward Man,
Leonard Harrison,
Hercules Collins.

London, July, 30, 1681.[2]

---

[2] This date is apparently a printer's error, and should be 1689. The "present liberty" mentioned in the summary and contents of the work points to a date after the accession of William and Mary to the English Throne.

~ The Gospel Minister's Maintenance Vindicated ~

The Contents of the chief Things insisted on in the ensuing Treatise.

A Regular Ministry Asserted. Pag.[3]

Christ himself in his own Person first settled the Ministry in a most solemn manner.

Power left to particular congregations to choose their own Ministers

Churches ought to take care that they choose Men to Office, that are competently qualified, according to 1 Tim. 3.1,2,3. *And* Tit. 1.6.9.

Churches after Election and Tryal of their Ministers ought solemnly to ordain them by Prayer and Imposition of Hands.

Churches undue Proceedings in the choice of Elders, dishonorable; and an hinderance to the Gospel.

Every Congregation that neglects their Duty in providing a fit Maintenance for their Pastors, is able, is dishonourable, and a scandal to Religion.

Ministers Maintenance Asserted, strange that any should doubt of it.

The Scriptures urged, to prove an indispensible Duty, to provide a comfortable Livelyhood for Faithful Ministers.

13 Arguments to prove this Duty.

1. *Christ would not have his Disciples when he first sent them out, waste their own Substance, whilst imployed in his Work.*

2. *God has positively ordained, or appointed his Ministers a comfortable Maintenance under the Gospel.*

  Ministers Maintenance not now by Tithes, as it was under the Law.

  No Denying or avoiding the Duty of Ministers Maintenance.

3. *Ministers commanded to attend wholly on their Work.*

  Nothing but real Necessity, will admit him to dispence with the contrary, all his time little enough.

  Pastors must visit their Members, go from House to House.

4. *Ministers that follow Trades, &c. exposes them to Reproach, therefore if possible to be avoided.*

5. *Ministers Maintenance, proved by the Law and Light of Nature, as well as by the positive Law of Christ.*

---

[3] In the original, each of these topics was followed by a pagination notation.

~ The Gospel Minister's Maintenance Vindicated ~

6. *Ministers not unable to follow Trades, some could do it, and provide for themselves, and get Estates as well as others; therefore ought not to suffer for taking that sacred work upon them.*

Ministers are as much bound to provide for their Families as other Men.

7. *Shewing what great Provision God made for his Ministers under the Law, proving the Equitableness of the same Law remains still.*

As great Reason for the People to provide for their Ministers under the Gospel; nay, greater in some Respects, than for them under the Law.

8. *Elders or Pastors must be given to Hospitality; therefore, if Churches are able, and they poor, they ought to put them into a capacity to shine in that Virtue.*

9. *This duty urged from the Honourableness of it, it frees Members from the sensure of Covetousness; one part of that double Honour due to Elders that Labour in the Word, proved to be Maintenance.*

10. *Argued for, from the said Effects and Inconveniences that attends the neglect of it.*

    It lays a Discouragement in the way of good Men, to give themselves to Study and Dedicate themselves to take part in the Ministry.

This neglect hinders Ministers in their Study, they having not time, and so preach no better, its necessary for Ministers to have store of Useful Books, and Time also.

11. *Neglect to Ministers and the concern of God's House, is a robbing of God, and may bring a blast upon Men's Estates.*

12. *A shame to God's People, to suffer the Heathens and Papists to do more to uphold Idolatry, than they do to uphold the true Worship of the Living God.*

13. *Ministers will be left wholly without excuse, if they do not faithfully fulfil their Ministry, when the Congregations sufficiently provide for them*

One Minister took off of Worldly Business, may do more in promulgating the Gospel, than several others who are not.

Motives to Press this duty.

Motive 1. *Ministers represent Christ, what done to them is done to him.*

Motive 2. *Ministers being intrusted with our Souls, we ought to take care they want nothing that is necessary for their Bodies.*

Motive 3. *Ministers being exposed to many Temptations and Discouragements, a great Motive why not to be left to serve in wants and necessities.*

Motive 4. *Ministers may forbear working if they will, provided the Church can provide for them, and they faithfully discharge their Duty.*

Quest. *May a Pastor make Terms with a Church about his Maintenance, before he take charge of them? A*nswered.

Quest. *What shall that Church do that is not able to provide for her Pastor?* Answered.

Quest. *Have not you disclaimed against such who Preach for Hire? A Threefold* Answer *given.*

Obj. *Is there any Reason that Rich Men that are Pastors should have an Allowance?* Answered.

Obj. *Our Church is Small, our Pastor cannot take up all his Time in Spiritual Service.* Answered.

The Reason why some Churches are small may be, because Ministers are no more Labourious in Preaching the Gospel up and down in the adjacent places where they Live, which some can't do because not in capacity. The present Liberty to be improved. Idle and Slothful Ministers not to be maintained.

Two Reasons of some Pastors Remisness in Preaching, or Labouring no more.

Ministers may Work with their Hands, and ought so to do when it will tend to the furtherance of the Gospel.

A great Harvest now, and good Weather therefore, Ministers ought to Labour hard.

Freely you have received, freely give. Answered.

Ministers not to Preach for Hire, i.e. *to propound that as their end.*

The Congregations ought to give the Ministers their Portion, with Respect and Honour.

*Ministers Work now as great and weighty as those was under the Law,
like Necessity of their Work, 'tis as Honourable, neglect as
dangerous as then: People now as great Benefit by the Ministry, or
more; from Hence, the same Reason for their Maintenance as
under the Law.*

*May he that Exercises his Gift but now and then, expect an Allowance
from the Church.* Answered.

The Weightiness of the Ministers Work opened.

*Their Work is Honourable, they are in a high Sphere, intrusted with
the big best concerns in the World.*

They Workers with Christ.

May be in danger of losing the Souls of Men.

They must have a Regular Call.

Ministers intrusted with the Charge of the Church.

Their Work difficult in 5 Respects.

Advertisement.

Reader,

Whereas, in the 38th *Article of Religion* (called *The Thirty Nine Articles* of the Church of *England*;) 'tis said, *The Riches and Goods of Christians are not common, as touching the Right, Title, and Possession of the same, as certain* Anabaptists *do falsly boast.*[4] We look upon ourselves to declare, (that if there were in the last Age, in *Germany*, or elsewhere, any People bearing that Name, who Asserted any such thing;) we know none called *Anabaptists* in *England,* nor anywhere else, who hold that absurd or rotten Principle; but do *testifie* our *dislike* and *abhorrence of it*, and verily believe, as 'tis intimated in the said *Article, That the Goods, Riches, and Possessions of all Christians, as touching the right and title of the same are their own,* as the Holy Scripture witnesses, *Acts* 5.4. Yet notwithstanding we also believe and teach, that *every man ought of such things as he possesseth liberally to give Alms to the poor according to his Ability,* as is also there asserted. Having this opportunity, we thought it not amiss to publish this to clear our selves and our Brethren, from the scandal, which possibly some may cast upon them since these Articles (by reason of a late Act of this present *Parliament*) are more generally known and examined by many People.

---

[4] The full text: Article XXXVIII. Of Christian Men's Goods, which are not common. The Riches and Goods of Christians are not common, as touching the right, title, and possession of the same; as certain Anabaptists do falsely boast. Notwithstanding, every man ought, of such things as he possesseth, liberally to give alms to the poor, according to his ability. See Thomas Rogers, *An Exposition of the Thirty-Nine Articles*, edited for the Parker Society by J. J. S. Perowne (Cambridge: University Press, 1854, first published in 1586), 352.

A Regular Ministry in the Church Asserted.

GOD in his Infinite Goodness having by his present Providences, not only given us respite from our former Sufferings, but we trust begun that great and glorious work of the Churches Deliverance, so long the hope and expectation of all that truly love and fear the Lord; we cannot but look upon our Selves concerned to endeavour to make a due improvement of that Mercy and Goodness that is attending us herein; and taking into consideration the Condition of the Church of Jesus Christ, we cannot but be concerned with, and afflicted for the late present wants She lies under in respect to the Ministry, God having of late Years removed so many able and pious Men, and seems to be near the removing many more by Age and Bodily Infirmities. This with other things put us upon the Consideration how much the honour of Christ, the reputation of his Glorious Gospel in the World; as likewise, the Good and Well-being of the Churches[5] depends upon a regular and orderly Ministry, and the Continuation thereof; And so the Churches[6] to be under a supine neglect herein is very sad.

First, *Either in not endeavouring after and calling forth such a regular and stated Ministry, according to Gospel Institution at all; or,*

Secondly, *To be so weak and inadvertent as to call forth such as are not so duly furnished and qualified for it; or,*

Thirdly, *Suffering such as are called forth to the great Work under competent abilities, to lye under unsupportable Burthens, must needs be greatly blameable before our Lord Jesus Christ, the great Bishop and Shepherd of our Souls, as well as highly negligent of their own Edification and Well-being.*

1. To proceed, it cannot be denied but Christ hath, and ought to have, a stated and regular Ministry in the Churches,[7] according to his own Institution: Who himself, when he entered upon his Ministry, here on Earth, did call forth Apostles and Disciples to bear that part of the

---

[5] *Errata*: original reads "Church."
[6] *Errata*: original reads "Church."
[7] *Errata*: original reads "Church."

Work with him, which he called them to, and fitted them for: See *Mark,* 3.13. to the 19. *Christ went up into a Mountain, and called to him whom he would, and they came to him, and he ordained Twelve that they should be with Him, and that he might send them forth to Preach; to whom He gave the Name of Apostles,* Mat. 10.2. Luke 6.13. Which he did with great Solemnity and Invocation to the Father (for *he continued all Night in Prayer to God*) *and when it was Day he chose the Twelve and Named them Apostles.* After which he appointed other Seventy, *and sent them forth by Two, and Two, before His Face, to every City and Place* &c. which were labourers with Him in the Harvest, V.2. And He commanded them to give themselves up to the Work he had called them to, and not take Care what they should Eat or Drink, *For the Labourer* (saith he) *is worthy of his hire.* Ver. to 14. Here our Lord Jesus Christ Himself did institute and lay the Foundation of the Gospel Ministry in His own Authority; and accordingly takes care for the continuance of it after His Death and Resurrection, and actual Investiture in our Nature of all Power in Heaven and Earth, *Matt.* 28.18.19.20. *And Jesus came and spake unto them, saying, All Power is given unto me in Heaven and in Earth. Go ye therefore Teach all Nations,* &c. *And lo I am with you always, even to the End of the World.* Amen. Also after His Blessed and Glorious Ascension,[8] and S*itting on the Throne of the Majesty in the Heavens.* Heb. 8.1. *Angels, and Authorities, and Powers being made subject unto him.* 1 Pet. 3. & 22.[9] Did by His Apostles give Commandment and Direction for the continuance hereof to the end of the World, and his Second *Coming without Sin unto Salvation.* Heb. 9.28. As *Acts* 14.21,22,23. After they had by their Ministry been blest with the Conversion of many Souls, they took care to direct them into the Duty of Church Communion; and by their Suffrages, *Ordained them Elders in every Church.* So the Apostle gives this as the Reason, Why he *left* Titus *in* Creete; (he not having opportunity after preaching the Gospel to them) to put things into due Order. *Tit.* 1.5. *That he should set in order the things that were wanting* (or left undone by the Apostle) *and Ordaine Elders in every City*: that is the[10] Church in every City, as

---

[8] *Sic.*

[9] *Sic.*

[10] *Errata*: original omits "the."

before, *Acts* 14 who are called *Elders, Bishops, or Pastors,* and *Teachers*; Names significative of the Authority, Office and Work.

2. Christ being now in Heaven, and an extraordinary Call being ceased, the Scriptures being a perfect and standing Rule to the Church through all Ages, he has committed this Care to her self, according to the Power given to her, who, is *the Pillar and Ground of Truth*, to provide Ministers, for her own Edification, in Obedience to his Command and Rules given in his word, as he shall see good to Bless her with Spiritual Gifts and Abilities, in order to the fitting them for this Work; the Father also has Covenanted to give his Spirit in the Gifts and Graces of it, and promised that the Words *he has put into Christ's Mouth, and the Spirit that is upon him, shall never depart from him, nor his see, for ever:* Likewise has according to the Circumstances of time the Church hath been under, blest her as with his Grace so with all needful Spiritual Gifts. *Eph.* 4.7.11. *For the perfecting the saints for the Work of the Ministry, for the Edifying the Body of Christ.* So that whilst there is a Church Millitant, Saints on this side Perfection, any of the Members of Christ Mystical Body on Earth, those Spiritual Gifts needful to their present State, shall be given, and be amongst them, for the Support of the great Ordinance of the Ministry, and for the good of the Church.

3. And as its the Duty of the Churches[11] to Seek these Spiritual Abilities, and to improve them when they are given to these great and Holy Ends; so they[12] must walk regularly herein, in obedience to the Rules given by Christ in this Case; who hath laid down the qualifications both Negative and Positive, of all such as ought to be called to this great work and Trust of Ministring by Office 1 *Tim.* 3.1. to 9. *Tit* 1.6.9. we have no warrant to put any into the Ministry otherwise, save such as are here discribed, and competently fitted for it: For as it was a sin of Old in the Church to put any into the Ministry, but those whom God appointed by the Rules given to them so it can be no less Evil for the Church now, to call forth into Office, but such who are qualified as God's Word directs; and now, as Christ hath made this grant of Power to the Churches[13] of choosing their[14] own Officers for

---

[11] *Errata*: original reads "the Churches duty."

[12] *Errata*: original reads "she."

[13] *Errata*: original reads "Church."

their[15] Edification; so he hath left Rules for her,[16] who, and how to chose, as we said before: So likewise he has laid down those special Duties of the Officers in the Church, who are to take the oversight, Feed, Govern, Go in and out before them. *Acts* 20.17,18. 1 *Pet.* 5. and 2.

4. When the Church has had a Tryal of the meetness and Abilities of any Person, or Persons, for this work and service, they are by Election and Choice solemnly to set him, or them apart, by Prayer, and Laying on of Hands. *Acts* 14.21,22,23. *Acts* 6. By which a new relation ariseth of an Elder, and a Church, a Pastor, and a Flock: This must be therefore by the mutual voluntary acts of each other, by which the Duties of each relation becomes binding upon them, according to the Laws of Christ: It is the Pastors Duty now to Watch, Feed, and Govern the Flock, and to give himself up to it; It is the Churches Duty to submit themselves to Him in the Lord; to Love, Reverence, and Administer freely to him. 1 *Pet.* 5.1,2,3,4,5. *Heb.* 13.7.17. How greatly then must those Churches be to blame, that unconcernedly live in neglect of so great a Duty, upon which the Edification of the Church, and her Well-being so much depends, as well as Gospel Order: For although the Essence and Being of a Church depends upon its Institution in respect both of Matter and Form: (A competent number of Believers may by mutual agreement lay the Foundation of the Being of a Gospel Church,) but they cannot be a Church Organical without Officers, which the Lord hath placed there for the orderly Exercises of his Authority committed to her; To neglect this, is to despise the Wisdom of Christ, who best knows what is for the good of His Church, and for Her Edification in this state. 2,[17] To slight His goodness in so useful and beneficial an Institution. 3, Its a contempt put upon his Authority, as King of Saints, who has in his Sovereign Right, in and over the Church, ordained it so to be, for the Churches Good and Well-being.

---

[14] *Errata*: original reads "her."

[15] *Errata*: original reads "her."

[16] No change is noted on the *Errata* page for this pronoun.

[17] This "2" appears unexpectedly in the text, but is not a typographic error, as a "3" shortly follows. Apparently a "1" is implied prior to the words "To neglect this, is to despise the Wisdom of Christ . . . ."

Secondly, As there should not be a neglect of this Duty, so there should be great care taken that we answer the Will of God herein, wherein His Name and Honour is so much concerned, in Respect of his Love to, and Care of his Church; therefore the greatest[18] diligence should be taken that the Rules He has given be duly observed, and Applications made of the Qualifications laid down, in respect of all such that are called unto Office: The outward Call is an Act of the Church; the acceptation of the Person so called, is an Obediential Act of him to the Will of God, but neither of these can be regular, where there is not a previous indication of the Mind of God, in bestowing those Spiritual Gifts and Qualifications, as may render him competently fit to the Discharge of his Office and Work.

Now in a Churches undue proceeding herein, they discover their own weakness, if not Ignorance, in respect of the Rule it self, and injure the Person so called, in laying the weight of so great a Work upon him, who is not furnished with Spiritual Abilities to discharge it, & thereby expose the Honour of Christ, and Reputation of His Gospel in the World, which should be dear unto us.

And we have reason to reckon that some Churches not walking so regular herein, has been one cause of the want of that Reputation, which otherwise they might have gained amongst the Saints, and in the World, observe what *Moses* said to *Israel, Deut.* 4.6. *Keep therefore, and do them, for this is your Wisdom and your Understanding in the sight of the Nations, which shall hear of all these Statutes; and say, Surely this great Nation is a wise and understanding People.* Who otherwise were the least of all Nations. We ought with far greater reason to take heed we deviate not from the Laws of the Son of God, who deserves greater Honour than *Moses*, which he hath given to His Church, under the Gospel Dispensation; If in the choice of Deacons, *Acts* 6.3. They were to look out *from amongst themselves Men of honest Report, full of the Holy Ghost and Wisdom,* to be set apart to that Work: How much more in the choice of Pastors or Elders whose Work requires greater spiritual Abilities to a right discharge thereof?

---

[18] Original reads "greaest."

For Churches therefore to be so unconcern'd, whether they have Officers or not, according to Gospel Rule, or so overly[19] in the Choice of those they call into such high stations amongst them whether they are competently qualified or not, are greatly blameable.

Thirdly, In the next place we conclude, It is very dishonourable to God, and a reproach to our *Sacred Religion* for the Churches when they have called forth such Pastors and Ministers, who are competently qualified according to the Rule of the Gospel, to let them lye under those unsupportable burdens, of worldly Snares and Incumbrances; without providing for them, according to the Ordination of our Lord Jesus Christ in the *New Testament.*

The Gospel Minister's Maintenance Vindicated.

And indeed, it seems to us a thing Grievous as well as Strange, that any People should be so clouded in their Understandings, as in the least to doubt, whether it should be a Duty or not that the Churches[20] should allow a Meet and Due Maintenance to their Faithful Pastors and Teachers: Yet, we hear there are not only some who have doubts about it, but others, who seem to Object, and stiffly argue against it as if it were Unlawful, if not Antichristian, for Ministers to receive a Yearly, or Quarterly Allowance from the Churches, amongst whom they are placed, and imployed as Labourers; which Conceit cannot be without its sad Effects and Consequences; and if they are not convinced of this Mistake and error the sooner, may in a little time appear to the more palpable Detriment, and Prejudice of the Gospel, and Reproach of Profession, which is indeed too Visible or Manifest already; therefore are we stirred up in Love, to Christ and his Blessed Interest, and as a Prevention of the Evil and Danger threatened upon the Account of this Defect and Remisness of Duty, to Write this short Treatise.

---

[19] The word "unconcern'd" may be implied at this place in this sentence. This would fit both the immediate context in the sentence, and the context of the section in which the statement is made.

[20] *Errata*: original reads "Church."

Our main Business at this time, is not only to Assert the Minister's Maintenance to be an Institution of Christ; but also, to prove it so to be, and that to with-hold it from them by a Church, who is able comfortably to provide for them, is a great and crying Sin, and will be attended (we fear unless prevented by an unfeigned Repentance and Reformation) with severe Judgment from the Holy God, who will not always bear with the Ignorant, much less the willful neglect of his own Holy Law, contained so expresly in his sacred Word, and that we may do this the more effectually, we shall in the first place cite those Scriptures upon which we ground the Truth of what we Assert and Plead for.

Matt. 10.9,10. *Provide neither Gold, nor Silver, nor Brass in your Purses—nor Scrip for your Journey, neither Two Coats, neither Shoes, nor Staves, for the Work-man is Worthy of his Meat.*

1 Tim. 5.17. *Let the Elders who Rule well be accounted worthy of double Honor, especially they who labour in the Word and Doctrine,* For the Scripture saith, *Thou shalt not muzzle the Mouth of the Ox that treadeth the Corn, for the Labourer is worthy of his Reward.*

Gal. 6.6. *Let him that is taught in the Word, communicate to him that teacheth him in all good Things; be not deceived, God is not mocked, for what a Man soweth, that shall he reap.* v.7.

1 Cor. 9.7. *Who goeth a warfare at anytime at his own Charge? Who planted a Vineyard, and eateth not of the Fruit thereof? Who feedeth a Flock, and eateth not of the Milk of the Flock?* V.9. *Is it not written in the Law of* Moses, *Thou shalt not muzzle the Mouth of the Ox that treadeth out the Corn, doth God take Care for Oxen?* V.10. *Or saith he it altogether for our sakes? For our sakes no doubt, this is Written, That he that Ploweth, shall Plow in Hope; and he which Thrasheth in Hope, shall be made partaker of his Hope.* V.11. *If we have sown unto you Spiritual Things, is it a great Thing, if we shall Reap your Carnal Things?* v.13. *Do you not know, that they which Minister about Holy Things Live of the Things of the Temple; and they that wait at the Altar, are partakers with the Altar.* v.14. *Even so hath the Lord ordained, that they which Preach the Gospel, should live of the Gospel.*

We will Appeal to all Mens Consciences in the Fear of God, whether there is any Duty lies more clear and evident in express

Words in the Holy Scripture than this doth; and yet how strangly are some good Christians at a loss about it, and are hardly brought to receive it as an indeispensible Duty, or else to a Faithful Discharge of their duty herein. Our Work is before us, we shall therefore proceed, to open (as the Lord may help us,) the Mind of God in these places of Holy Scripture, and give you the Sense of them, First, *it appears that as soon as our blessed Saviour sent forth his Ministers to Preach the Gospel, as we have shewed,* Matt. 10.7,8,9,10. *He Discovered this part of His Will and Pleasure. I.e. That they should not spend, or waste their own Substance;* they are forbid to take either Gold or Silver, &c. which Words clearly intimate, that they might have both Gold and Silver, and more Coats, and Shoes too; but they were not to take them with them, in their Journey, being sent forth to Preach the Kingdom of God.

Obj. *But some possibly may Object it was but a temporary Precept, being the Will of God concerning them, for that short Journey at that time.*

Answ. We Answer, it seemeth to us manifestly to declare the absolute Will and Pleasure of Christ, that his Faithful Labourers should be provided for by the People with all things Necessary appertaining to this Life, and not only then, but also in all succeeding Ages; and we find our Worthy *Annotators* directly agree with us herein, though may be, some things contained in the place might be temporary: Take what our late *Annotators* say upon the Text,[21] *Our Saviour designed to give them* (saith he) *an Experience of the Providence of God, and to teach them to trust in it; as also, to teach People that the Labourer is worthy of his hire, and that God expecteth, that his Ministers should not live of their own, but upon the Altar, which they serv'd; so as at once he taught his Disciples not to be Covetous, nor overmuch Sollicitous, and the People to provide for those who Ministred to them in things Spiritual.* Besides those other absolute Precepts of like Nature, given to all by the Spirit of Christ in the Apostles, contained in several Epistles, to sufficiently prove this to be the Mind and Intention of our Saviour in this place.

---

[21] In Margin: "Continuation of Mr. *Poole's* Annotations." The quotation may be found in context in Poole on Matt. 9:10.

~ *The Gospel Minister's Maintenance Vindicated* ~

Secondly, *That we may put it out of all doubt, We shall now come to consider of the sacred Appointment of God in this matter:* If it appear to be nothing less, nor more, than what the Lord has Ordained, *viz.* That his servants who are called forth to Preach the Gospel and take Care of his Churches, should have a fit and suitable Maintenance (according as the State and Ability of the Churches may be, to whom they belong, and whose Servants they are) than we hope there is none will object or argue against it any More.

And that this is the Will, and Sacred Appointment of the Lord, is very evident in the fore-cited place. 1 *Cor.* 9.14. and in diverse others. *Even so hath the Lord ordained that they that Preach the Gospel, should live of the Gospel.* Truly the Lord hath not Ordained that his Servants and Ministers under the Gospel should have Tythes, or the Tenth of every Members increase, as he formerly appointed under the Law; yet nevertheless he hath taken Care of them and Ordained that they *should live of the Gospel,* not (unless Necessity requires) that they should live on the *Labor* of their Hands, in common with other Men, and pray observe, 'tis not said the Church has Ordained it, nor we the Apostles have Ordained it; but the Lord hath Ordained it, or it is the Holy Appointment or Sacred Precept of Jesus Christ, for the Support and Comfort of his Painful and Faithful Servants; he and his People have called forth to Preach his blessed Gospel , but some may yet say, *how has he Ordained it.*

Answ. Pray observe, So hath the Lord Ordained, let us look a little back, and take notice of the Scope and Coherence of the place; the Apostle hath a Reference to what preceeds, *Do ye not know, that they that Minister about Holy things, live of the things of the Temple; and they which wait at the Altar, are partakers with the Altar: So hath the Lord Ordained,* &c. That is, 'tis God had a Ministry under the Old Testament. Namely, *the Priest of the tithe of* Levi; and he Ordained and appointed a Comfortable Livelyhood for them, as *Numb.* 18.20. *Deut.* 10. 9. And 18.1. So as they needed not to Labor (as other Men) with their hands to get Bread to eat; even so hath the Lord Ordained and appointed, that those who Preach the Gospel should have likewise a Comfortable Livelyhood or Maintenance now under this Dispensation, that they may be delivered from the Incumbrances of this life, and so not hindered or obstructed in their Holy and most

Sacred Imployment, with secular Affairs. *God's Will* (saith our late *Annotators*) *is the same, under the New Testament, that is also under the Old,* i.e. *It is not as to the People a matter of Liberty, so as they may chuse whether they will maintain their Ministers or no, there is an Ordinance of God in the Case, it is the Will of God, that those who are taken off from Worldly Imployments, and spend their time in the Study and Preaching of the Gospel should have a livelyhood from their Labours.*[22]

This also agrees with what the same great Apostle saith, Gal. 6.6. *Let him that is taught in the Word Communicate to him that Teacheth in all good Things.* Is not this think ye a Precept? Is not this directly laid down, as other great and indispensable Precepts and Duties are, see Ephes. 4.23. *Let him that stole, steal no more; but rather, let him Labour with his Hands: Let no corrupt Communication proceed out of your Mouths,* &c. and again, *Ephes.* 5.33.—*Let every one of you in particular so Love his Wife,* &c. You can under no pretence avoid these great Duties; nor can you plead to be excused; and pray doth not the same Holy Spirit, and ever blessed God, injoin and require you (in the same form of Speech) who are taught in the Word to Communicate to him that Teacheth in all good Things. Shall such who have always shewed much Zeal for the sacred Ordinances and Institutions of Jesus Christ, and plead for a Universal Obedience; justifie themselves in the neglect of so plain a Precept, Christ saith, *then are ye my Friends, if you do whatsoever I have commanded you*; pray ye this great Ordinance then be thought upon, and have equal regard by you; 'tis a Gospel Institution and Appointment of Jesus Christ we argue for *that so you may stand compleat in the whole Will of God: You know what* David saith, *then I shall not be ashamed when I have a respect to all thy Commandments. Let him that is taught in the Word, Communicate to him that teacheth in all good things,* that is, every one according as God hath blessed him with the good things of this World; God would not have his Faithful Ministers want any good thing to make their Lives comfortable to them. *The Precept* (saith our late *Annotators*) *is concerning the Maintenance of Ministers, which is fitly expressed by the* Term *Communicate because, as the People distribute to their*

---

[22] Cf. Poole on 1 Cor. 9:14.

Ministers things Temporal, so the Ministers distribute things Spiritual: the good things here mentioned are Temporal good things such as may be Useful to the Teacher for to uphold Himself and Family. The text teacheth us, that it is the Will of God that Ministers should be maintained as the Charge of the Church, to which they Administer; and it is but an Act of Justice, for they do but Communicate temporal things, to those who Communicate to them much more valuable things: Be not deceived, God is not mocked, &c. *The* Apostle *addeth this* (saith our *Annotators*) *to terrify those who find out vain and false Excuses to save their Purses; he adviseth them not to cheat themselves, for tho they might deceive Men, yet they could not deceive the All-seeing, and Heart-searching God, &c.*[23]

Thirdly, But to proceed, *Ministers are commanded to attend wholly, upon their Sacred Calling in their Ministry, and are required not to intangle*[24] *themselves in the Affairs of this Life*; for certainly, what *Paul* willeth *Timothy* to do in this respect, in him he requireth all Ministers to do the like; and altho' every Christian in many respects may be compared to a Souldier, yet in this place, 2 *Tim.* 2.4. The Apostle only alludes to those in the Ministry, or such who are Spiritual Officers in Christ's Army, they ought to take heed who go forth in that Warfare, they intangle not themselves with the affairs of this Life, *i.e.* in Trades and Callings, which other Christians are allowed to follow: and the reason is offered *that they may please him who hath chosen them to be Soldiers.* And hence 'tis that same Apostle in another place exhorts *Timothy*, and so all other Ministers (who the Church calls forth to that great Work) to *give himself up to Reading, to Exhortation, to Doctrine, and to the Study of the Word; Meditate on these things* (saith he) *give thy self* wholly *to them,* that they[25] *profiting may appear to all.*

Nothing doubtless, but real necessity may dispense with the contrary, but whole time and strength is little enough to be imployed in the Work and Service he is called to. *Let these things be the business of thy Thoughts, and take care of them, be in them; so it is in the* Greek

---

[23] Cf. Poole on Gal. 6:6 and 7.

[24] *Errata*: original reads "contangle."

[25] *Sic.*

(as our Annotators observe), *Let them be thy whole Work.*[26] He must, saith one, give himself up to the Ministry of the Word and Prayer, and continue in reading Meditation, &c. as a Man wholly devoted unto Gospel Service; and is therefore by his Call to the Ministry secluded from those ways and means of providing for his own Subsistance, as Trades and Secular Employments of others furnish them with; that his Mind by the cares of Worldly Business may not be diverted from the Study of God's Word, and care of Souls, which the duty of his Station engageth him to. And if he may not expose himself to the careful Thoughts that accompany worldly Business, though tending to his Profit; certainly it is no way meet that he should be left to conflict with the Thorny Cares of a necessitous Condition, whilst those he Ministers to have means to prevent it: doubtless the Holy God Ordained the Ministers Maintenance upon the most weighty Grounds and Reasons; some of which, blessed be His Name, he hath not concealed or hid from us; and this we say seem to us to be one among the rest, *viz. That his Mind and Thoughts might not be diverted from his Work with Earthly Things.*

Fourthly, *And not in respect of himself upon this account only, but also to prevent that occasion of Scandal,* that we see daily is ready to attend Men who follow Trades and Secular Employments in the World; for let Christian Men be never so careful and circumspect in their Callings and Commerce with Men, we find by daily experience how subject they are to fall under the clamours of some ungodly and envious People, they lying in wait for their halting; and if it be a Minister or Pastor of a Church that is a Trading Person, be sure they will (if be possible) watch him so that he shall not escape their reproachful Tongues though it be not in the least deserved and hereby his Hands are not only made weak, but his Spirits are grieved, and his Ministry made (tho unjustly) contemptible. We find from hence very necessary, that the Pastors of our Churches and Teachers too if possible, should be freed from all such Insnarements; and cannot but observe the Wisdom of God in respect of His Holy Ordinance: *i.e.* in ordaining a Support and Livelyhood for His Servants another way, so that they might not be brought under Infamy and reproach; and that

---

[26] Cf. Poole on 1 Tim. 4:15.

~ The Gospel Minister's Maintenance Vindicated ~

thereby also the Word of God might the better Run and be Glorified. These two Arguments we cannot but Judge are weighty, namely; 1. The work of the Ministry, especially in the Hands of a Pastor, being so great, that it doth require his utmost attendance, or all his whole time and strength, as it must needs appear to every Man who soberly and seriously considers it in its Parts: 'Tis true a Man may bear that Name, and Discharge that Sacred Office in part, nay, and as well as he can, considering his circumstances in the World, and thereby have in part peace in his Mind; but tis another thing to discharge the duty of this Calling as he ought and as the *Sanction* of the Office calls for, to the Honour of the Holy Name of God, and Credit of religion; for we conclude to Preach one or two Sermons in a Week is the least part of his Work, and the least indeed if his matter be not so well prepared and digested; that he may *shew himself a Workman that needeth not be ashamed, rightly dividing the Word of Truth, that so every one may have their portion of Meat in due Season*; which *Timothy* might do, St. *Paul* advises him to careful and diligent Study: But how such poor Men can do this, who are forc'd to follow their Trades hard every Day in the Week, to get Bread for their Families, we see not? But besides the great Work of giving themselves up to Reading, Meditation, and labourious and diligent Study and Preaching of God's Word. There is another great Duty lyes upon them which is, Visiting the Members of the Church under their Care, so that they may *know that State of their Flock*; yea go from House to House: And if this be not done, How can they so well know what Food to Administer or Hand forth unto some poor Souls they have committed to their Charge? Where the Work of Visiting is neglected, we conclude one main Part of the Pastors Business lies undone; and what an account they will have to give of the Souls of Men and Women to Jesus Christ, We know not, if they be amiss here: or what an account the Church can give if they are out of a capacity to discharge this great Trust, through neglect of their Duty to them. *They* (saith the Apostle) *Watch for your Souls, as such as must give account.* Heb. 13.17. And then Secondly, the Credit and Honour of their Ministry, in respect of what we before mentioned, ought to be considered; for if the Preacher hath Blots and Stains upon him, through the necessities he may be in, in respect of the things of this World, by not having his wants supplyed, but it is involved in Debt, or exposed to the breach of his Word in the way of Trading. What weight or power think you, will his Ministry have upon the Consciences of Men? For it necessarily makes room for the old Proverb, *Physician heal thy self*; and it is as a prevention of those evils, *i.e.* for the good, Health, and Well-being of the Souls both of Pastors and People here and hereafter. We conclude that God has been pleased to Ordain and so to provide for his Servants in the Ministry, as we have shewed; but this is not all; For

Fifthly, *According to the Law and Light of Nature, the Church is obliged to provide for her[27] Ministers*, as to the matter of Equity and Justice; and from hence the Apostle argues the Point with the Corinthians 1 *Cor.* 9.7. &c. *Who goeth a Warfare at any time at his own Charge? Who Planteth a Vaineyard, and eateth not of the Fruit thereof? Or who Feedeth a Flock, and eateth not of the Milk of the Flock.* None that Lifts an Army expects that his Souldiers[28] should maintain themselves without Pay: The Ministry is a Spiritual Warfare, undertaken at the Command of Christ, and by the Call of the Church for the service of their Souls; and 'tis as reasonable that Ministers should receive a supply of outward things from them as that a Soldier should receive Pay from his Captain at the charge of the Common-wealth, for whose Good and Safety he enters upon that Military Employment. Again the Apostle argues the equitableness of it further; *Shall a Man Plant a Vineyard and not Eat of the Fruit thereof?* The Preaching of the Gospel is like a man planting a Vineyard; the Church is compared thereto in Scripture, *Isa.* 5.1.2. The Plants are the Lords, but he useth Ministers Hands in the Planting of them and none planteth a Vineyard but expectation of some Fruit from thence, none Imployeth his Servant to Plant but he doth (and 'tis but Just he should) uphold him with Food and Raiment, he doing his Work. The Church also, as the Apostle intimates, is compared to a Flock; And now who Feedeth a Flock, either personally, or by his Servants, but he eateth, or alloweth his Servant to eat of the Milk of the Flock, which it is his Work to keep and feed? By these three Instances commonly known to Men, the Apostle sheweth the reasonableness that the Ministers of the Gospel should be maintained by the People to whom they Minister; he plainly

[27] *Errata*: original reads "their."
[28] *Sic.*

intimating that it is inconsistent with common Justice to deprive a man of the Fruit of that Vineyard which is planted and manured by his own Labour. And such is the case between a Minister and his People; it is not (as one well observes)[29] your Charity that we ask for them, but Justice and Right, which the very Light of Nature as well as God's Word clearly sheweth: They are Imployed in your Service, and do that Business for you in which your Eternal Happiness is concerned; they take care to provide Bread for your Souls, and of right therefore should live upon your charge, and you ought to see that neither they, nor their Families want Bread, nor any thing necessary for their Bodies: Nay, and since *they Sow or Impart unto you Spiritual Things, Is it a great thing if they shall reap your carnal things?* Have you not (as if the Apostle should say) better things from them, than they partake of from you? St. *Paul* (as our Annotators note) argueth the reasonableness *of Ministers maintenance from their People, they giving them* quid pro quo, *a just Compensation for such allowance, yea that which is of much more value; for there is a great disproportion between things Spiritual and things Carnal; the former much excelling the latter, so that the People have the advantage, they receiving things far more excellent from Christ's Ministers, than his Ministers receive of them:*[30] They communicate Gold and precious Stones, and Pearl; and do receive from the People that which comparatively is but as Brass or Copper; And yet shall this seem a great thing? Will you, as if the Apostle should say, Grudge them a due portion of your Temporals, when you receive so plentifully from them of choice Heavenly or Spiritual things? How unreasonable a thing is this?

Obj. *But some may be will Object the things they communicate,* viz. *Those Spiritual Things are not their own but the Lords, and*

---

[29] Much of this section is taken over from N[ehemiah] C[oxe], *A Sermon Preached at the Ordination of an Elder and Deacons in a Baptized Congregation in London* (London: Tho. Fabian, 1681). See for example pp. 38-39. The material is rearranged to some degree in *The Gospel Minister's Maintenance Vindicated*, but much of it is taken *verbatim* from Coxe.

[30] Cf. Poole on 1 Cor. 9:11. The author(s) of *The Gospel Minister's Maintenance Vindicated* seem to have altered the latter part of the comments of Poole.

imparted to them to hand out for the good of others; And therefore the Case is different.

Answer. It is against the Apostle you raise this *Objection*: But will you see how you are mistaken? Pray what more Right or Property have you to your Carnal Things, than they have to their Spirituals? Are not their Spiritual Things their own as much as your Carnal Things are your own? Hath the Lord made you any other than Stewards of your worldly Things; And must not you be Accountable to him for them, if you do not lay them out as he hath Commanded you? For the good of others come your Carnal Things, even *your Wooll and your Flax*. Hos. 2.9. is as much the Lords, as the Ministers. Knowledg, and other Spiritual Gifts are the Lords; and it doth as much behove you to see that you Communicate to others of your Worldly or carnal Things: We mean to the Poor Saints and Ministers of the Gospel, as it behoveth them to Preach or Communicate Spiritual Things to you; and therefore the Case is not different: Besides, you forget how poor Ministers oft times wast their strength, and consume their Bodies, being brought to utter Weakness in their outward Man, in their painful Studies and Labours, in Preaching the Word, thereby Communicating Spiritual Things to you: And is not that (we mean health &c.) more in worth (and their own too) than all you have or can Communicate to them? Sure their strength, and the health of their Bodies together with the expence of their Time, you will say, is as much their own, as any thing you can call yours; And is it then a great thing they should be supplyed from you with all things necessary for this Life Besides, in point of Equity our Saviour as well as the Apostle calls Ministers Labourers; and you all will readily say, *The Labourer is worthy of his Hire*. How then is it that any should seek ways, and excuses to avoid their Duty herein to their Spiritual harvest Men? we must tell you again, tis Jesus Christ who saith tis their due, and that they are worthy of it and He hath Ordained that they should have it; so that you cannot with hold it from them without Sin, nay such Sin that it is not only against the Law and Light of Nature, but the express Law of Jesus Christ: And we must tell you, That if the keeping back, or defrauding the Hire of your Labourers who have Reaped down your Corn Fields, be so great an Evil, that their Cry enters into the Ears of the Lord of Sabbaths, and doth provoke and stir up the justice of God to a severe vengeance, for their daring Boldness and cruel Oppression of the poor: What think you will be the Effects of the Cry of Christs painful Spiritual Harvest-men, who Labour to gather in his Divine Corn, should you withhold from them their just Right upon this Account; by which means they may be exposed, especially some of them, to Heart Disquieting, and Soul Afflicting Snares in the World, and their poor families want such things as are necessary for them, when it is in the power of the Peoples hands plentifully to supply them: We must in discharge of our Duty at this time be plain with every Man, that we may deliver our own Souls and theirs too, from so great a Sin as such an neglect as that is does appear to us to be, and will to all, if seriously Consider'd, and laid to Heart.

Object. *May be some will Object our Ministers do not need it, nor desire it of us, they can live without it.*

Answ. So perhaps some *of your Harvest-men that Reap down your Fields* may be well to pass in the World and can live without their Hire and just due &c. Yet will that be a good Plea (think you) to seek ways or means to with-hold their wages from them? So, and in like manner say we the Ability of your pastors in respect of the things of the Worlds, doth not excuse you from the discharge of your duty to them, according to the Just Law of God, and Equitableness of the Case. Yet certainly they (if of *Paul's* Spirit) will refuse to receive any thing lest it should lessen their esteem in their Ministry; tis left to their Liberty, they may chuse whether they will receive it or not: But though they may dispence with their Right if they please, as *Paul* did sometimes through his great Zeal and Love to the Gospel; yet cannot you dispence with your Duty, you have no Warrant so to do: Yet we can't but greatly commend those Pastors of the Churches, who can and do without receiving any thing, serve Christ and his People, and resolve (being Blessed with the good things of the world) not to make the Gospel Chargeable, or a Burden to any; but yet we would have you sensible of your Duty, and look upon your selves to be Debtors to them, and esteem of them the more: But do these Pastors who are Rich, Able, and Willing to serve the Churches for nothing, sequester or give themselves up to the Work of the Ministry, and faithfully discharge that Trust, as another who is taken off of Secular Employment? But may be, though they do[31] like other *Labourers*, yet if they did not receive it from you, they could Distribute it to the Needy, or to help other poor Ministers who serve other Churches, whose Poverty may be such, that they cannot allow a sufficient Maintenance to their Pastor. And therefore whether it may be necessary for you to with hold it from them, or for them to refuse it, is worth Consideration.

Sixthly. But to proceed. (*Since we are pleading the case in point of Equity and just Right, let it be Considered:) You do not chuse such men to be your Pastors or Ministers, who are of the lowest of the People*; but such as may be allowed to have ashare[32] of Parts, Common Prudence, and Abilitys for Business with other Persons; and some of them could manage Trades or fall into other Imployments, and get Estates as well as you, if they were not Devoted to a better Service: And must (as one observeth)[33] they needs be devoted to Necessities and Miseries, in the same Hour that they enter upon the Ministry. This ought not to be; GOD hath Ordered the Case otherwise in his Wisdom. Certainly (all will Confess) tis the Duty of a Minister, as well as other men to provide for his Family, as much as lies in him; or take Care of his Wife and Children that they may not be exposed to a Thousand Miseries and Temptations when he is gone: For though a Covetous raking Temper, worse becomes a Minister of all Men in the World (yet as the Author before cited Noteth) we greatly mistake ourselves to think he must divest himself of that due Affection of an Husband to his Wife, or of a Father toward his Children; or that those Fruits thereof which are Justly esteemed Commendable in others, should be thought in him to be a Fault: And is it not sad (Judge you) That they must be constrained to one of these *Dialema's? i.e.* Either to neglect the full and Faithfull Discharge of their Duty to Christ and his Church, or else

---

[31] *Errata*: original reads "are."

[32] *Sic.*

[33] Cf. Coxe, *Ordination Sermon*, 39 and 37. The material is rearranged to some degree in *The Gospel Minister's Maintenance Vindicated*, but much of it is taken *verbatim* from Coxe.

Neglect their poor Families by fulfilling their Ministry, and doing the work of Pastors, according to the Nature of that Sacred Office. But as to him who is poor (and must get his Bread before he Eats it) who thinks he can Discharge both these Duties well enough, tis to be feared he does never a one of them as he ought: Moreover, 'tis good for him to consider the reason of that Law of the ever Blessed God, who hath otherwise Ordained. Yet let every Servant of Christ use his own Freedom, and act and do, as he thinks may most promote the Glory of God, and Good of the Church, and the Increase thereof; so that he may give a good account of himself in the Day of Christ.

Seventhly, *The Lord hath not left me to argue this only from general Principles of Reason, and common Equity, but to put the Matter beyond dispute* (as we have already shewed) hath subjoyned *His express Command.* And may not *in the next place, that Provision which God was pleased to make for his Ministers in the time of the Law,* be of great use to us, and full of Instruction upon this account? Nay, and ought we not to consider it, sith the Apostle argueth 1 *Cor.* 9.13. for a Gospel Maintenance from thence. *Do ye not know, that they which Minister about Holy things, live of the Things of the Temple; and they which serve at the Altar, are partakers with the Altar?* It appears this is a duty still; and tho' the mode or manner of the Maintenance of the Ministers of God under the Law, was quite different to this under the Gospel, yet the reason and equitableness of the thing abides: Ministers were then provided for by the Lord; so he has ordered they should Live comfortably now under the Gospel. We find God did then no sooner separate the *Levites* to the Service of the Sanctuary, but he by Law provided for their Subsistence: And though they were but one Tribe in Twelve, yet the *Tenth* of the Increase of the whole Land was given to them, besides the first Fruits and Offerings, and diverse other Advantages; so that their Lot and Portion might equal, yea exceed that of their Brethrens. This indeed is Abrogated; Gospel Ministers have no Divine Right to the *Tenths* of men's Increase; nor can it be thought to be any Burden to provide a comfortable Livelyhood for our Ministers, were but our Senses rightly exercised to discern how Good and Gracious God appears to us under the Gospel Dispensation, in easing our People from those vast and great Expence and Charges which the Lord's People were required to be at under the Law: For we shall soon perceive if we consider, that the charge of the Worship of God, and the Ministry &c. now is comparitively little or nothing, to what there was under that Dispensation; though Men did endeavour now to come up to their duty for as one observes,[34] he thought he could make it appear, *That the Fifth Part of their Estates was Yearly to be spent in Things relating to Temple Service.* And we know not but he might say right: And yet we cannot be unsensible of the excellency of the Gospel Ministry, above the Ministry, of the Law; And what great Blessings and Priviledges upon many Accounts we have above them? One would think these things were enough to stir up all Faithful Christians to leave their Disputings, and heartily with a cheerful Mind be ready to contribute towards the defraying the moderate Charge of a Gospel Ministry, in such a manner it may give reputation to our Sacred Profession; certainly the Labourer is still worthy of his Hire; and every one will say, not less worthy because he Labours under the Gospel, than they who Laboured under the Law.

Eighthly, *An Elder, or a Pastor of a Church, is under a special Charge to Use Hospitality, and to set*[35] *himself a Pattern of Charity, and other good Works,* that so he may better adorn his Profession. This is his Duty, and if he fails herein, he loses some part of those most excellent Virtues in which he ought to shine: but if he be Poor, and left to the thorny cares of this World, and the Church not administring so to him, as to put him into a Capacity to answer this requirement of the Gospel, where will the fault and blame lie? Therefore since he ought to be a patern[36] of Hospitality and Charity; we argue, 'tis doubtless the indispensible Duty of the People to whom he Ministers, to be concerned to the uttermost of their Abilities to make him capable of giving Proof of this Grace, by the Exercise of it as there may be Occasion.

Ninthly, *We also argue for this Duty from the Consideration of the Honourableness of it, when 'tis faithfully discharged;* it being one of those things, which is *Honest, Just, Pure, Lovely,* and of *good Report,*

---

[34] Coxe, *Ordination Sermon*, 41.

[35] *Errata*: original reads "let himself be." This is a direct quotation from Coxe's *Ordination Sermon*, 38, where the phrase reads "to set in himself a pattern . . . ."

[36] *Sic.*

there is both *Vertue* and *Praise* attends it, *Phil.* 4.8. First of all, How can Men think you are the People you profess your selves to be, *viz.* Such who endeavour to Walk Blamelessly in observing all the Ordinances and Commandments of the Lord Jesus whilst you neglect this so plain and undeniable an Institution, even such a one, that 'tis expresly said, *So God hath Ordained it,* &c. Why are you so Zealous for some other Precepts and Remiss Here? Doth not the same God who commandeth you to Repent, to Believe, and to be Baptiz'd, and to Love one another; command you also to Communicate to your Ministers in all good things? How is it then? that any can be so partial in the Law of Jesus Christ.

2.[37] This will in a great measure deliver you from that reproach of Covetousness: What can any People think should be the cause why Christians should suffer their Ministers to want what is necessary for them, when they themselves are so full? Unless it be from the Spirit of this World; which is a Sin too often laid at the doors of the Professors of this Age: Would to God there was no cause or ground for it.

3. Hereby the People will also raise the Reputation and Honour of the Ministry, and shew their great esteem of them, which well agrees with the Exhortation of the Apostle; *Let the Elders that Rule well be accounted worthy of double Honour, especially they who Labour in the Word and Doctrine. For the Scripture saith, Thou shalt not Muzzle the Mouth of the Oxe that treadeth out the Corn: For the Labourer is worthy of his Reward.* 1 Tim. 17.18.[38]

By double Honour here is meant as some conclude, *Reverence or Honourable Esteem* for Christ's Sake whose Ambassadors they are said to be, and so represent His Most Sacred Majesty.

2.[39] *Maintenance.* And 'tis evident this cannot be excluded in this place considering the Connextion of the Words following; for the Scripture saith, *Thou shalt not muzzle the Oxe that Treadeth out the Corn, and the Labourer is worthy of his Reward.* This verse, saith our *Annotators*, maketh evident, *That Maintenance is part of the double*

---

[37] This "2." and the following "3." evidently refer to the second and third implications of the heading "ninthly."

[38] *Sic.* The proper reference is 1 Tim. 5:17 and 18.

[39] This "2." evidently refers to the second implication drawn from the cited text.

Honour that is due to such as Labour in the Word and Doctrine.[40] This
then must be granted it tends to the Honour of Christ's Ministers; but
'tis so evident to all, that those Persons, let them be of what
Perswasion soever, if they should leave their Ministers to the wide
World to shift for themselves, and though Poor, take no care of them;
instead of honouring of them, they would cast a slight and contempt
upon them: and hence 'tis that others also for their following of some
Trades, do lay them under great reproach, which the Churches to
whom they belong, if able, might and ought[41] to deliver them from.
We are perswaded there are some rich Members in most
Congregations, that would not indure that any of their near Relations
should fall under such, or the like Circumstances, or be exposed to
such Inconveniences, because of the Dishonour they Judge it would be
to them; People knowing they are Wealthy and Great in the World,
and able to do considerable for such near Kindred, or else all would
say they have no favour nor esteem for them. And shall Men shew
greater favour and respect to their Carnal relations than to Christ's
Ambassadors? This surely ought not to be.

Tenthly, Further to Evince this great Duty, *It may not be amiss to
consider of other great Inconveniences that do follow the neglect of it.*
There are some Ministers in the Churches who were brought up to
Learning, and who are utterly uncapable to follow Secular Trades and
Callings: now if Provision be not made for these men what will
become of them? How is it possible they and their Families should
live? Besides, what Incouragement is here given to others who are
Young, whom God hath Graciously indowed with considerable Gifts
and are willing to give up themselves to the Ministry? And for their
better Accomplishment endeavour after a Knowledg of the Tongues,
&c. which we all confess is very good and serviceable, though not of
absolute necessity in a Minister: Who will apply himself (we say) to
gather, and lay up those stores of solid Learning, which oft-times in
the Defence of the Truth against Opposers, has been found very
profitable, when he can expect nothing but Poverty and Distress
thereby: Nay furthermore, may not this neglect quite deter any Godly
Young Men to exercise their Gifts, in order to serve the Churches in

---

[40] Cf. Poole on 1 Tim. 5:18.
[41] Original reads "ough."

after times, when Death shall call away those Labourers the Churches have now amongst them, should they see the present Ministry slighted, and not provided for: Or what ground have we to expect a Blessing by the Providence of God, to attend the Churches in respect of an Able and Honourable Ministry in time to come, when His great Ordinance is slighted and neglected, which He in Wisdom hath Ordained for an Encouragement upon this very account. In his own Way we may look for a Blessing, but not out of it.

Nay to be plain with you, Have not some in a few Years last past seen to their great trouble and grief, how this neglect and ommission of Duty hath laid (divers hopeful young Men who were indued with excellent Gifts for the Ministry) under great Temptations, even so far as to refuse utterly the exercise of their Gifts to the Profit and Edification of the Churches; lest in process of time they should be called forth to a Pastoral Charge, and thereby be exposed to Snares and Poverty in the World; as perhaps some poor Ministers and Pastors have been and may be daily still are; especially they considering and laying to Heart the Care and Charge their Parents have been at with them, in putting them forth to good Trades and Callings, whereby they knew with the Blessing of God they might (if they gave themselves up with a due and necessary Diligence and Industry to follow those Trades) live well in the World, and sufficiently provide for themselves (and their Wives and Children, if they saw good to Marry) in after-times? And by this very means the Churches (may be to their great loss and detriment) have been deprived of those great helps which a faithful discharge of Duty to the present Ministry, may prevent for time to come. Also, do we not see at this very time what a sad pass some Congregations are come to already, for want of useful helps in the Ministry, both in City and Country; some Pastors (nay many of them) being grown very Ancient, and almost become unserviceable, and not like to continue long: And though the Harvest is great, yet O! how few are the Labourers amongst us, and fewer they are like to be, if care be not taken in the discharge of this indispensible Duty to the present Ministry: Nor is it a strange thing that Godly Men should fall under such a Temptation which we before mentioned, considering this great Evil and neglect of Duty herein: Since we find of Old in the *Holy Scripture* the very same Snare and Temptation many of the Priests and

Ministers of the Lord fell under. Pray read and carefully consider *Nehemiah* 13.8,9. especially the 10 Verse. *And I perceived that the Portions of the Levites had not been given them; for the Levites and the Signers that did the Work, were Fled every one to his Field.* Now 'tis evident that through the like Evil and Neglect of the People to the Levites and Ministers of God, in not giving them that due allowance or maintenance God had Ordained for them, they left their work and service every one of them, and betook themselves to secular Employments, *viz.* To labour in the Fields and manure their Land, or gather in their Corn, which according to the *Law* others were to do for them. Nor did *good Nehemiah* (as we can find) reprove or blame the *Levites* for so doing: Nor indeed, what reason was there he should? Considering 'tis a Moral Duty for every Man to provide for himself and Family; and he that does not do it, the Apostle shews *is worse than an Infidel, and hath denyed the Faith.* But he contended sharply with the People, especially with the Rulers; saying *Why is the House of God forsaken?* That is, the Work of the House of the Lord: *And he gathered them together and set them in their place.* Verse 11. They had not only injured the *Levites*, as our A*nnotators* observe upon the place, in withholding their Dues, but also occasioned the neglect of GOD's House and Service, &c.[42] *And he gathered them together*: That is, say they, from their several Possessions in the Country, in which they were dispersed, and restored them to the Exercise of their Office. And *Them*, saith the Text, *brought all* Judah *the Tithe of the Corn, and the new Wine, and the Oyl unto the Treasuries.* Verse 12. We cannot slightly pass by this matter, for the Evil and danger of the Sin of the Churches upon this account, doth as palpably appear in this Case, as in any we have mentioned. How can we expect in ordinary way to have an Able *Ministry* raised up; or those who are now imployed in the Work of the Gospel carry on that Work, to the Honour of GOD, Comfort of His People, and to the Credit or our Sacred religion, if a Gospel Incouragement be not given them? True, we may perhaps have Preachers; some may be willing to Exercise their Gifts, but is it fit think you, to call such to Preach publickly, who have scarcely one Hours time to prepare themselves for the Work; or may be have not

---

[42] Cf. Poole on Neh. 13:11.

~ The Gospel Minister's Maintenance Vindicated ~

meet and proper Indowments or Qualifications for that Holy and Sublime Service. What is it (Judge you) that causes the Ministry to be slighted and neglected in some places, but the want of such a *Ministry* that may honourably carry it on? And who shall we blame? What would you have poor men to do, that have (may be) no time to spare to give themselves up to the Study of the Scriptures, nor no useful Books and proper helps to improve and assist them in their Study: or if they have, yet their circumstances in the World will not afford them so much leisure from their worldly Business, to read and meditate upon the Word, so as well to digest what they have to deliver to the People. Come, think and say what you please; tis not without diligent and continued Study, that the deep things of God can be searched out, and so proposed, as to inrich the minds of people with clear and solid Knowledge: He that is not indowed with the clear Light and Understanding of Divine Truths, or the mystery of the Gospel himself, How can he Feed others as they ought to be Fed with the Knowledg of those Sublime and Soul inriching *Mysteries*? A little Knowledg and Study 'tis true (as one observes) may furnish a man with such a Discourse as may please some weak Christians that Judg of a Sermon by the loudness of the Voice and affectionate Sentences, or can fancy themselves to be Fed with good Doctrine, when perhaps 'tis but with the Ashes of Jingling Words and cadency of Terms. But alas! (saith he) the seeming warmth of Affection that is stirred up by such means, is as short Liv'd as a Land Flood that hat no Spring to Feed it.[43] He that will do the Souls of his people good, and approve himself a Pastor after God's own Heart, must endeavour to Feed them with Knowledg and Understanding, that the people may learn and come to understand those things which were hid, and not opened or known to them before; and so strive to maintain a constant Zeal and Affection in them, by well informing their Judgments, and such an opening of the mind of God from the Scriptures, as may command their Consciences. And this is not to be expected, but from him that Labours in his Study, as well as in the Pulpit: But (saith He) mistake me not; we know the success and fruit of all Studies and Labours of men that preach the Gospel, is from the Grace and Power of the Holy Ghost, but the assistance of the

---

[43] Cf. Coxe, *Ordination Sermon*, 42-43.

Spirit is to be expected by the use of means, and in the way of our Duty. And now from the whole, this is that we say, 'Tis not to be thought men can arrive to that degree of Light and Knowledg in the deep things of God, and mystery of Christ, so as to preach the Gospel as they ought, unless they dedicate and give themselves up by *Prayer* and *Meditation* to the dilligent search and Study of the Word of GOD, which cannot be done unless some time be spent, which divers men cannot spare without a due Allowance for their pains and loss of time. And this we say too, is nothing less nor more than what God has Ordained and directly Appointed in this *Matter* in the *New Testament*, as we have sufficiently proved: But to proceed,

Eleventhly, *The great Duty of the People to contribute towards the publick Worship of God, and the Ministry may be further demonstrated and the Evil and Sin in their neglect of it evinc'd, from the Consideration of that sharp reproof, and severe Judgments of God, brought against, and denounced upon the People of Old,* upon this very account, so *Mal.* 3.8. *Will a Man rob God? Yet ye have robbed me*: The evil of this People lay in this, *i.e.* In that they did not faithfully bring into his House all those Riches and good Things, which by the Law and Requirement of God they ought to have done, for the carrying on and management of the Service of the Temple, and publick Worship of God; they through Covetousness, or a base Carnal and Self-seeking Spirit, did retain and keep back part of these Tythes and Offerings for their own Use, or to inrich themselves, and did not yield them up to the Use and End God had appointed them: And this the People might do, *i.e.* rob God, *viz.* In with-holding from the Priests of the Lord what was appointed or ordained for them: And also this the Priests might do, whilst they took too much, and more than what was their due Allowance, or take the Wages, and not do the Work which was appointed for them. However, to keep back, or retain part, or the whole, of what God has ordained and commanded to be brought into his House, for the carrying on, and well Management of the publick Worship, *The Lord calls it a robbing of him*: And certainly God hath as great Care, and has made as Honourable Provision for the Gospel Church, and his Worship and Interest now, under this Dispensation, as he had then; and has appointed or ordained that his People bring into his House now, so that nothing may be wanting for the Honourable management and carrying on the Work of the Gospel, and the Ministration therefore, in any Respect: Nor can this be done without Charge; And if the Lords People shall so seek their own Things, as not to concern themselves for the Interest of Christ, but retain, or through Covetousness, keep back that which his Church, Worship, and publick Interests calls for, and by which means, his blessed Interest should sink and languish in their Hands, who were intrusted with it; certainly, they will be, and are looked upon, as great robbers of God now, as those were then, of whom the Prophet speaks.

Would to God this were considered; which if the Nations (as if God should say) have robbed their Gods: But blush ye *Jews*, for ye have robbed me, and therefore ye are cursed with a curse; your Sin, your Sacriledg, of which you are guilty hath so provoked me, and the curse shall abide upon you, so long as ye abide, and continue in this sinful Course; strange that you dare Sin, whilst I am punishing you for this Iniquity (so the *Annotators*) will you go on in your Sin, whilst you are under the Judgment and Curse of your God?[44] *Bring ye all the Tithes into my Store-house, that there may be Meat in mine House, and prove me now herewith, saith the Lord of Hosts; If I will not open the Windows of Heaven, and pour you out a Blessing that there be not room enough to receive it,* vers. 10. (Though we do not say) God hath brought the like curse now; yet we fear the Lords People in *England*, both in City and Country, are under just Rebuke in retaining that from God, for the Use of his Publick Worship, Service and Ministry, which he Requires and Commands them to bring in, and lay up in his Spiritual House; and hence it is he is provoked, and seems to bring a blast instead of a blessing upon us; we fear we have Cause to say, and cry out with our Apostle, *All seek their own, and none the things that are Jesus Christs, Phil.* 2.21. Do you think the Service of Gods House can be carryed on without any Charge, or is God less careful of his Church and Ministry under the Gospel, than he was under the Law. The first Church that was planted after the Ascension of Christ, were so Zealous and Piously inclined to the Service of the Gospel, that they seemed to give up all they had for the publick Interest of Christ, and sole their Possessions, which thing you are not required to do; you

---

[44] Cf. Poole on Mal. 3:9.

may keep your own Propriety in your Goods, Lands and Possessions; but yet, nevertheless ought you to consider your ways, and not let the Interest of Christ, and the Gospel to sink under your Hands: *Will you dwell in your Ceiled Houses; and let the House;* i.e. *The Lord's House lye wast*? Especially, considering 'tis the Lord's Time, we are verily perswaded in which he is going about to build it, and add to the glory of it; What proof have you given, O ye Christians and Members of the Churches! That you love Jesus Christ more than Father or Mother, yea, more than Son and Daughter? Which if you do not, our Saviour saith ye are not worthy of him; and what Demonstration can we see of this thing, whilst you thus pursue the World, and indeavour to lay up, nay, and daily do part with so many Hundred of Pounds, to such a Son, and to such a Daughter; and yet can't spare the Twentieth Part thereof for Christ his Church and Publick Ministry? Our Souls mourn and grieve to see what an Earthly and Covetous Spirit is got into the Professors of this Age, and fear that that Zeal is much gone; for the Truth and fervent Love to Christ, which was once amongst those who were his People; does it not appear so? Whilst some of the Churches seem to be contented with any, nay, the meanest Gifts that are amongst them, provided they can have them without any Charge, rather than they will seek out, and indeavour for an Able and Honourable Ministry, because of that great experience and cost they fear then they shall be at: As also, whilst Careless and mind not what want of faithful Labourers there may be abroad in other Places and Churches, so that they are provided themselves: As likewise, do not give proper and meet Incouragement for the raising up, and continuing of an Able Ministry for the time to come. These things are Lamentable and great ground of Mourning and Bitter Tears: Know ye therefore this, and believe it, that God is offended, and may justly blast you in your Trades, and Worldly Substance, if he hath not already, because you do not lay this evil to Heart; and that which you think ye saye this way, may bring a blast upon all you have; and while you look for much, ye may carry in little, and that which you do gain and bring home, may be put into a Bag with Holes, *Hag.* 1.6. pray Read the 6.v.[45] *Ye looked for much, and lo it came to little, and when ye brought it home, I did blow upon it. Why,*

---

[45] The text clearly states the "6" verse, but the verse quoted is the 9th verse. It may be that the 9 was inverted by the printer in the original.

~ The Gospel Minister's Maintenance Vindicated ~

*saith the Lord of Hosts? Because of mine House that is waste, and ye
run every Man to his own House.* Many Persons we have amongst us,
meet us daily with great Disappointments, Losses, and manifold
Afflictions, diverse manner of ways, and wonder at it, and are troubled
at the Thoughts; but we fear do not lay to Heart, nor consider from
whence it is, nor the chief Cause thereof; which possibly may be,
because you have not discharged your Duty to Christ, for the
promoting of his blessed Gospel, and Interest in the World; but have
shewed much more Love to, and Care of your own Houses, and
Concerns than for the House and Church of God: God may say of you,
O ye Professors! You have toiled and been at great Cost and Labour;
and have expected, hoped, and promised your selves great Increase;
but you have clearly discerned, and were sensible that it answered not
your Expectation, much of it dwindled into very little; you were
loosers,[46] and went backward still, which you have not regarded nor
laid to Heart; but have let my House lie as it were waste; nothing was
too much in your Eyes to lay out on your own Houses and Buildings to
Adorn and Beautifie them; nor did you grudge to provide Sumptuous
Provision and Apparel for your Selves, and for your Sons, and
Daughters: Nay, have idly and in superfluities expended much
Treasure to gratifie your Lust, and yet have let my poor Children and
Faithful Ministers want such things that were Necessary for them, and
not been concerned to encourage and able and painful Ministry, that
the perishing Souls of Sinners up and down in the Nation might have
the Bread of Life; and from hence is it that your Trades fail, and your
Labours bring in but little increase. But if once you reform your doings
or[47] shew your Zeal for the Gospel and Love to me, and act as
becomes a People professing my Name; you shall see you shall not be
losers by it; for *I will open the Windows of Heaven, and pour you out a
blessing, that there shall not be room enough to receive it:* Nay saith
he, *Prove me now if I do not do it.*

We conclude, the Judgment on the one hand for such an Evil and
Neglect of Duty herein, and Mercies and Blessings promised on the
other hand, may be a great Argument to provoke you to a Faithful
Discharge of those Obligations that lye upon you in this matter. If you

---

[46] *Sic.*
[47] *Errata*: original reads "and."

have a Dasire to be blest in your Bodies, Souls, and Estates, take Care of God's House, and bring in your Stores, that there may be Provision for his Poor, and for his Ministers. But if you neglect this Duty, and persue the World, and prefer your own Houses and Things above those great Things of God and his Gospel, you may look for a blast.

Twelfthly, *Consider the Zeal of the Heathen of Old, and that of the Antichristian Party of latter Times*; the former spared no Cost nor Pains to Beautify and Garnish their Idols, *they lavish Gold out of the Bag*, &c. *Isa.* 46.[48] They took it by handfuls as it were, and never sold it, as some conceive, not mattering what Cost or Charge they were at; sith[49] it was for the Adorning of their Gods: *The Goldsmith spreadeth it over with Gold, and casteth Silver Chains.* Isa. 40.10.[50] *He is* (saith the Prophet) *so impoverish'd that he hath no Oblation*, that he can hardly procure Money sufficient to buy the meanest Sacrifice for his Gods; he is so Zealous for his Idols that he will one way or another find Money to procure the choicest Materials, saith the Annotators, and get the help of the best Artist to make it, &c.[51] Did they shew such Zeal for, and Love to them who were no Gods: And shall not such be ashamed and blush, who have been so niggerly[52] and sparing to help on the Service and Worship of the True and Living God? They would have the *best Artist*, and most *Curious Workman* to do their Business, though they impoverished themselves; but some of you, we fear, can be contented with *very unskilful Men*, to carry on the Work of the God of Heaven, rather than be at the Charge to distribute of your Treasure for the better Improvement of them which you imploy, or to procure such who you have not amongst your selves; and as for the *Papists*, you cannot be Ignorant what vast Treasure they have from time to time freely bestowed on their Church, and large Revenues appointed for their Priests &c. and have they not commonly when they come to dye; besides all this, left large Legacies for Spiritual Uses, as they call them, and all to carry on their filthy Idolatry. But how little hast thou,

---

[48] Properly Isa. 46:6.

[49] "Sith" is an archaic form of "since."

[50] The reference is incorrect. The correct reference is Isa. 46:19.

[51] Cf. Poole on Isa. 40:20.

[52] According to the *Oxford English Dictionary*, this is an obsolete form of "niggardly."

O Professor parted with to this day, for the upholding the Church of God, and carrying on the Ministration of the Gospel of Jesus Christ? Thou hast shewed that Zeal for the True God, which some have shewed for a False One: For that Care of, and Love to the True Worship of God, which others have shewed for Idolatry: May not these Carnal and Antichristian heathens one Day rise up in Judgment against you?

Obj. *But may be you will Object and say, 'tis no marvel the Papists give so plentifully because they think to merit Heaven thereby.*

Answ. What Then? Will not you do as much for the Honour of God, and to promote his Interest in the World, as thou wilt do for the Salvation of thine own Soul? If thou hast Eternal Life meerly of Grace, or through the Favour and Mercy of God, and Merits of Jesus Christ? How much the more should this lay thee under an Obligation to be Bountiful and Liberal, to further and carry on, and promote the Gospel and the Glory of God in the World? Or have you a mind to betray your own Sincerity? Doth not Grace teach you better Doctrine, even to prefer the Honour of God, above whatsoever is dear to you on Earth.

Thirteenthly, This will render your Ministers inexcusable, if they do not faithfully discharge their Duties in every Respect, to God and his People; we mean, when you discharge your Duties to them, according to the Law of Christ, and Rule of Justice and Righteousness: What will they have to say, to excuse their Remisness and Omissions in a painful studying Meditation, and preaching the Word, and in visiting the Flock, when you have freed them from all manner of worldly Snares and Incumbrances, and comfortably provided for them all good things? But on the contrary, if they come forth unprepared, and feed you with Food that hath little Soul Nourishment in it: How can you blame them? For if they never go about all the Year to know the State of the Flock as their Duty is, have they not a ready Answer and Excuse? *i.e.* What shall become of our poor Families? What can you say to them? Can you excuse them from indispensible Duties? And say we will be contented with what Service you are able to do, and all to save your Purses: the Lord open your understandings, and shew you the great Evil there is in this neglect, in not complying with the Will of God, in communicating all good Things to them, who Preach the Gospel to you. And is it not from hence there is such a complaint in some parts of the Country, for want of the *saving Food of God's Word?* We hear daily what a blessing those Elders and Ministers are of to the People whereabouts they live, who are provided for by the Churches, over what others be who are not taken off of their secular Affairs, being not maintained by the People; one Minister may do more than several such do or can do. Besides when once you come to acquit yourselves, as good Christians ought in this Case; with what Comfort may you be able to give up your Account to Christ? And with Joy and much Soul Peace lye down, not only in your Beds; but also in your Graves, when you come to Dye.

Motives to press the Duty of the Ministers Maintenance, with an Answer to other Objections.

1. **C**onsider well, and remember that your Pastors are the Ministers; nay, the Ambassadors of Jesus Christ; such who represent his Sacred Majesty, and have his Commission, for what they act and do in his Name; and dispense the Mysteries of God to you, according to their Duty; therefore the Lord Jesus will account that done to Himself, which is done to his Ministers: *He that receiveth you* (saith he) *receiveth me, and he that despiseth you, despiseth me, Mat.* 10.40. *Luke* 10.16. If the Name and Authority of Christ will beget an aw[53] in you, or his Matchless and Unspeakable Love Influence your Souls; there is no doubt but his word will abide upon you, and cause you to discharge the Duty we have pressed upon your Spirits. If you acknowledge a Religious Respect and Reverence due to the Son of God, exercise it in a humble Obedience to his word; and if you Love him and value his Gospel, treat not his Ministers in an unworthy manner: Have you not called them off from other Business? And are they not your Servants? And is not from thence a Gospel Maintenance due to them from you, as is the wages of your other Servants? Tho we fear some give more to the meanest Servants in their House, than they to give to the Ministers of Christ.

2. 'Tis evident, they have a great Charge committed to their Trust, *they watch for your Souls, as they who must give an account, Heb.* 13.17. And therefore you ought to consider them, and pity them, and endeavour to assist them, and put them into the best Capacity you are able to do, that they may make full proof of their Ministry, and *be free from the Blood of all Men*; 'tis the Business of your own Salvation, and concern of your precious and immortal Souls, that your ministers are imployed in; and therefore 'tis much more your own interest than his, and from hence ought to make Conscience of your Duty; for if they can't *give their account with Joy, that will not be profitable for you*: And how can they give an account of Joy concerning you, when you have neglected one great and indispensible Duty, by which means

---

[53] *Sic.*

they were rendered unable to perform their Work, as became them? Nor can indeed the Ministry ever be effectual to your Souls, if you be not sincere in Obedience under it: Besides, as one observes, will you be less Carefull for your Souls, and their Eternal wellfare, than for your Bodies, and the Comforts of a Temporal Life? Can you be content to lay out your Strength and Substance to provide for these, and neglect the other? Is it not sad, saith one to consider, *How many there are among Professors, that live in this World, as if there were no Truth in the report of that which is to come, and have the meanest esteem of the most necessary means of Salvation?* viz. *The Word and Ordinances of Christ, and a Gospel Ministry; some can expend perhaps an hundred Pounds* per Annum, *more or less, for Ornaments or Delights to Adorn a frail Carcase, but will grudg half so much for the poor Saints, or to the support of the Worship of the Gospel, and his sinking Interest.*[54]

3. Consider how many Temptations and Soul discouraging Weaknesses your Ministers lye under continually, both from within and without, if sensible of the greatness of their Work, and of their own insufficiency: You know not their Fears, their Cares, their Tears, and how hard they are put to it to keep up in their Work finding such strong Oppositions made against them by the Enemy, and continually so that you had need to Strengthen, Comfort, and Incourage them, as much as you can; and not to add to their Sorrow, and make them serve you in wants and necessities.

4. We might tell you also what the Apostle says in respect of his Liberty as a Minister, in forbearing to Work at all: Will any of you say your Ministers must labour and provide for themselves, when God hath Ordained the contrary; and also when the Apostle saith, he had power to forbear Working? See 1 *Cor.* 9.6. *Or I only and* Barnabas, *Have we not power to forbear Working? We certainly* (as well as the rest of Christ's Ministers) *if we will run out to the utmost end of the Line of our Liberty in things, without having regard to your Circumstances, might forbear Working with our Hands, and expect that those among whom we Labour should maintain us.* So the

---

[54] Cf. Coxe, *Ordination Sermon*, 44-45. The first part of the quotation is exact, the latter part is slightly paraphrased.

Annotators render it.[55] Now, you would think this a hard thing, should any of your Pastors make use of their Liberty; yet if they should do it, provided they were Faithful in their Work and Office, knowing also your Ability, we would know whether any of you could charge them with Sin, as we know you may and ought other Persons, who work not and though the Apostle did sometimes Work, it was of choice, and to prevent the glorying of those false Apostles, and for some other Reasons, which upon special Circumstances for that time he mentioneth, and yet he accounts it amongst his Afflictions.

Quest. *Ought a Pastor or Minister to make Terms with the Church about his Maintenance, before he take the Charge of them?*

Answ. We assert for no such thing, he is to take the Charge freely, and of a ready Mind: But we say there is as indispensable a Duty lies upon the People to provide Carnal or Temporal good Things for him, as there lies upon him to provide Spiritual good Things for them, and to give him Grounds to Believe they will be Faithful to Christ and to him, in their duty upon that account.

Quest. *But what shall that Church do, who are not able to allow a sufficient Maintenance to their Pastor?*

Answ. We have a Three-fold Answer to this Question.
First, If through the Poverty of the Church they cannot provide for their Minister, they may make their Case and Circumstance known to other Sister Churches, and desire their Aid and Assistance herein; but if they can have none, and the Church do their Duty to the utmost themselves, and yet they are not able to supply his Necessities, then he must be contented to suffer with the Church. But
2. If God Bless a Congregation with a plentiful Portion of the Worlds Good, it is their Duty to make their Ministers a Party with them in their Flourishing Condition (and as a late Author saith) *Considering the Place and Imployment he is in, and the Service he attends, it would be extreamly unworthy to think they have done*

---

[55] Cf. Poole on 1 Cor. 9:6.

enough, if his pressing Necessities be answered; whilst they themselves abound in Superfluities. But if the Congregation be poor, and there is no helps to be had, then their Minister must and ought to be content to be poor with them; yea, rejoyce to approve himself a Minister of Christ, (as *Paul* did) by Hunger and Nakedness, if the Providence of God call him thereto; but whilst it is in the power of their Hands to provide better for him, God expects it from them; and let none deceive themselves, *GOD is not mocked,* nor will he suffer his Commands to be slighted and evaded, without rendering a just rebuke to the Offender, *For whatsoever a Man Soweth that shall he Reap.*[56] Yet necessity is laid upon Christ's Ministers, and woe be to them if they Preach not the Gospel.

3. It may deserve our most mature Consideration, whether a People may safely continue themselves in a Church State, when not able to provide for a Ministry, especially as the Case may be circumstanced; for, possibly they might very well joyn themselves to another Congregation near unto them, and be a great help to such a Church, being Imbodied with them, And this we do say, For a People to put themselves into a Church State, is one of the most weightiest Things in the World, and ought with as great Care and Consideration to be done; we concluding in some places where there are many Churches near to each other, it would be far better for some of those small and insufficient Societies to unite themselves to some other Congregation; and by that means the weight of those Indispensible Duties and Obligations that are incumbent on them, would with much more ease be borne and answeres, to the Honour of Christ, reputation of the Gospel, and their own Edification: Moreover, if all Christians ought to consider whether they may or ought to put themselves into a Church State, except they have Persons fitly qualified and furnished with Gifts and Graces for the Ministry; which if they may not safely do, then by the same parity of reason ought they to consider whether they may proceed therein, if they know their own Insufficiency in respect of their making a Gospel Provision for their Maintenance, unless they live remote from any other Church, and so necessity put them upon their so doing.

---

[56] Cf. Coxe, *Ordination Sermon*, 36. All of the material after 2. up to this point is from Coxe.

~ The Gospel Minister's Maintenance Vindicated ~

Obj. *But is not this to build, that which you yourselves have destroyed, viz. Have you not disclaimed against such who Preach for Hire?*

Answ. We never went about we hope to destroy any Institution or Ordinance of Jesus Christ, as the Ministers Maintenance is, as has sufficiently been proved. But for men to Preach for Hire, to make that their End, we mean in Preaching the Gospel, we still utterly disclaim any such Practice, and say 'tis a low, carnal, and base End and Design, and unworthy of any Christian Man.

2. We have always disowned, or do disclaim against *Tythes* or the *Tenths* of Mens Increase, declaring that *they* are not the right of any Gospel Ministers by the *Law of Jesus Christ*, or the due of the Ministers of the *New Testament*, by the appointment of the Lord Jesus; being only a *Mosaical Rite*, and that Law to be Abrogated, as *Aarons* Priesthood is.[57]

3. We have always disowned and declared against such Ministers, who use to strive to compell Men by outward force to Pay them what they call their dues, it looking so much like an Antichristian Spirit and Practice, and not agreeable to the Gospel of Jesus Christ; were Love to Christ, and the sence of Duty, we find ought to be the only prevailing Argument to excite and provoke every Man to his Duty in this great Case. Moreover you must take heed you are not prejudiced against your Dutys from mistaken Conclusions; because some will not Preach unless you put into their Mouths, and so make a meer Trade of Preaching. Will you not answer the requirement of God to those who are the faithful Ministers of his Word? Because some will not receive their Poor, unless they are forced to do it, Will you disown your Duty to the poor Saints, and not relieve them, but Object and say, 'tis too much like the National practice? Or, do you not like *Preaching* after that manner, *i.e.* with a Text, Doctrine, Reasons and Application; because such, and such do so, whom you disown, and cannot have

---

[57] This objection is made against the State system of supporting the ministers of the Church of England by means of an obligatory tithe, collected as a tax from the citizens. For an early expression of the Particular Baptists' rejection of this practice, see Benjamin Coxe's letter to Richard Harrison, printed in *Association Records of the Particular Baptists of England, Wales and Ireland to 1660*, ed. B. R. White (London: The Baptist Historical Society, 1971), 43-50.

Communion with. Let all such weak *Objections* be avoided, and mentioned no more forever.

Object. *You have we fear ever done it; for though we do believe 'tis the duty of the Churches to allow to their Pastors a comfortable Maintenance, who are low in the World, and so exposed to the distracting Cares of this Life, and thereby hindred in the discharge of their Duty in the Ministry. Yet for rich Men who need it not; who have an allowance, we see no reason for that.*

Answ. We Answer, It is not an act of Charity (to Ministers that are poor) we plead for, But we have proved it is an Ordinance of God, he hath been pleased *to Ordain, that those who Preach the Gospel should live of the Gospel*: 'Tis their due as they are *Christs* Ministers; He is their Portion now, as well as formerly under the Law, and have therefore as much right to it, as you have to your Inheritance; and from hence he willed them when he first sent them out, *to take no Money in their Purses*, &c. And therefore the State of such you speak of, can't exempt you from that Ordinance, nor your duty to them; besides, is it fitting (think you) that such Ministers who have Estates should waste their Substance, and injure their Children in their Faithfulness to Christ in Preaching the Gospel, and in the services of your Souls: For their Work is such, that it calls for all their time and uttermost dilligence (in a right discharge of their Duty therein) and therefore thereby they are prevented of Improving what they have, for the future comfort and advantage of their Families: Nay, and we have heard to our great trouble, how some worthy Men, who have Laboured fully to improve their Ministry (through the Peoples neglect of their duty to them) have in process of time sunk in their Estates, and in Truth have been brought to a low Condition; for 'tis rare to see a Pastor of our Churches to abound in Riches: Tho some (Blessed be God) may be indifferent well to pass in the World: now to expose a rich man to Poverty, or to let a poor man shift for himself under wants and necessities, are Evils much of the like nature: and for a prevention of both, God hath ordered it so, that neither of these things should, or ought to be. Therefore this neglect (in short) exposeth Ministers to Temptations (concerning the moral Duty that lies upon them, in

~ The Gospel Minister's Maintenance Vindicated ~

common with other men to provide for their Families) namely, to content themselves in doing but one part of their Work, *viz*. To Preach a Sermon or two in the Week, &c. Now our desires are that they may all be wholly sequestred to the Lord's Work and Service; and not be other ways imploying themselves, when they should be Preaching the Kingdom of God, but to Labour to fulfill their Ministry they have received of the Lord, so that they may have their Accounts to give up with Joy in the Day of Christ.

Object. *But our Church is small, and our Pastor can't take up all his time in the Lord's Work.*

Answer. We Answer, If he wants work, who will hinder him from following of his secular Business, provided he doth faithfully and fully discharge every part of the duty of his Place and *Function*? But do not the Neighbouring Villages, and places adjacent want the Gospel, having no Bread for their Souls, and this too by reason such Pastors are unconcerned in this matter? and by which means 'tis doubtless that the Glorious Gospel is no more promulgated up and down in dark and blind corners of this Nation, nor the Church increases no more; Besides do not many poor Sinners daily perish hereby for want of Knowledg? Brethren, 'tis not for our selves, but for the Lord, and his sinking Interest that we plead for; it grieves our Souls to hear what cries there are in many parts of this Kingdom for want of Bread, some being forc'd, we hear, to go twelve or sixteen Miles to hear a Sermon; now if Ministers of Churches made it their whole Business to Preach the Word, and concern themselves for the promoting of the Truth, it would not be as it is as this very time; nor can we think it should be otherwise, unless we had a travelling Ministry (which we fear we shall hardly find) unless Pastors and Teachers in the respective Churches were taken off of all Incumbrances, and so give themselves up to the Ministry of the Word.

God has done great things for us, and hath opened a mighty door, and shall not we do some great thing for Him? The Case, Blessed be the Lord, is much altered: You may come now into any Town and none dare forbid you, (if any one will but entertain you) and Preach the Gospel; And shall we not take care to answer this Mercy; and do what we can that the poor Blind World may be Inlightened, and brought to the saving Knowledge of Jesus Christ? If the present *Providence* of God be not answered by a due Improvement to his Glory, and the furtherance of the Gospel: We may say with *Solomon, Why is there a price in the Hand of a Fool, seeing he hath no Heart to it,* Prov. 17.16. By this time we hope you may more clearly understand us, and what we drive at, and earnestly desire to see accomplished, *viz.* That Ministers may not only bear that Name, but with all Faithfulness do the Work, they are called to; 'tis not to press our People to Minister to such Preachers who are Idle and Negligent in their Business, whose Hearts and Hands are in the World, and eagerly pursue their own secular Affairs, and matter not what becomes of the Interest of Jesus Christ.

No, 'tis to encourage the Faithful and Labourous Person, who is willing to give himself up to the Lord, in the Discharge of that great Trust committed to him, and to Labour in Christ's Vineyard; it is in truth a shame for a Minister to receive the Lord's Wages, and not do the Lord's Work; for some there are in the World that do not deserve the Name of Ministers they doing the Work of the Lord so deceitfully.

Our Churches also are 'tis like in some places in the Country but small, and are like to be smaller, if the Ministry is not awakened to become more Labourous: Are there not such in some Towns, who are hardly known by the Inhabitants to be Ministers at all, they are so little concerned in Preaching, they are better known to be *Farmers, Yeomen,* and *Tradesman,* then[58] Preachers of the Gospel; they are intangled so in the Affairs of this Life, that they have little time to mind the great Work they are called to: We would ask some Ministers, whether they could not do much more. Preach oftener, and in more Places, and take greater Pains, to promote the Gospel, and gather in Souls to Christ, than they do? Certainly they will and must say, yea, we might; Why what is the reason of your not doing it? Ought we not with *Mary* to do what we can?[59] We conclude, this Omission of Duty either arises from the evil of your own hearts, or else from the Remisness and Neglect of the People, in Respect of their Duty to you. (1.) It may arise from the Evil in your own Hearts, in that you have not or do not espouse the

---

[58] *Sic.*

[59] Presumably, this is a reference to Luke 10:38-41.

Interest of Jesus Christ equal with, or above your own: Can any be contented in doing a little Service for Christ, tho his Interest sinks in their Hands; whilst they thrive in their own concerns, and grow Rich in the World: Lord, what will be come of such Ministers in the Day of Judgment? Can they think to look Christ in the Face with Comfort, that have been such slothful Servants; but God forbid there should be any among us who mind more their own trifling Affairs, than the great Work and Business of their blessed Lord and Master? Is this *the making full Proof of your Ministry you have received of the Lord?* Christ's Ministers are called *Labourers*, but we fear some Labour but little, unless it be at their own work: should you be as Remiss in your own Affairs, as possibly you are in the Lords, you would find quickly a decay in your Estates, and be in a sinking Condition in the World; which 'tis like, would soon startle you, and stir you up to greater Care and Industry; and ought you not to be as considerate in the great concernment of Christ, his Gospel and Churches? We take it not upon us to reprehend any of you but in Love (as fellow Servants may do) to caution you; pray remember, you have the most sacred Interest and Matters of Jesus Christ committed to your Trust; 'tis the greatest Charge in the World, and you and we must be called to an Account, if Souls perish in their Sins, and *the Watchman gives not suitable warning, the Blood of those Sinners God will require at the Watchman's Hands*, Zeck. 3.[60] Ministers ought to be the Light of the World, they should shine therefore in Life and Doctrine, to all round about where they live, that the People may know they have a *Noah*, a Preacher of Righteousness amongst them. But

2. This grand fault may arise from the Peoples Remisness of Duty to their Ministers; for hark, do we not hear many worthy and faithful Pastors crying out? Alas Brethren, we are no more in the Lord's Work, no more in Preaching, in Visiting, &c. Because our Families would suffer want, and what is necessary for them; we should gladly make the Gospel our whole Business, and not only watch over, and feed our own Flocks, but Preach the Gospel up and down in Towns and Villages, lying near us, if we knew how our Wives and Children might be provided for; for should we neglect that great Moral and

---

[60] *Sic.*

indispensible Duty, how would the Holy Name of God be reproached? Alas, our souls are bowed down in us, we must confess, we have daily calls to Preach, in this and that place, where to this day there has hardly been any Meeting; but we are not able to do it, and therefore, we are forc'd to send to *London*, that some Ministers might come down into our Parts, to Answer that great Call and Cry of Men and Women, for want of the Bread of Life.

This is a hard Case indeed, *i.e.* for the Servants of Christ to have the due sense of the greatness of their work upon their Hearts, but cannot discharge it according as they see there is a Call and Occasion, by Reason the People neglect their Duty to them: But however, do what you can, and venture out, God will provide for you, and move upon the Hearts of such you Preach the Gospel to, or some other Way provide for you: Improve this present Liberty, and do not *let the Lord's House lie waste*: Remember, *Necessity is laid upon you, and wo be to you, if you Preach not the Gospel*, be not Unbelieving, but trust the Providence of God; great things he expecteth from us, who has so gloriously and graciously appeared for us, and for the Land of our Nativity.

Nevertheless, Let none mistake us; we do not say, 'tis unlawful for Preachers to Work or follow Callings; but as Preaching doth not make Working unlawful, neither should any Worldly Business hinder Preaching, therefore when working with our Hands will further the Gospel, we may Work; we have a Call so to do (which was once Paul's case) but when working at Trades and Callings, does palpably tend to the hinderance of the Promulgation of the Gospel: we must give over such Working, and wholly give up our selves to Preaching &c. 'Tis but to make an Expediment, if the People should fail you: You know your Liberty, he that Laboured with his Hands, hath by that Example set the Consciences of Ministers at Liberty, to provide for the Necessities of this Life, by other Imployments, when they cannot Live of the Gospel; but this very thing *Paul* accounted amongst his Afflictions; and certainly, it must needs be a sore Grief and Exercise to any Godly Preacher in this respect, *i.e.* when he hears People calling him, one Day to this Town to Preach, and another Day to that, and he finds he cannot Answer neither of their Calls, through the Necessities of his Family[61]; and the truth is, all do readily grant, that no Positive Duty can Discharge a Man from the Obligations of that pure Moral and Universal Duty of providing for his Families.

Brethren, you know when the Harvest proves catching, and the Painful and Laborious Harvest-men are taken off of their Business, then they may do a little Work for themselves, but when 'tis good Harvest weather, and the Harvest is great, and the Labourers but few, they must stick to it and Labour hard.

Even so when the late *Storms of Persecution* were upon us, many of *Christ's Spiritual Harvest-men* were much hindred[62] and taken off of their Work, and did may be imploy themselves otherwise, in their other Affairs (few being willing to open their Doors to them;) but now the Providence of God has opened a great Door for the Gospel, and sent us Blessed Harvest Weather, and the Labourers alas! being also very few, though the Harvest is very great: How ought we to stick to our Business?

There was never certainly such a Call to Ministers to Work for God as there is now; therefore that Servant that will not do his *best* at such an Hour, is like *the Son* (that *Solomon* speaks of) *that Sleeps in Harvest and so causeth Shame*. And as a wise Husband-man will not neglect a fit opportunity of gathering in his Corn, upon presumption of much fair Weather to come: So ought not we to lose the present Season for gathering in Souls to Christ, not knowing how soon Clouds may rise, and another Storm overtake us, when we cannot Work for God as now we may; and if you have not such Incouragement[63] as you ought to have from the People, yet remember when Night comes, the Lord Jesus will well reward you for all the pains you take in his Work; yet since our Saviour saith the Labourer is worthy of his Hire, we can't think any (when they consider the Matter a little better) will any way obstruct, or hinder you in your Business through their neglect of Duty to you.

Object. *But doth not Christ tell his Disciples? As they had freely received, so they should freely give.*

---

[61] *Errata*: original reads "famly."

[62] *Sic.*

[63] *Sic.*

Answ. We believe this Text is not taken, or understood according to the meaning of our Saviour; for it cannot mean that Christ's Ministers should receive neither Money, Meat or Clothes, whilst they are imploy'd[64] in his Work and Service, because in the very next Verse he bids them *Provide neither Gold nor Silver, nor Brass in their Purses, nor two Coats, nor Scrip for their Journey*; because he plainly intimates all such things they are worthy of, and might expect them from the People to whom they Preached. Therefore 'tis an horrible abuse put upon the Text, to take that Words in that Sense; as if our Blessed master should forbid his Servants to receive a Maintenance from the People; for then indeed they might have said, Lord, If we must Preach so freely as not to receive any thing, it behoveth us to provide well for our Journey; but since they were forbid to do so, it is clear that could not be our Saviours meaning: Besides, such a Sence[65] is directly opposite or repugnant to those other Precepts the Lord Jesus hath laid down by his Apostles in the *Epistles*; wherein it is positively asserted (as you have heard) that *He that is taught in the Word ought to Communicate to him that Teacheth in all good things,* 1 Tim. 5.18. *And that they who Minister at the Altar should partake of the Altar; God having Ordained that he that Preaches the Gospel, should live of the Gospel,* 1 Cor. 9.14. Therefore we rather are of the Opinion (in respect to this Text) with a late worthy Writer; *The Doctrine* (says he) *they were to Preach, they were Impowered*[66] *to Confirm with Miracles; which*[67] *He gives them a Charge they should Work freely, without receiving any Reward for them; that the Miracles might not be used to their private Profit, but to the End they were appointed of God, which was the Confirmation of their Doctrine.*[68]

2. It may also teach us that Ministers ought not to make a Bargain with the People, or desire to know what they shall have before they enter on their Work; for he who would approve himself a true Minister of Jesus Christ ought not to Preach for Hire or filthy Lucres sake, *i.e.,* that ought not to be the thing he aims at; that's a low and base design,

---

[64] *Sic.*

[65] *Sic.*

[66] *Sic.*

[67] *Errata*: original adds "say they."

[68] Cf. Poole on Matt. 10:8. The quotation is slightly altered.

but as you know Churches provide and ought to provide for the Poor; yet should any seek to come into your Communion meerly for a Maintenance, you would say he or she that did so, were no better than Hypocrites, and (may say truly) yet that would not free you from communicating to poor Faithful Christians. Even so, if some deceitful and carnal Persons should undertake the Work of the Ministry for filthy Lucres sake, and not in Love to Christ, and to promote his Interest and Glory, they, doubtless act contrary to this Precept of Christ's. But yet nevertheless, the Church is bound to communicate and allow a comfortable Maintenance to her Faithful Ministers; and as he freely, and of a ready Mind, and for Christ's sake, Preaches the Gospel, and is bound so to do if he will approve himself Faithful; so in like manner are the People and Churches of God bound freely and of a ready mind to Minister to them, if they would shew to all they are Faithful Christians, such who have an equal respect to all Christs Commands and Desire, to the utmost of their Abilities, to further and not hinder the promulgation of the Gospel in the World.

But by the way it is plain, had it not been the practice of the Gospel Churches in the Apostles time, to allow their Pastors a Maintenance, what room was there for the Apostle to caution any Minister or Elder not to undertake the Work for filthy Lucres sake, but of a ready mind. Moreover, very remarkable is it to consider how the *Priests of God under the Law* were to receive *that Portion Jehovah gave them*: They were not (as Mr. *Ainsworth* noteth) *To receive it after a base or servile manner, but as Gifts due to the Lord, and to them from him: The* Hebrew Canons (saith he) *shew the Israelites were to give them their Portion with Honour; and it was unlawful for the* Priests *or* Levites *to snatch away the Heave-Offering, or the Tithes; yea,* saith he, *if they did but ask their Portion with their Mouth it was unlawful.* Read his Annotation on *Numb.* 18. v. 12. And then on *Deut.* 18.3. He saith again, *the Priest might not violently take the Gifts, nor ask them with his Mouth, but he received them when they were given him with Honour.*[69]

---

[69] Henry Ainsworth, *Annotations upon the Five Bookes of Moses, The Booke of the Psalmes, and the Song of Songs* (London: John Bellamie, 1627) on Numbers 18:12 and Deuteronomy 18:3.

~ The Gospel Minister's Maintenance Vindicated ~

This may teach us two things. First, that Christ's Servants ought to take heed they shew all true and real Zeal and Love to Christ, when they undertake his Work and Service; and not to shew such a servile and base Spirit as to demand their Portion that God has Ordained for them, but leave it to the free will Offering of the People. Secondly, It may also teach Churches to see they do neither withhold the Ministers Portion from them, nor give it them grudgingly, or in an unbecoming manner, but to hand out to them what they need with due respect and honour, they being worthy of it, and are to receive it as their part and portion from God, and as they are His Stewards and Faithful Labourers, by Virtue of a Divine and Holy Law: Nay, and the Lord's People ought to be as careful in discharge of this Duty to Christ's Ministers now, as the *Israelites* were to the *Levites*; tho' as we have already said, their Portion is not the *Tithes of Mens Increase*, nor *the First Fruits*, which Law is Abrogated. Yet saith *reverend Ainsworth*, "The Equity of that Law remaineth perpetually, as the Apostle observeth, *Do you not know that they which Minister about Holy things, live of the things of the Temple; and they that wait at the* Altar*, are partakers with the* Altar: *Even so hath the Lord Ordained,* &c. 1 Cor. 13.14. Because the Ministers of God then were injoyned to attend on his Service, he would not have them cumbred with worldly Affairs, 'least (saith he) they should be hindred from doing their Duties; as it is Written, *No Man that Warreth intangleth himself with the Affairs of this Life, that he may please him who hath called him to be a Soldier.* From hence God hath ordered it thus for them." Moreover, *The Hebrews say from hence 'twas* Levi *was not counted meet to have Inheritance in the Land of* Israel*, or Spoils with his Brethren, because he was separated to Serve the Lord, and to Inherit him, and to teach his strait Ways, and his Just Judgments unto the People: therefore was he separated from the ways of the World; they wage not War, as the rest of* Israel *do; neither do they Inherit nor earn for themselves with the Strength of their Bodies, but they are the Lords Power (or Substance) as it is Written,* Deut. 13.11. Bless Lord his Power; *and the Blessed God earneth for them, as it is Written* Numb. 18.20. *I am thy*

Part and thine Inheritance. Maim. Treat. Of the Release and Jubilee, *c.* 13.*f.*12.[70]

The reason of the same Law, 'tis evident of necessity does remain; the Work of Ministers is great now, and 'tis as Holy as Honourable as ever, and the neglect of a faithful discharge herein, as great a Sin as it was then; and God's People have as great, nay, greater Benefit and Divine Profit by the Ministry of the Gospel, than those had who lived under the Law; besides Christ's Servants have the same need of it: moreover, our People are delivered from other great Burdens and vast Charges that the People of *Israel* were continually at; and therefore how unjust and unreasonable a thing it is to with-hold a fit and convenient Lively-hood from them. Nay, and we must say, that which any with-hold from the Servants of God, is the Lord's, and none of theirs; for he lays claim to part of their Substance, as that which He has Ordained to his own special service and use of His Faithful Ministers.

Quest. May every one then that Preaches expect an Allowance, though they Preach but now and then.

Answ. That must be left to the Wisdom and Consideration of the Church; who ought to consider the Persons Circumstances with the Call he hath to Preach, &c. But principally it belongs to those who are set a part to that Work, whose Strength and Time is taken up about the great Affairs of Christ and the Gospel.

Thus we have indeavoured to discharge our Duty as touching this great Work, and have we hope Answered all the material Objections any have to bring, or urge against the Ministers Maintenance: But since we have a little Room we shall add some brief hints further, to shew the great charge and work of a true Gospel Minister, and so conclude; that all may see how needful a thing it is, that every one take

---

[70] This is a confusing collation of passages from Ainsworth. The reference within the quotation marks is incorrect and should read "1 Cor. 9.13.14." The quotation marks above are as in the original text, ending in a strange place, not after the first citation from Ainsworth, but in the middle of the second. "Maim." is the Jewish author Maimonides.

care to discharge their Duty in this matter to them, whereby also the Justness and Righteousness of the Law, and appointment of God herein, may yet further appear to all.

The Great and Weighty Work of a True Gospel Minister opened.

The Nature and Weightiness of the Work of the Faithful Servant of Christ, together with the necessity and difficulty of it, we shall consider in its parts in a brief and compendious manner.

First, 'Tis a Holy and sublime Office; he is placed in a very high Sphere[71] and Station, hence called the Ambassador of Christ; What higher Dignity can be conferred on Man? The greatness of the Prince whose Messengers they are, sets forth their Dignity; they are in Christ's stead Imployed in the great Affairs of His Spiritual Kingdom; and have received Authority from Him, and are also prepared and qualified for this Sacred Work by Him, and indeed therefore ought to be blameless, *as the Stewards of God*: And hence it is that those who are said to receive them, receive Him; and those who despise them, despise Him. O! with what Holy Fear, Dread, and Reverence ought they to enter upon this Work and Office, least they should dishonour their great and glorious Prince and Heavenly Soveraign, whom they represent! Is it not a weighty thing to be made the Mouth of Christ?

2. Nay, and this is not all, they are intrusted with matters of the highest moment in the World, Christ having committed the Management of his Glorious Interests, and great concerns he has on

---

[71] In the original, the heading at the top of pages 1-13 reads "*A Regular Ministry Asserted*"; on pages 14-113, the left pages are headed by the words "*The Gospel Minister's*" and the right pages by the words "*Maintenance Vindicated*." From page 114 (which begins at this point in the text) through the end of the book (page 132), all pages are headed by the words, "*Minister's Work is Great*." Page 116 is an exception, reading "*The Gospel Ministers*." The word "*Ministers*" on pages 115, 117-31 is printed without the apostrophe.

Earth into their Hands; they are sent to treat with poor Sinners about Eternal Matters, even the Eternal Life, or Eternal Death and Damnation of their Precious and Immortal Souls, in and about these things Ministers of the Gospel are Fellow Workers together with Christ. 2 *Cor.* 6.1. Though but as Instruments, serving him as the principal Agent, and efficient Cause: *He trod the Wine-Press of his Fathers Wrath alone*; but in the Application of the purchase of Man's Salvation, he admits of Fellow-workers, tho the internal Work be his, *i.e.* the effects of his Spirits upon the Souls of those whose Hearts are changed; yet there is a Ministerial part which lyeth on the faithful Discharge of the Minister's Duty, which consisteth partly in *Exhortations, Motives* and *Arguments*, by the Ear conveyed to the Soul; and thus Ministers may be said to be Workers together with Christ, and without him they can do nothing, they are Workers, but they must have Christ Work with them, or they will find that they Labour in Vain.

But is it not think you a high and most sacred Place and Office thus to be imployed? May not every one of us say, who are sufficient for these things, *for we are unto God* (saith the Apostle) *a sweet savour of Christ in them that are saved, and in them that perish*, 2 *Cor.* 2. for that God whom we serve, will not Judge of us, nor reward us according to our Success (as a worthy Author observes) but according to our Faithfulness and Diligence in his Work, we give (as if *Paul* should say) a good savour by our Doctrine unto all, and our Labours are a sweet savour in the Nostrils of God, whatever effects they have upon the Souls of Men; God accepteth of our Labours, as to good Men, to whom we are Instruments of Eternal Life and Salvation; and though others despise the Gospel, and refuse the sweet sound thereof; yet as to them also, we are a sweet savour in the Nostrils of God, tho *Israel* be not saved, saith the Prophet, yet I shall be glorious; it is not through any neglect in us, as to our duty if any perish, but from their own Willfulness and Rebellious Hearts. *To the one, we are the savour of Death unto Death, and to the other, the savour of Life unto Life. And who is sufficient for these things.* ver. 16.

As sweet smells, which are to some pleasant and comfortable (saith a Worthy Author) yet are to others pernicious and deadly; so it is with the sweet savour of the Gospel; the report which we in all places make of Christ, to some (through their unbelief, and hardness of their Heart, and fondness of their Lusts) proveth; but the Savour of *Death unto Death*, hardning their Hearts to their Eternal Ruine and Destruction; but to such who (being ordained to Eternal Life; believe our Report, and) imbrace the Gospel, and give up to the Precepts and Rule thereof; our Preaching proves a Cause of Spiritual and Eternal Life to which that leadeth; but O how great a work is this! What Man? What Angel, is sufficient for it? O it is a mighty Work to Preach the Gospel, as we ought to Preach it;[72] it is that by which Faith cometh, *How shall they believe on him, of whom they have not heard? And how shall they hear, without a Preacher? And how shall they Preach, except they are sent?* Rom. 10.14. *i. e.* Unless they have an extraordinary or ordinary Mission, *i.e.* either from God more immediately (which Call is long since ceased) or else, by the Election of the Church, and Ordination of the Elders, or Presbytery; this is necessary in all Regular Ministers: How else can they duly or profitably in the Name and Authority of Christ, preach the Word of Life? Brethren, (you who are Christ's true Ministers being orderly called to this sacred Work,) your Preaching hath attendancy, either to save, or eternally to condemn the Souls of Men; and with what trembling then, ought this work to be undertaken and performed; you are intrusted with Men's Souls, and must be accountable for them; especially, such who are committed to your Charge; did we consider it, and duly ponder upon it in our Minds, certainly, we should have little else to think upon, nor trouble our Heads and Hearts about, it would be sure cause us to be more Serious, and Laborious, we are perswaded, then we are: What shall we do, if through our Neglect and Remisness in this great Work, any should die and perish in their Sins? Mind what God saith in that of *Ezek.* 3.18. Unto his Watchmen, *When I say unto the wicked, thou shalt surely dye, and thou givest him not warning, nor speakest to warn the wicked from his way, to save his Life, the same wicked man shall die in his Iniquity, but his Blood I will require at thine Hand*; tho some do prophanely scoff and deride, yet must we speak to them, and warn them, until it do appear they are such as *will*

---

[72] Cf. Poole on 2 Cor. 2:15-16. The quotation is slightly altered at several points. All of the material from the words "2 *Cor.* 2" in the preceding paragraph is closely based on Poole.

~ *The Gospel Minister's Maintenance Vindicated* ~

turn again and rend us, Men must be told their Sins, and their Dangers, that so we (as instruments in God's Hand) may preserve their Souls, and recal them at once from Sin and Death, the Man who is not warned, will certainly die in his Sins, his Ignorance will not be sufficient to prevent his Ruin and Damnation; but if Ministers admonish him not, warn him not, that will involve them also under Guilt and Danger, God will punish such Ministers and Watchmen, who possibly might have saved those perishing Sinners, however they ought to have warned them, And

Hence how Careful was St. *Paul*, see *Acts* 20.26. that ye might be pure from the Blood of all Men; he appeals to the Church of *Ephesus*, in that matter, they knowing his great Care, Faithfulness, and unwearied Industry, upon every Respect; and shews that no Soul had been lost through his default, he having sincerely, and in all simplicity declared to them the way of Life, and perswaded them to walk therein, and had not kept back any part of the Will and Mind of Christ from them, but had shewed them the whole Counsel of God, *and ceased not* for three Years (which was all the whole time he was amongst them) *to warn every on Night and Day with Tears.* Acts 20.31. The precious Worth of the Immortal Souls of Men lay upon the Spirit and Conscience of this Blessed Apostle: And in this he laid forth himself as an Example for all true and faithful Ministers, who are injoyned elsewhere to follow his Steps. If one Soul be worth more than all the World; How great is the charge of Christ's Ministers, that have many souls committed to their Care and Trust? But

2. This is not all, they are Intrusted with that Holy, High, and Peculiar Interest which Jesus Christ hath here below, which is dearer to him than Ten Thousand Worlds; He is gone into Heaven, and hath left His great Concerns He hath here on Earth to them to mind and look after and take the care of: For the good of which, and to carry it on, and for the perfecting of it: He hath shed His most Precious Blood, and given His Holy Spirit to them in the Gifts and Graces of it, and appointed them a Livelyhood, without being incumbred with worldly Business; and hath also promised them a Crown of Glory at last, if they abide Faithful to the end, assuring them that they, and all others who turn many to Righteousness, shall shine as the Stars for ever more. *Dan.* 12.2,3.

3. They are not only *Stewards of the Mysteries of God*, 1 Cor. 4.1. But also Intrusted with the charge and care of his Churches, and Holy Doctrine of the Gospel; Ministers are the Stewards of Christ's House: Moreover, *It is required in Stewards, that a Man be found Faithful,* 1 Cor. 4.2. Especially such Servants who are entrusted with their Masters Goods, to be dispenced out to others: Now the Faithfulness of such Stewards lies in their giving to every one their due Portion, according to their Masters order, and not detaining any thing from others which he hath ordered them to have; the same in quality, not *Water instead of Wine, nor Dross instead of Gold:* not *Mens Inventions and Traditions, instead of his Holy Sacraments and Sacred Institutions.* And the same for quantity; not now and then a small Portion, but as Christ hath provided plenty, so they should plentifully hand forth to all His Servants: And they also must be Faithful to cherish and strengthen the Weak, and heal with all Skill and Tenderness the wounded and sickly Ones of Christs Family, and every way improve their Masters Money, and do what they can to gather in Souls to him: For one chief End of Gospel Ministry is for the gathering together of the Saints; as well as for the Edifying the Body of Christ; therefore in every place where there is a Door opened for them, they must work hard whilst there are any Sinners to be called into the Vineyard, and must not leave their Masters Business to follow their own; especially when they know not but Christ hath much People in and about the place where they live, who are to be brought into His Fold.

Secondly, The necessity and usefulness of their Work and Ministration is opened by divers other *Metaphors*: *viz.* They are called *Shepherds*; What would soon become of the Sheep, if the Shepherd should be careless, they will quickly go astray, &c. the Wolf would devour them. They are called also Guides, and of Old *Seers* and *Watchmen*; being set to discover and give warning of approaching danger.

The Greatness and Labouriousness of their Work, is set forth by their being called *Planters, Builders,* and *Labourers.*

The *Dignity* and *Honourableness* of their Work and Office is set forth by their being called *Fathers, Angels, Ambassadors, Stars and Rulers*: Now from the whole it must needs appear to all, that the

Ministers Work is hard and difficult: We may well say, *Who is sufficient for these things*? 'Tis such a Work that it caused some of God's Servants of Old, to undertake it with much Trembling; nay it made *Moses* to cry out, *Send by whom thou wilt send.* Exod. 4.13.

'Tis so hard and difficult, that a man with all his acquired Parts is not sufficient for it; nay, a Saint with all his Spiritual Gifts and Graces is not able to perform it without fresh supplies of renewed Strength every Day.

But to proceed, the difficulty of the Ministers Work lies in these respects following.

First, In regard of themselves who are Imployed in it.

1. They are but Men; *Son of Man I have made thee a Watchman.* And as they are men, so commonly they are not the wisest and most learned in respect of humane Parts and Knowledg neither. *You see your Calling Brethren.*

2. Man at best is but a Worm, he is a poor dark-sighted Creature, *we* (saith the Apostle) *know but in part.*

3. Man at best with all his Accomplishments, is attended with Weakness and carries about with him, *a Body of Sin and Death.* Rom. 7.

4. Man at best with all his Heavenly Graces, hath but small Skill, and short Experiences.

5. Man at best is subject to great Discouragements, and lyable to many grievous Temptations.

Secondly, The difficulty of their Business, lies in the Work it self, the Ministers Imployment is hard, and no ways easie. Because,

1. 'Tis a Mysterious Work, what Mysteries are greater than those a Minister is to study, and dive into? *Without Controversy, great is the Mystery of Godliness.* 1 Tim. 3.16. *But we speak the Wisdom of God in a Mystery, even the hidden Wisdom.* 1 Cor. 2.7.

That which the most wise, and knowing in the same Art, can reach or understand but part of, must needs be a great Mystery; but so it is here, for the Apostles who had the greatest and clearest Knowledge of these Mysteries, as any ever had in the World; yet declare, they *knew but in part, and saw but in part, darkly, as through a Glass. ver.* 13.9.12. 'Tis such a Mystery, that *he that thinks he knows any thing, knows nothing, as he ought to know.*

What a Mystery is that of the Incarnation of our Lord Jesus? That the Nature of Man should be joined to the Divine Nature of God, and both make but one Christ.

What a Mystery is there in the Doctrine of Faith? 1. That a Man should go out of himself, and be carried above himself, to believe things impossible to Man's Natural Reason, that he should seek for Justification, by the Righteousness and Obedience of another; for a Man (as one would think) to have a great store of Holyness, and good Works, and yet throw it (as it were) all away, and be dead to it in point of Trust, and Dependance, is to Natural Men a strange Mystery. 2. To believe when every thing is opposite to it: To Work for Life, and oppose some Sin, a Natural Man is ready to do; but to believe in Christ, for Life and Holyness, to rely on his Doings, his Works, his Merits; this the Heart of Man can't understand, but is naturally averse to; nay, and Satan also opposeth it, and the World mocks at it, and accounts it Foolishness. 3. That a Man should believe and not see; nay, believe as *Abraham* did, in hope, against hope is a Mystery.

Yet, may be there are some greater Mysteries than this which a Minister is to Study, in respect of Christ the Mediator; his Work, Offices, Glorious Covenant, Ordinances, and Providences of God in the World, and therefore his Work is a difficult Work.

2. 'Tis difficult, in that it calls for the greatest Care and Exactness imaginable, every thing must be done according, to the Holy Pattern set by Christ in the Gospel; there must be no adding to, no diminishing from, nor altering of anything in the least, without eternal hazard and danger.

3. 'Tis difficult and very hard in that it calls for the greatest strength that the most strong Grace and Wisdom can arrive unto, it requires all the Powers of the whole Soul to be exerted or put forth to a right Discharge thereof.

4. It calls not only for all our strength, but also all our Time and Diligence; a slothful or Idle Person is not fit to be a Minister, 'tis a work that must be followed continually, let the times be what they will; *Preach the Word, be instant in season, and out of season, reprove, exhort, with all long Suffering, and Doctrine*; be not Slothful, but Diligent, fear no Faces, regard no Threats, respect no Mans Person, reprove all impartially, be no fawning nor flattering Preacher; nor like

those who rather vent their own Passion, than persue the end of Instruction, and Reformation of Souls; and this is a hard Work to do.

5. 'Tis difficult Work, in respect of the opposition that is made against them, and the Grand Obstructions they meet withal.

1. *From their own Hearts, the Flesh is weak, tho the Spirit indeed is willing,* many times, that it is ready to say with *Peter, Master, pity thy self;* Why dost thou spend thy Time, thy Strength, and ware out thy poor Body at this sort? Less may do &c.

Besides, the Heart of a Minister (who is sensible of the Nature of his Work) causes him oft to tremble, in Consideration of his Unfitness, and Unworthiness for such a sacred Undertaking and Imployment.

2. *From Sin,* in dwelling Sin, and other Humane Frailties; alas, they are Men of like Passion and Infirmities with others.

3. *From Satan,* he is an Implacable Enemy to them, and to their Work; hence he raises up all the Opposition against them imaginable, to hinder them in their Business, or take them off of it, or make them Remiss and Negligent in doing it, *we are not Ignorant* (saith *Paul*) *of his devices.* 2 Cor. 2.11.

4. *From the World,* 1. By Reproaches and Contradictions of Ungodly Men, 2. By Hereticks and False-Teachers, with these they are forc'd to fight, and many times are hard put to it, as *Paul* when he ingaged those evil Beasts in Ephesus.

5. Lastly, *By Persecutors,* allways the heat of this Battle falls upon Christ's poor Ministers; they are the Mark these wicked Archers shoot at; hence they like *Paul* are oft in Bonds, and Prisoners for Christ's sake.

Now, put all these things together, and it is needful (think you) that your poor Ministers be thought upon, and incouraged by you, as Christ hath appointed? But we shall say no more, only, conclude all with one Word to our *Fellow Labourers.* Brethren, let us strive to double our Diligence, and shew to all the sense of the greatness of our work is upon our Spirits; and tho we have not that incouragement from the People that God has Ordained; yet, remember we serve a good Master: Besides, a Necessity is laid upon us, we must Preach the Gospel; and let us, be contented, with that State and Portion we meet with in the World; 'tis our great Business to approve our selves the Ministers of Christ, *in Labours, in Watchings, in Fastings, by Pureness, by*

Knowledge, by the Holy Ghost, by Love unfeigned, by the Word of Truth, by the Power of God, by the Armour of Righteousness, on the Right Hand, and on the Left; by Honour, and Dishonour; by evil Report and good Report, 2 Cor. 6.5,6,7,8. Possibly, we may be reproached, and sensured for what we have done, and said, in this small Tract. But should it be so, we matter it not, since we have the Testimony of our Consciences, that our Design is the Glory of God, and the promoting his Blessed Gospel in the Nation, and the good of his poor Churches; and also, because we know we have the sure Word of God to confirm the Truth of what we plead for: Wherefore, whilst we make it appear to all, 'tis not the Hire, the Wages, &c. that we aim at, but contrariwise, the Honour of the ever blessed God, and to Witness to the Sanction of every one of his Just and most Holy Precepts, we cannot be without Peace in our Souls.

FINIS

8

A Confession of Faith

Introduction

It is strange that many today refer to the following document as the 1689 Confession, when it was not in fact published in that year, but twelve years earlier in 1677, and again in 1688. The reason for the designation '1689' is simple—the Confession is closely identified with the London General Assembly of that year.[1]

The Particular Baptists had published an earlier general confession in 1644 (significantly revised in 1646, and again slightly in 1651[2]). Intending to demonstrate their orthodoxy, that Confession was largely based on the 1596 *True Confession* issued by English separatists in the Netherlands, supplemented by material from William Ames' *Marrow of Sacred Divinity* and other material. Following the same methodology, the 1677 *Confession* likewise relied heavily on previous English Puritan Confessions, namely the *Westminster Confession of Faith* of 1647/48 and the *Savoy Declaration and Platform of Polity* issued in 1658.[3] In the epistle "To the Judicious and Impartial Reader," the editors state that this dependence is purposeful, demonstrating that these Baptists consented to "hearty agreement with them, in that wholesome Protestant Doctrine." In both of their general Confessions, the Particular Baptists purposely used extant documents to

---

[1] See the notice included in the *1689 Narrative* above.

[2] The 1651 printing is labeled "The third Impression corrected." A "fourth Impression corrected" was issued in 1652, and another bearing the label "fourth Impression corrected" in Leith, Scotland, in 1654.

[3] The texts of these confessions, as well as their source documents, may be consulted in James M. Renihan, *True Confessions: Baptist Documents in the Reformed Family* (Palmdale, CA: RBAP, 2004).

demonstrate their concurrence with the theological convictions of their Puritan contemporaries.

We do not know the precise origins of the 1677 *Confession*. The first known literary reference to it is found in the manuscript church book from London's Petty France congregation. The entry for 26 August 1677 reads "It was agreed that a Confession of faith, wth the Appendix thereto having bene read & considered by the Bre: should be published."[4] This has led some to conclude that the pastors of this church, Nehemiah Coxe and William Collins, were responsible for the editing of the document. This is a reasonable assumption.[5]

Modern versions commonly omit the epistle "to the Judicious and Impartial reader" as well as the Appendix. The Appendix was published with the 1677 and 1688 editions, but not with that of 1699. It is an important document, serving an apologetic purpose for the Baptist practice. The fact that it is an appendix is important to note. This was a purposeful choice, allowing the Baptists to address the important matter under consideration while at the same time separating it from the more significant matters in the Confession itself.

There is no question that this Confession has had immense influence on Baptists around the world. It became the standard confession of American Baptists, having been published by Benjamin Franklin for the Philadelphia Association in 1742 and followed in rapid succession by editions authorized by other Associations throughout the Colonies.

---

[4] Petty France Church Minute Book 1675-1727, London Metropolitan Archives, 5.

[5] See Renihan, *Edification and Beauty*, 22ff.

~ A Confession of Faith (Introduction) ~

A

CONFESSION

OF

FAITH

Put forth by the

Elders and *Brethren*

Of many

CONGREGATIONS

OF

CHRISTIANS

(Baptized upon Profession of their Faith)

in

London and the *Country*.

With an

APPENDIX concerning Baptism.

With the Heart man believeth unto Righteousness, and with the Mouth
  Confession is made unto Salvation, Rom. 10.10
Search the Scriptures, John 5:39

London: Printed for *John Harris*, at the *Harrow* against the *Church* in
the *Poultrey*, 1688

To the Judicious and Impartial Reader
Chapter 1. Of the Holy Scriptures
Chapter 2. Of God and of the Holy Trinity
Chapter 3. Of God's Decree
Chapter 4. Of Creation
Chapter 5. Of Divine Providence
Chapter 6. Of the Fall of Man, of Sin, and of the Punishment Thereof
Chapter 7. Of God's Covenant
Chapter 8. Of Christ the Mediator
Chapter 9. Of Free Will
Chapter 10. Of Effectual Calling
Chapter 11. Of Justification
Chapter 12. Of Adoption
Chapter 13. Of Sanctification
Chapter 14. Of Saving Faith
Chapter 15. Of Repentance Unto Life and Salvation
Chapter 16. Of Good Works
Chapter 17. Of The Perseverance Of The Saints
Chapter 18. Of the Assurance of Grace and Salvation
Chapter 19. Of the Law of God
Chapter 20. Of the Gospel, and of the Extent of the Grace Thereof
Chapter 21. Of Christian Liberty and Liberty of Conscience
Chapter 22. Of Religious Worship and the Sabbath Day
Chapter 23. Of Lawful Oaths and Vows
Chapter 24. Of the Civil Magistrate
Chapter 25. Of Marriage
Chapter 26. Of the Church
Chapter 27. Of the Communion of Saints
Chapter 28. Of Baptism and the Lord's Supper
Chapter 29. Of Baptism
Chapter 30. Of the Lord's Supper
Chapter 31. Of the State of Man After Death, and of the Resurrection
            of the Dead
Chapter 32. Of the Last Judgment
An Appendix

TO THE
Judicious and *Impartial*
READER

Courteous Reader,

It is now many years since divers of us (with other sober Christians then living and walking in the way of the Lord that we professe) did conceive our selves to be under a necessity of Publishing a *Confession of our Faith*, for the information, and satisfaction of those, that did not throughly understand what our principles were, or had entertained prejudices against our Profession, by reason of the strange representation of them, by some men of note, who had taken very wrong measures, and accordingly led others into misapprehensions, of us, and them: and this was first put forth about the year, 1643. in the name of seven Congregations then gathered in *London*; since which time, diverse impressions thereof have been dispersed abroad, and our end proposed, in good measure answered, inasmuch as many (and some of those men eminent, both for piety and learning) were thereby satisfied, that we were no way guilty of those Heterodoxies and fundamental errors, which had too frequently been charged upon us without ground, or occasion given on our part. And forasmuch, as that *Confession* is not now commonly to be had; and also that many others have since embraced the same truth which is owned therein; it was judged necessary by us to joyn together in giving a testimony to the world; of our firm adhering to those wholesome Principles, by the publication of this which is now in your hand.

And forasmuch as our method, and manner of expressing our sentiments, in this, doth vary from the former (although the substance of the matter is the same) we shall freely impart to you the reason and occasion thereof. One thing that greatly prevailed with us to undertake this work, was (not only to give a full account of our selves, to those Christians that differ from us about the subject of Baptism, but also) the profit that might from thence arise, unto those that have any account of our labors, in their instruction, and establishment in the great truths of the Gospel; in the clear understanding, and steady belief of which, our comfortable walking with God, and fruitfulness before him, in all our ways, is most neerly concerned; and therefore we did conclude it necessary to expresse our selves the more fully, and distinctly; and also to fix on such a method as might be most comprehensive of those things which we designed to explain our sense, and belief of; and finding no defect, in this regard, in that fixed on by the assembly,[1] and after them by those of the Congregational way,[2] we did readily conclude it best to retain the same *order* in our present confession: and also, when we observed that those last mentioned, did in their confession (for reasons which seemed of weight both to themselves and others) choose not only to express their mind in words concurrent with the former in sense, concerning all those articles wherein they were agreed, but also for the most part without any variation of the terms we did in like manner conclude it best to follow their example in making use of the very same words with them both, in these articles (which are very many) wherein our faith and doctrine is the same with theirs, and this we did, the more abundantly, to manifest our consent with both, in all the fundamental articles of the Christian Religion, as also with many others, whose orthodox confessions have been published to the world; on behalf of the Protestants in divers Nations and Cities: and also to convince all, that we have no itch to clogge Religion with new words, but do readily acquiesce in that form of sound words, which hath been, in consent with the holy Scriptures, used by others before us; hereby declaring before God, Angels, & Men, our hearty agreement with them, in that wholesome Protestant Doctrine, which with so clear evidence of Scriptures they have asserted: some things indeed, are in some places added, some terms omitted, and some few changed, but these alterations are of that nature, as that we need not doubt, any charge or suspition of unsoundness in the faith, from any of our brethren upon the account of them.

In those things wherein we differ from others, we have exprest our selves with all candor and plainness that none might entertain jealousie of ought secretly lodged in our breasts, that we would not the world

---

[1] I.e., the Westminster Assembly.

[2] I.e., *The Savoy Declaration and Platform of Polity* issued by the congregationalists of the Savoy Synod in 1658.

~ To the Judicious and Impartial Reader ~

should be acquainted with; yet we hope we have also observed those rules of modesty, and humility, as will render our freedom in this respect inoffensive, even to those whose sentiments are different from ours.

We have also taken care to affix texts of Scripture, in the margin for the confirmation of each article in our confession; in which work we have studiously indeavoured to select such as are most clear and pertinent, for the proof of what is asserted by us: and our earnest desire is, that all into whose hands this may come, would follow that (never enough commended) example of the noble *Bereans*, who searched the Scriptures daily, that they might find out whether the things preached to them were so or not.

There is one thing more which we sincerely professe, and earnestly desire credence in, *viz.* That contention is most remote from our design in all that we have done in this matter: and we hope the liberty of an ingenuous unfolding our principles, and opening our hearts unto our Brethren, with the Scripture grounds on which our faith and practise leanes, will by none of them be either denyed to us, or taken ill from us. Our whole design is accomplished, if we may obtain that Justice, as to be measured in our principles, and practise, and the judgement of both by others, according to what we have now published; which the Lord (whose eyes are as a flame of fire) knoweth to be the doctrine, which with our hearts we must firmly believe, and sincerely indeavour to conform our lives to. And oh that other contentions being laid asleep, the only care and contention of all upon whom the name of our blessed Redeemer is called, might for the future be, to walk humbly with their God, and in the exercise of all Love and Meekness towards each other, to perfect holyness in the fear of the Lord, each one endeavouring to have his conversation such as becometh the Gospel; and also suitable to his place and capacity vigorously to promote in others the practice of true Religion and undefiled in the sight of God and our Father. And that in this backsliding day, we might not spend our breath in fruitless complaints of the evils of others; but may every one begin at home, to reform in the first place our own hearts, and wayes; and then to quicken all that we may have influence upon, to the

~ To the Judicious and Impartial Reader ~

same work; that if the will of God were so, none might deceive themselves, by resting in, and trusting to, a form of Godliness, without the power of it, and inward experience of the efficacy of those truths that are professed by them.

And verily there is one spring and cause of the decay of Religion in our day, which we cannot but touch upon, and earnestly urge a redresse of; and that is the neglect of the worship of God in Families, by those to whom the charge and conduct of them is committed. May not the grosse ignorance, and instability of many; with the prophaneness of others, be justly charged upon their Parents and Masters; who have not trained them up in the way wherein they ought to walk when they were young? but have neglected those frequent and solemn commands which the Lord hath laid upon them so to catechize, and instruct them, that their tender years might be seasoned with the knowledge of the truth of God as revealed in the Scriptures; and also by their own omission of Prayer, and other duties of Religion in their families, together with the ill example of their loose conversation, have inured them first to a neglect, and then contempt of all Piety and Religion? we know this will not excuse the blindness, or wickedness of any; but certainly it will fall heavy upon those that have thus been the occasion thereof; they indeed dye in their sins; but will not their blood be required of those under whose care they were, who yet permitted them to go on without *warning*, yea led them into the paths of destruction? and will not the diligence of Christians with respect to the discharge of these duties, in ages past, rise up in judgment against, and condemn many of those who would be esteemed such now?

We shall conclude with our earnest prayer, that the God of all grace, will pour out those measures of his holy Spirit upon us, that the profession of truth may be accompanyed with the sound belief, and diligent practise of it by us; that his name may in all things be glorified, through Jesus Christ our Lord, *Amen.*

~ To the Judicious and Impartial Reader ~

CHAP. I.
Of the Holy Scriptures.

1. The Holy Scripture is the only sufficient, certain, and infallible (*a*) rule of all saving Knowledge, Faith and Obedience; Although the (*b*) light of Nature, and the works of Creation and Providence do so far manifest the goodness, wisdom and power of God, as to leave men unexcusable; yet are they not sufficient to give that knowledge of God and His will, which is necessary unto Salvation. (*c*) Therefore it pleased the Lord at sundry times, and in divers manners, to reveal himself, and to declare that His will unto his Church; and afterward for the better preserving, and propagating of the Truth, and for the more sure Establishment, and Comfort of the Church against the corruption of the flesh, and the malice of Satan, and of the World, to commit the same wholly unto (*d*) writing; which maketh the Holy Scriptures to be most necessary, those former ways of Gods revealing his will unto his people being now ceased.

a 2 Tim. 3 15,16,17. Isa. 8. 20. Luk. 16. 29,31. Eph. 2. 20.
b Rom. 1. 19,20,21. &c. ch 2. 14,15. Psal. 19. 1,2,3.
c Heb. 1. 1.
d Pro. 22. 19,20,21. Rom. 15. 4. 2 Pet. 1. 19,20.

2. Under the Name of Holy Scripture or the Word of God written; are now contained all the Books of the Old and New Testament which are these,

Of the Old Testament.

Genesis, Exodus, Leviticus, Numbers, Deuteronomy, Joshua, Judges, Ruth, 1 Samuel, 2 Samuel, 1 Kings, 2 Kings, 1 Chronicles, 2 Chronicles, Ezra, Nehemiah, Esther, Job, Psalms, Proverbs, Ecclesiastes, The Song of Songs, Isaiah, Jeremiah, Lamentations, Ezekiel, Daniel, Hosea, Joel, Amos, Obadiah, Jonah, Micah, Nahum, Habakkuk, Zephaniah, Haggai, Zechariah, Malachi.

Of the New Testament.

Matthew, Mark, Luke, John, The Acts of the Apostles, Pauls Epistle to the Romans, 1 Corinthians, 2 Corinthians, Galatians, Ephesians, Philippians, Colossians, 1 Thessalonians, 2 Thessalonians, 1 Timothy, 2 Timothy, to Titus, to Philemon, the Epistle to the Hebrews, the Epistle of James, The first and second Epistles of Peter, The first, second and third Epistles of John, the Epistle of Jude, the Revelation. All which are given by the (*e*) inspiration of God, to be the rule of Faith and Life.

   e 2 Tim. 3. 16.

3. The Books commonly called *Apocrypha* not being of (*f*) Divine inspiration, are no part of the Canon (or rule) of the Scripture, and therefore are of no authority to the Church of God, nor to be any otherwise approved or made use of, then other humane writings.

   f Luk. 24. 27.44. Rom. 3. 2.

4. The Authority of the Holy Scripture for which it ought to be believed dependeth not upon the testimony of any man, or Church; but wholly upon (*g*) God (who is truth it self) the Author thereof; therefore it is to be received, because it is the Word of God.

   g 2 Pet. 1. 19,20,21. 2 Tim. 3. 16. 2 Thes. 2. 13. 1 Joh. 5. 9.

5. We may be moved and induced by the testimony of the Church of God, to an high and reverent esteem of the Holy Scriptures; and the heavenliness of the matter, the efficacy of the Doctrine, and the Majesty of the stile, the consent of all the parts, the scope of the whole (which is to give all glory to God) the full discovery it makes of the only way of mans salvation, and many other incomparable Excellencies, and intire perfections thereof, are arguments whereby it doth abundantly evidence it self to be the Word of God; yet notwithstanding; our (*h*) full perswasion, and assurance of the infallible truth, and divine authority thereof, is from the inward work of the Holy Spirit, bearing witness by and with the Word in our Hearts.

   h Joh. 16. 13,14. 1 Cor. 2. 10,11,12. 1 John 2. 2.20.27.

6. The whole Councel of God concerning all things (*i*) necessary for his own Glory, Mans Salvation, Faith and Life, is either expressely set down or necessarily contained in the *Holy Scripture*; unto which nothing at any time is to be added, whether by new Revelation of the *Spirit*, or traditions of men.

Nevertheless we acknowledge the (*k*) inward illumination of the Spirit of God, to be necessary for the saving understanding of such things as are revealed in the Word, and that there are some circumstances concerning the worship of God, and government of the Church common to humane actions and societies; which are to be (*l*) ordered by the light of nature, and Christian prudence according to the general rules of the Word, which are always to be observed.

i 2 Tim. 3. 15,16,17. Gal. 1. 8,9.

k John 6. 45. 1 Cor. 2. 9,10,11,12.

l 1 Cor. 11, 13,14. & ch. 14. 26. & 40.

7. All things in Scripture are not alike (*m*) plain in themselves, nor alike clear unto all; yet those things which are necessary to be known, believed, and observed for Salvation, are so (*n*) clearly propounded, and opened in some place of Scripture or other, that not only the learned, but the unlearned, in a due use of ordinary means, may attain to a sufficient understanding of them.

m 2 Pet. 3. 16.

n Ps. 19. 7. and 119. 130.

8. The Old Testament in (*o*) *Hebrew*, (which was the Native language of the people of God of old) and the New Testament in *Greek* (which at the time of the writing of it) was most generally known to the Nations being immediately inspired by God, and by his singular care and Providence kept pure in all Ages, are therefore (*p*) authentical; so as in all controversies of Religion the Church is finally to appeal unto them (*q*.) But because these original tongues are not known to all the people of God, who have a right unto, and interest in the Scriptures, and are commanded in the fear of God to read (*r*) and search them, therefore they are to be translated into the vulgar language of every Nation, unto which they (*s*) come, that the Word of God dwelling (*t*)

plentifully in all, they may worship him in an acceptable manner, and through patience and comfort of the Scriptures may have hope.

o Rom. 3. 2.
p Isa. 8. 20.
q Act. 15. 15.
r John 5. 39.
s 1 Cor. 14, 6.9.11,12.24.28.
t Col. 3. 16.

9. The infallible rule of interpretation of Scripture is the (*u*) Scripture it self: And therefore when there is a question about the true and full sense of any Scripture (which is not manifold but one) it must be searched by other places that speak more clearly.

u 2 Pet. 1. 20,21. Act. 15. 15,16.

10. The supream judge by which all controversies of Religion are to be determined, and all Decrees of Councels, opinions of antient Writers, Doctrines of men, and private Spirits, are to be examined, and in whose sentence we are to rest, can be no other but the Holy Scripture delivered by the Spirit, into which (*x*) Scripture so delivered, our faith is finally resolved.

x Mat. 22. 29.31. Eph. 2. 20 Acts 28. 23.

~ Chapter I. Of the Holy Scriptures ~

CHAP. II.
Of God and of the Holy Trinity.

1. The Lord our God is but (*a*) one onely living, and true God; whose (*b*) subsistence is in and of himself, (*c*) infinite in being, and perfection, whose Essence cannot be comprehended by any but himself; (*d*) a most pure spirit, (*e*) invisible, without body, parts, or passions, who only hath immortality, dwelling in the light, which no man can approach unto, who is (*f*) immutable, (*g*) immense, (*h*) eternal, incomprehensible, (*i*) Almighty, every way infinit, (*k*) most holy, most wise, most free, most absolute, (*l*) working all things according to the councel of his own immutable, and most righteous will, (*m*) for his own glory, most loving, gracious, merciful, long suffering, abundant in goodness and truth, forgiving iniquity, transgression and sin, (*n*) the rewarder of them that diligently seek him, and withall most just, (*o*) and terrible in his judgements, (*p*) hating all sin, and who will by no means clear the (*q*) guilty.

a 1 Cor. 8.4 6. Deut. 6.4.
b Jer 10.10. Isaiah 48.12.
c Exod 3.14.
d Joh. 4.24.
e 1 Tim. 1.17. Deut. 4.15,16.
f Mal. 3.6.
g 1 King. 8.27. Jer. 23.23.
h Ps. 90.2.
i Gen. 17.1.
k Isa. 6.3.
l Ps. 115.3. Isa. 46.10.
m Pro. 16.4. Rom. 11.36.
n Exod. 34.6,7. Hebr. 11.6.
o Neh. 9.32,33.
p Ps. 5.5,6.
q Exod. 34.7. Nahum. 1,2,3.

2. God having all (*r*) life, (*s*) glory, (*t*) goodness, blessedness, in and of himself: is alone in, and unto himself all-sufficient, not (*u*)

standing in need of any Creature which he hath made, nor deriving any glory from them, but onely manifesting his own glory in, by, unto, and upon them, he is the alone fountain of all Being, (x) of whom, through whom, and to whom are all things, and he hath most soveraign (y) dominion over all creatures, to do by them, for them, or upon them, whatsoever himself pleaseth; in his sight (z) all things are open and manifest, his knowledge is (a) infinite, infallible, and independant upon the Creature, so as nothing is to him contingent, or uncertain; he is most holy in all his Councels, in (b) all his Works, and in all his Commands; to him is due (c) from Angels and men, whatsoever worship, service, or obedience as Creatures they owe unto the Creator, and whatever he is further pleased to require of them.

r Joh. 5.26.
s Ps. 148.13.
t Ps. 119.68.
u Job, 22.2,3.
x Rom. 11.34.35,36.
y Dan. 4.25. and v.34,35.
z Heb. 4.13.
a Ezek. 11.5 Act. 15.18.
b Ps. 145.17.
c Rev. 5.12,13,14.

3. In this divine and infinite Being there are three subsistences, (d) the Father the Word (or Son) and Holy Spirit, of one substance, power, and Eternity, each having the whole Divine Essence, (e) yet the Essence undivided, the Father is of none neither begotten nor proceeding, the Son is (f) Eternally begotten of the Father, the holy Spirit (g) proceeding from the Father and the Son, all infinite, without beginning, therefore but one God, who is not to be divided in nature and Being; but distinguished by several peculiar, relative properties, and personal relations; which doctrine of the Trinity is the foundation of all our Communion with God, and comfortable dependance on him.

d 1 Joh. 5.7. Mat. 28.19. 2 Cor. 13.14.
e Exod. 3.14. Joh. 14.11. 1 Cor. 8.6.
f Joh. 1.14.18.
g Joh. 15.26. Gal. 4.6.

~ *Chapter II. Of God and of the Holy Trinity* ~

CHAP. III.
Of Gods Decree.

1. God hath (*a*) *Decreed* in himself from all Eternity, by the most wise and holy Councel of his own will, freely and unchangeably, all things whatsoever comes to passe; yet so as thereby is God neither the author of sin, (*b*) nor hath fellowship with any therein, nor is violence offered to the will of the Creature, nor yet is the liberty, or contingency of second causes taken away, but rather (*c*) established, in which appears his wisdom in disposing all things, and power, and faithfulness (*d*) in accomplishing his *Decree*.

    a Is. 46.10. Eph. 1.11. Heb. 6.17. Rom. 9.15,18.
    b Jam. 1.15,17. 1 Joh. 1.5.
    c Act 4.27,28. Joh. 19.11.
    d Numb. 23.19. Eph. 1.3,4,5.

2. Although God knoweth whatsoever may, or can come to passe upon all (*e*) supposed conditions; yet hath he not *Decreed* anything, (*f*) because he foresaw it as future, or as that which would come to pass upon such conditions.

    e Act. 15.18.
    f Rom. 9.11.13.16.18.

3. By the *decree* of God for the manifestation of his glory (*g*) some men and Angels, are predestinated, or fore-ordained to Eternal Life, through Jesus Christ to the (*h*) praise of his glorious grace; others being left to act in their sin to their (*i*) just condemnation, to the praise of his glorious justice.

    g 1 Tim. 5.21. Mat. 25.41.
    h Eph. 1.5,6.
    i Rom. 9.22,23. Jud. 4.

4. These Angels and Men thus predestinated, and fore-ordained, are particularly, and unchangeably designed; and their (*k*) number so certain, and definite, that it cannot be either increased, or diminished.

    k 2 Tim. 2.19. Joh. 13.18.

5. Those of mankind (*l*) that are predestinated to life, God before the foundation of the world was laid, according to his eternal and immutable purpose, and the secret Councel and good pleasure of his will, hath chosen in Christ unto everlasting glory, out of his meer free grace and love; (*m*) without any other thing in the creature as a condition or cause moving him thereunto.

> *l* Eph. 1.4.9.11. Rom. 8.30. 2 Tim. 1.9. 1 Thes. 5.9.
> *m* Rom. 9.13.16. Eph. 1.6.12.

6. As God hath appointed the Elect unto glory, so he hath by the eternal and most free purpose of his will, fore-ordained (*o*) all the means thereunto, wherefore they who are elected, being faln in Adam, (*p*) are redeemed by Christ, are effectually (*q*) called unto faith in Christ, by his spirit working in due season, are justified, adopted, sanctified, and kept by his power through faith (*r*) unto salvation; neither are any other redeemed by Christ, or effectually called, justified, adopted, sanctified, and saved, but the Elect (*s*) only.

> *o* 1 Pet. 1.2. 2 Thes. 2.13.
> *p* 1 Thes. 5.9,10.
> *q* Rom. 8.30. 2 Thes. 2.13.
> *r* 1 Pet. 1.5.
> *s* Joh. 10.26. Joh. 17.9. Joh. 6.64.

7. The Doctrine of this high mystery of predestination, is to be handled with special prudence, and care; that men attending the will of God revealed in his word, and yeilding obedience thereunto, may from the certainty of their effectual vocation, be assured of their (*t*) eternal election; so shall this doctrine afford matter (*u*) of praise, reverence, and admiration of God, and (*x*) of humility, diligence, and abundant (*y*) consolation, to all that sincerely obey the Gospel.

> *t* 1 Thes. 1.4,5. 2 Pet. 1.10.
> *u* Eph. 1.6. Rom. 11.33.
> *x* Rom. 11.5,6.
> *y* Luk. 10.20.

~ *Chapter III. Of God's Decree* ~

CHAP. IV.
Of Creation.

1. In the beginning it pleased *God* the Father, (*a*) Son, and Holy Spirit, for the manifestation of the glory of (*b*) his eternal power, wisdom, and goodness, to *Create* or *make* the world, and all things therein, (*c*) whether visible or invisible, in the space of six days, and all very good.

 a John 1.2,3. Heb. 1.2. Job 26.13
 b Rom. 1.20.
 c Col. 1.16. Gen 2.1,2.

2. After God had made all other Creatures, he *Created* (*d*) man, male and female, with (*e*) reasonable and immortal souls, rendring them fit unto that life to God; for which they were *Created*; being (*f*) made after the image of God, in knowledge, righteousness, and true holiness; having the Law of God (*g*) written in their hearts, and power to fulfill it; and yet under a possibility of transgressing, being left to the liberty of their own will, which was (*h*) subject to change.

 d Gen. 1.27.
 e Gen. 2.7.
 f Eccles. 7.29. Gen. 1.26.
 g Rom. 2.14,15.
 h Gen. 3.6.

3. Besides the Law written in their hearts, they received (*i*) a command not to eat of the tree of knowledge of good and evil; which whilst they kept, they were happy in their Communion with God, and had dominion (*k*) over the Creatures.

 i Gen. 6.17. & ch. 3.8,9,10.
 k Gen. 1.26,28.

CHAP. V.
Of Divine Providence.

1. God the good *Creator* of all things, in *his* infinite power, and wisdom, doth (*a*) uphold, direct, dispose, and govern all Creatures, and things, from the greatest even to the (*b*) least, by *his* most wise and holy providence, to the end for the which they were *Created*; according unto *his* infallible foreknowledge, and the free and immutable Councel of *his* (*c*) own will; to the praise of the glory of *his* wisdom, power, justice, infinite goodness and mercy.

> *a* Heb. 1.3. Job 38.11. Isa. 46 10,11. Ps. 135.6.
> *b* Mat. 10.29,30,31.
> *c* Eph. 1.11.

2. Although in relation to the foreknowledge and *Decree* of *God*, the first cause, all things come to pass (*d*) immutably and infallibly; so that there is not any thing, befalls any (*e*) by chance, or without *his* *Providence*; yet by the same *Providence* he ordereth them to fall out, according to the nature of second causes, either (*f*) necessarily, freely, or contingently.

> *d* Act. 2.23.
> *e* Pro. 16.33.
> *f* Gen. 8.22.

3. God in *his* ordinary *Providence* (*g*) maketh use of means; yet is free (*h*) to work, without, (*i*) above, and (*k*) against them at *his* pleasure.

> *g* Act. 27.31.44. Isa. 55.10 11.
> *h* Hos. 1.7
> *i* Rom. 4.19,20,21.
> *k* Dan. 3.27.

4. The Almighty power, unsearchable wisdom, and *infinite* goodness of *God*, so far manifest themselves in *his* *Providence*, that *his* determinate Councel (*l*) extendeth it self even to the first fall, and all other sinful actions both of Angels, and Men; (and that not by a bare permission) which also he most wisely and powerfully (*m*) boundeth,

and otherwise ordereth, and governeth, in a manifold dispensation to *his* most holy (*n*) ends: yet so, as the sinfulness of their acts proceedeth only from the Creatures, and not from *God*; who being most holy and righteous, neither is nor can be, the author or (*o*) approver of sin.

l Rom. 11 32,33.34. 2 Sam. 24 1. 1 Chro. 21.1.

m 2 Kings 19.28. Ps. 76.10.

n Gen. 50 20. Isa. 10 6,7.12.

o Ps. 50.21 1 Joh. 2.16.

5. The most wise, righteous, and gracious *God*, doth oftentimes, leave for a season *his* own children to manifold temptations, and the corruptions of their own heart, to chastise them for their former sins, or to discover unto them the hidden strength of corruption, and deceitfulness of their hearts, (*p*) that they may be humbled; and to raise them to a more close, and constant dependence for their support, upon himself; and to make them more watchful against all future occasions of sin, and for other just and holy ends.

So that whatsoever befalls any of his elect is by his appointment, for his glory, (*q*) and their good.

p 2 Chro. 32.25,26.31. 2 Sam. 24 1. 2 Cor. 12.7,8,9.

q Rom. 8.28.

6. As for those wicked and ungodly men, whom God as a righteous judge, for former sin doth (*r*) blind and harden; from them he not only withholdeth his (*s*) Grace, whereby they might have been inlightned in their understanding, and wrought upon in their hearts: But sometimes also withdraweth (*t*) the gifts which they had, and exposeth them to such (*u*) objects as their *corruptions* makes occasion of sin; and withall (*x*) gives them over to their own lusts, the temptations of the world, and the power of Satan, whereby it comes to pass, that they (*y*) harden themselves, even under those means which God useth for the softning of others.

r Rom. 1.24.26.28. ch. 11.7,8.

s Deut. 29.4.

t Mat. 13.12.

u Deut. 2.30. 2 King. 8.12,13.

x Psal. 81.11,12. 2 Thes. 2.10,11,12.

y Exod. 8.15.32. Is. 6.9,10. 1 Pet. 2.7,8.

~ *Chapter V. Of Divine Providence* ~

7. As the *Providence* of *God* doth in general reach to all *Creatures*, so after a most special manner it taketh care of his (*z*) Church, and disposeth of all things to the good thereof.

 z 1 Tim. 4.10. Amos 9.8.9. Isa. 43.3,4,5.

CHAP. VI.
Of the fall of Man, of Sin, and of the Punishment thereof.

1. **A**lthough *God created Man* upright, and perfect, and gave him a righteous law, which had been unto life had he kept it, (*a*) and threatned death upon the breach thereof; yet he did not long abide in this honour; (*b*) Satan using the subtilty of the serpent to seduce *Eve*, then by her seducing *Adam*, who without any compulsion, did wilfully transgress the Law of their *Creation*, and the command given unto them, in eating the forbidden fruit; which *God* was pleased according to *his* wise and holy *Councel* to permit, having purposed to order it, to *his* own glory.

    a Gen. 2.16,17,
    b Gen. 3.12,13. 2 Cor. 11 3.

2. Our first *Parents* by this *Sin*, fell from their (*c*) original righteousness and communion with *God*, and we in them, whereby death came upon all; (*d*) all becoming dead in *Sin*, and wholly defiled, (*e*) in all the faculties, and parts, of soul, and body.

    c Rom. 3.23.
    d Rom 5.12 & c.
    e Tit. 1.15 Gen. 6.5. Jer. 17 9. Rom. 3.10-19.

3. They being the (*f*) root, and by *Gods* appointment, standing in the room, and stead of all mankind; the guilt of the *Sin* was imputed, and *corrupted* nature conveyed, to all their posterity descending from them by ordinary generation, being now (*g*) conceived in *Sin*, and by nature children (*h*) of wrath, the servants of *Sin*, the subjects (*i*) of *death* and all other miseries, spiritual, temporal and eternal, unless the *Lord Jesus* (*k*) set them free.

    f Rom. 5.12-19. 1 Cor. 15.21,22.45.49.
    g Ps. 51.5. Job 14.4.
    h Eph. 2.3.
    i Rom. 6.20. & ch. 5.12.
    k Heb. 2.14. 1 Thes. 1.10.

4. From this original *corruption*, whereby we are (*l*) utterly indisposed, disabled, and made opposite to all good, and wholly inclined to all evil, do (*m*) proceed all actual transgressions.

  l Rom. 8.7. Col. 1.21.
  m Jam. 1 14,15. Mat. 15.19.

5. The *corruption* of nature, during this Life, doth (*n*) remain in those that are regenerated: and although it be through *Christ* pardoned, and mortified, yet both it self, and the first motions thereof, are truely and properly (*o*) *Sin*.

  n Rom. 7.18.23. Eccles. 7.20. 1 Joh. 1.8.
  o Rom. 7.24.25. Gal. 5.17

CHAP. VII.
Of Gods Covenant.

1. **T**he distance between *God* and the *Creature* is so great, that although reasonable *Creatures* do owe obedience unto him as their *Creator*, yet they could never have attained the reward of Life, but by some (*a*) voluntary condescension on *Gods part*, which he hath been pleased to express, by way of *Covenant*.

    a Luk. 17.10. Job 35.7.8.

2. Moreover *Man* having brought himself (*b*) under the *curse* of the Law by his fall, it pleased the *Lord* to make a *Covenant* of *Grace* wherein he freely offereth unto *Sinners*, (*c*) Life and Salvation by *Jesus Christ*, requiring of them Faith in him, that they may be saved; and (*d*) promising to give unto all those that are ordained unto eternal Life, his holy *Spirit*, to make them willing, and able to believe.

    b Gen. 2.17. Gal. 3.10. Rom. 3.20,21.
    c Rom. 8.3. Mark 16.15.16. Joh. 3.16.
    d Ezek. 36.26,27. Joh. 6.44 45. Ps. 110.3.

3. This *Covenant* is revealed in the Gospel; first of all to *Adam* in the promise of Salvation by the (*e*) seed of the woman, and afterwards by farther steps, untill the full (*f*) discovery thereof was compleated in the new Testament; and it is founded in that (*)[1] Eternal *Covenant* transaction, that was between the *Father* and the *Son*, about the Redemption of the *Elect*; and it is alone by the Grace of this *Covenant*, that all of the posterity of fallen *Adam*, that ever were (*g*) saved, did obtain life and a blessed immortality; *Man* being now utterly uncapable of acceptance with *God* upon those terms, on which *Adam* stood in his state of innocency.

    e Gen. 3.15.
    f Heb. 1.1.
    *2 Tim. 1.9. Tit. 1.2.
    g Heb, 11.6.13. Rom. 4.1,2, & c. Act. 4.12. Joh. 8.56.

---

[1] The "*" is original. It may indicate an insertion supplied after the text had been set, so also at Chapters 8.6 and 14.2.

CHAP. VIII.
Of Christ the Mediator.

1. **I**t pleased *God* in his eternal purpose, to chuse and ordain the *Lord Jesus* his only begotten *Son*, according to the *Covenant* made between them both, (*a*) to be the *Mediator* between *God* and *Man*; the (*b*) Prophet, (*c*) Priest and (*d*) King; Head and Saviour of his Church, the heir of all things, and judge of the world: Unto whom he did from all Eternity (*e*) give a people to be his seed, and to be by him in time redeemed, called, justified, sanctified, and glorified.

    a Is. 42.1. 1 Pet. 1.19,20.
    b Act. 3.22.
    c Heb. 5.5,6.
    d Ps. 2.6, Luk. 1.33 Eph. 1.23 Heb. 1.2. Act. 17.31
    e Is. 53.10. Joh. 17.6. Rom. 8:30.

2. The *Son* of *God*, the second Person in the *Holy Trinity*, being very and eternal *God*, the brightness of the Fathers glory, of one substance and equal with *him*: who made the World, who upholdeth and governeth all things he hath made: did when the fullness of time was come take unto him (*f*) mans nature, with all the Essential properties, and common infirmities thereof, (*g*) yet without sin: being conceived by the *Holy Spirit* in the *Womb* of the *Virgin Mary*, the *Holy Spirit* coming down upon her, and the power of the most *High* overshadowing her, (*h*) and so was made of a *Woman*, of the Tribe of *Judah*, of the Seed of *Abraham*, and *David* according to the *Scriptures*: So that two whole, perfect, and distinct natures, were inseparably joined together in one *Person*: without *conversion*, *composition*, or *confusion*: which *Person* is very *God*, and very *Man*; yet one (*i*) *Christ*, the only *Mediator* between *God* and *Man*.

    f Joh. 1.1.14. Gal. 4.4.
    g Rom. 8.3. Heb. 2.14.16,17. ch. 4.15.
    h Luk. 1.27,31.35.
    i Rom. 9.5. 1 Tim. 2.5.

3. The *Lord Jesus* in his humane nature thus united to the divine, in the Person of the *Son*, was sanctified, & anointed (*k*) with the *Holy Spirit*, above measure; having in him (*l*) all the treasures of wisdom and knowledge; in whom it pleased the *Father* that (*m*) all fullness should dwell: To the end that being (*n*) holy, harmless, undefiled, and full (*o*) of *Grace*, and *Truth*, he might be throughly furnished to execute the office of a *Mediator*, and (*p*) *Surety*; which office he took not upon himself, but was thereunto (*q*) called by his *Father*; who also put (*r*) all power and judgement in his hand, and gave him Commandement to execute the same.

k Ps. 45.7. Act. 10.38 Joh. 3.34.

l Col. 2.3.

m Col. 1.19.

n Heb. 7.26.

o Joh. 1.14.

p Heb. 7.22.

q Heb. 5.5.

r Joh. 5.22.27. Mat. 28.18. Act. 2.36.

4. This office the *Lord Jesus* did most (*s*) willingly undertake, which that he might discharge he was made under the Law, (*t*) and did perfectly fulfill it, and underwent the (*u*) punishment due to us, which we should have born and suffered, being made (*x*) *Sin* and a *Curse* for us: enduring most grievous sorrows (*y*) in his Soul; and most painful sufferings in his body; was crucified, and died, and remained in the state of the dead; yet saw no (*z*) *corruption*: on the (*a*) third day he arose from the dead, with the same (*b*) body in which he suffered; with which he also (*c*) ascended into heaven: and there sitteth at the right hand of *his Father*, (*d*) making intercession; and shall (*e*) return to judge *Men* and *Angels*, at the end of the World.

s Ps. 40.7,8. Heb. 10.5-11. Joh. 10.18.

t Gal. 4 4. Mat. 3.15.

u Gal. 3.13. Isa. 53.6. 1 Pet. 3.18.

x 2 Cor. 5 21.

y Mat. 26.37,38. Luk. 22.44. Mat. 27.46.

z Act. 13.37.

a 1 Cor. 15.3,4.

~ *Chapter VIII. Of Christ the Mediator* ~

b Joh. 20.25.27.
c Mark 16 19. Act. 1.9,10,11.
d Rom. 8.34. Heb. 9.24
e Act. 10.42. Rom. 14.9,10. Act. 1.10.

5. The *Lord Jesus* by his perfect obedience and sacrifice of himself, which he through the Eternal *Spirit* once offered up unto *God*, (*f*) hath fully satisfied the Justice of *God*, procured reconciliation, and purchased an Everlasting inheritance in the Kingdom of Heaven, (*g*) for all those whom the *Father* hath given unto him.

f Heb. 9.14. ch. 10.14. Rom. 3.25,26.
g Joh. 17.2. Heb. 9.15.

6. Although the price of Redemption was not actually paid by *Christ*, till after his *Incarnation*, (*) yet the vertue, efficacy, and benefit thereof were communicated to the Elect in all ages successively, from the beginning of the World, in and by those Promises, Types, and Sacrifices, wherein he was revealed, and signified to be the Seed of the *Woman*, which should bruise the Serpents head; (*h*) and the Lamb slain from the foundation of the World: (*i*) Being *the same yesterday, and to day, and for ever*.

*1 Cor. 4.10. Heb. 4.2. 1 Pet. 1.10,11.
h Rev. 13.8.
i Heb. 13.8.

7. Christ in the work of *Mediation* acteth according to both natures, by each nature doing that which is proper to it self; yet by reason of the Unity of the Person, that which is proper to one nature, is sometimes in *Scripture* attributed to the Person (*k*) denominated by the other nature.

k Joh. 3.13. Act. 20.28.

8. To all those for whom Christ hath obtained eternal redemption, he doth certainly, and effectually (*l*) apply, and communicate the same; making intercession for them, uniting them to himself by his spirit, (*m*) revealing unto them, in and by the word, the mystery of salvation; perswading them to believe, and obey; (*n*) governing their hearts by his word and spirit, and (*o*) overcoming all their enemies by his

Almighty power, and wisdom; in such manner, and wayes as are most consonant to his wonderful, and (*p*) unsearchable dispensation; and all of free, and absolute Grace, without any condition foreseen in them, to procure it.

l Joh. 6.37. ch. 10.15.16. & ch. 17.9. Rom. 5.10.

m Joh. 17.6, Eph. 1.9. 1 Joh. 5.20.

n Rom. 8.9.14.

o Ps. 110.1. 1 Cor. 15.25,26.

p Joh. 3.8 Eph. 1.8.

9. This office of Mediator between God and Man, is proper (*q*) onely to Christ, who is the Prophet, Priest, and King of the Church of God; and may not be either in whole, or any part thereof transfer'd from him to any other.

q 1 Tim. 2.5.

10. This number and order of Offices is necessary; for in respect of our (*r*) ignorance, we stand in need of his prophetical Office; and in respect of our alienation from God, (*s*) and imperfection of the best of our services, we need his Priestly office, to reconcile us, and present us acceptable unto God: and in respect of our averseness, and utter inability to return to God, and for our rescue, and security from our spiritual adversaries, we need his Kingly office, (*t*) to convince, subdue, draw, uphold, deliver, and preserve us to his Heavenly Kingdome.

r Joh. 1.18.

s Col. 1.21. Gal. 5.17.

t Joh. 16.8. Ps. 110.3 Luk. 1.74.75.

~ *Chapter VIII. Of Christ the Mediator* ~

CHAP. IX.
Of Free Will.

1. **G**od hath indued the Will of Man, with that natural liberty, and power of acting upon choice; that it is (*a*) neither forced, nor by any necessity of nature determined to do good or evil.

   a Mat. 17.12. Jam. 1 14. Deut. 30.19.

2. Man in his state of innocency, had freedom, and power, to will, and to do that (*b*) which was good, and well-pleasing to God; but yet (*c*) was mutable, so that he might fall from it.

   b Eccl. 7.29.
   c Gen. 3.6

3. Man by his fall into a state of sin hath wholly lost (*d*) all ability of Will, to any spiritual good accompanying salvation; so as a natural man, being altogether averse from that good, (*e*) and dead in *Sin*, is not able, by his own strength, to (*f*) convert himself; or to prepare himself thereunto.

   d Rom. 5.6. ch. 8.7.
   e Eph. 2.1.5.
   f Tit. 3 3,4,5. Joh. 6.44.

4. When God converts a sinner, and translates him into the state of Grace (*g*) he freeth him from his natural bondage under sin, and by his grace alone, enables him (*h*) freely to will, and to do that which is spiritually good; yet so as that by reason of his (*i*) remaining corruptions he doth not perfectly nor only will that which is good; but doth also will that which is evil.

   g Col. 1.13. Joh. 8.36.
   h Phil. 2.13.
   i Rom. 7.15.18,19 21.23.

5. The Will of Man is made (*k*) perfectly, and immutably free to good alone, in the state of Glory only.

   k Eph. 4.13.

CHAP. X.
Of Effectual Calling.

1. Those whom God hath predestinated unto Life, he is pleased in his appointed, and accepted time, (*a*) effectually to call by his word, and Spirit, out of that state of sin, and death, in which they are by nature, to grace and Salvation (*b*) by Jesus Christ; inlightning their minds, spiritually, and savingly to (*c*) understand the things of God; taking away their (*d*) heart of stone, and giving unto them an heart of flesh; renewing their wills, and by his Almighty power determining them (*e*) to that which is good, and effectually drawing them to Jesus Christ; yet so as they come (*f*) most freely, being made willing by his Grace.

a Rom. 8.30. Rom. 11.7. Eph. 1.10,11. 2 Thes. 3.13,14.
b Eph. 2.1-6.
c Act. 26.18. Eph. 1.17.18.
d Ezk. 36.26.
e Deut. 30 6. Ezek. 36.27. Eph. 1.19.
f Ps. 110.3. Cant. 1.4.

2. This Effectual Call is of God's free, and special grace alone, (*g*) not from any thing at all foreseen in man, nor from any power, or agency in the Creature, coworking with his special Grace, (*h*) the Creature being wholly passive therein, being dead in sins and trespasses, until being quickned & renewed by the holy Spirit, he is thereby enabled to answer this call, and to embrace the Grace offered and conveyed in it; and that by no less (*i*) power, then that which raised up Christ from the dead.

g 2 Tim. 1.9. Eph. 2.8.
h 1 Cor. 2.14. Eph. 2.5. Joh. 5.25.
i Eph. 1.19,20.

3. Elect Infants dying in infancy, are (*k*) regenerated and saved by Christ through the Spirit; who worketh when, and where, and (*l*) how he pleaseth: so also are all other elect persons, who are uncapable of being outwardly called by the Ministry of the Word.

k Joh. 3.3 5,6.
l Joh. 3.8.

4. Others not elected, although they may be called by the Ministry of the word, (*m*) and may have some common operations of the Spirit, yet not being effectually drawn by the Father, they neither will, nor can truly (*n*) come to Christ; and therefore cannot be saved: much less can men that receive not the Christian Religion (*o*) be saved; be they never so diligent to frame their lives according to the light of nature, and the Law of that Religion they do profess.

    m Mat. 22 14. ch. 13.20,21. Heb. 6.4,5.

    n John 6.44,45.65. 1 Joh. 2.24,25.

    o Act. 4.12. Joh. 4.22. ch. 17.3.

~ Chapter X. Of Effectual Calling ~

CHAP. XI.
Of Justification.

1. Those whom God Effectually calleth, he also freely (*a*) justifieth, not by infusing Righteousness into them, but by (*b*) pardoning their sins, and by accounting, and accepting their Persons as (*c*) Righteous; not for any thing wrought in them, or done by them, but for Christ's sake alone, not by imputing faith it self, the act of beleiving, or any other (*d*) evangelical obedience to them, as their Righteousness; but by imputing Christs active obedience unto the whole Law, and passive obedience in his death, for their whole and sole Righteousnnss, they (*e*) receiving, and resting on him, and his Righteousness, by Faith; which faith they have not of themselves, it is the gift of *God*.

a Rom. 3.24. ch. 8.30.
b Rom. 4.5,6,7,8. Eph. 1.7.
c 1 Cor. 1.30,31. Rom. 5.17 18,19.
d Phil. 3.8,9. Eph. 2.8,9,10.
e Joh. 1.12. Rom. 5.17.

2. Faith thus receiving and resting on Christ, and his Righteousness, is the (*f*) alone instrument of Justification: yet it is not alone in the person justified, but is ever accompanied with all other saving Graces, and is no dead faith, (*g*) but worketh by love.

f Rom. 3.28.
g Gal. 5.6 Jam. 2.17 22.26.

3. Christ by his obedience, and death, did fully discharge the debt of all those that are justified; and did by the sacrifice of himself, in the blood of his cross, undergoing in their stead, the penalty due unto them: make a proper, real and full satisfaction (*h*) to *Gods* justice in their behalf: yet inasmuch as he was given by the Father for them, and his Obedience and Satisfaction accepted in their stead, and both (*i*) freely, not for any thing in them; their Justification is only of Free Grace, that both the exact justice and rich Grace of *God*, might be (*k*) glorified in the Justification of sinners.

h Heb. 10.14. 1 Pet. 1.18,19. Isa. 53.5,6.
i Rom. 8.32. 2 Cor. 5.21.
k Rom. 3.26. Eph. 1 6,7. ch. 2.7.

4. God did from all eternity decree to (*l*) justifie all the Elect, and Christ did in the fulness of time die for their sins, and rise (*m*) again for their Justification; Nevertheless they are not justified personally, untill the *Holy Spirit*, doth in due time (*n*) actually apply *Christ* unto them.

l Gal. 3.8. 1 Pet. 1.2. 1 Tim. 2.6.
m Rom. 4.25.
n Col. 1.21;22. Tit. 3.4,5,6,7.

5. God doth continue to (*o*) Forgive the sins of those that are justified, and although they can never fall from the state of (*p*) justification; yet they may by their sins fall under *Gods* (*q*) Fatherly displeasure; and in that condition, they have not usually the light of his Countenance restored unto them, untill they (*r*) humble themselves, confess their sins, beg pardon, and renew their faith, and repentance.

o Mat. 6.12. 1 John 1.7.9.
p Joh. 10 28.
q Ps. 89.31,32,33.
r Psal. 32:5. & 51. Mat. 26.75.

6. The Justification of Believers under the Old Testament was in all these respects, (*s*) one and the same with the justification of Believers under the New Tement.

s Gal. 3.9. Rom. 4.22,23,24.

CHAP. XII.
Of Adoption.

All those that are justified, *God* vouchsafed, in, and for the sake of his only *Son Jesus Christ*, to make partakers of the Grace (*a*) of *Adoption*; by which they are taken into the number, and enjoy the Liberties, and (*b*) Priveledges of Children of *God*; have his (*c*) name put upon them, (*d*) receive the *Spirit* of *Adoption*, (*e*) have access to the throne of Grace with boldness, are enabled to cry *Abba, Father*, are (*f*) pitied, (*g*) protected, (*i*) provided for, and (*k*) chastned by him, as by a Father; yet never (*l*) cast off; but sealed (*m*) to the day of Redemption, and inherit the promises, (*n*) as heirs, of everlasting Salvation.

    a Eph. 1.5. Gal. 4.4,5.
    b Joh. 1.12 Rom. 8.17
    c 2 Cor. 6.18. Rev. 3.12.
    d Rom. 8.15.
    e Gal. 4.6. Eph. 2.18
    f Ps. 103.13.
    g Prov. 14 26.
    i 1 Pet. 5.7.
    k Heb. 12.6.
    l Is. 54.8,9. Lam. 3.31.
    m Eph. 4.30.
    n Heb. 1.14. ch. 6.12.

CHAP. XIII.
Of Sanctification.

1. They who are united to *Christ*, Effectually called, and regenerated, having a new heart, and a new *Spirit created* in them, through the vertue of *Christ's* death, and Resurrection; are also (*a*) farther sanctified, really, and personally, through the same vertue, (*b*) by his word and *Spirit* dwelling in them; (*c*) the dominion of the whole body of sin is destroyed, (*d*) and the several lusts thereof, are more and more weakned, and mortified; and they more and more quickened, and (*e*) strengthned in all saving graces, to the (*f*) practice of all true holyness, without which no man shall see the Lord.

    a Act. 20.32. Rom. 6.5,6.
    b Joh. 17.17. Eph. 3.16,17,18,19. 1 Thes. 5.21,22,23.
    c Rom. 6.14.
    d Gal. 5.24.
    e Col 1.11.
    f 2 Cor. 7.1. Heb. 12.14.

2. This Sanctification is (*g*) throughout, in the whole man, yet imperfect (*h*) in this life; there abideth still some remnants of *corruption* in every part, whence ariseth a (*i*) continual, and irreconcilable war; the Flesh lusting against the Spirit, and the Spirit against the Flesh.

    g 1 Thes. 5.23.
    h Rom. 7.18,23.
    i Gal. 5.17. 1 Pet. 2.11.

3. In which war, although the remaining *corruption* for a time may much (*k*) prevail; yet through the continual supply of strength from the sanctifying *Spirit* of *Christ* the (*l*) regenerate part doth overcome; and so the Saints grow in Grace, perfecting holiness in the fear of God, (*m*) pressing after an heavenly life, in Evangelical Obedience to all the

commands which *Christ* as *Head* and *King*, in his *Word* hath prescribed to them.

> *k* Rom. 7.23.
> *l* Rom. 6.14.
> *m* Eph. 4.15.16. 2 Cor. 3.18. ch. 7.1.

~ Chapter XIII. Of Sanctification ~

CHAP. XIV.
Of Saving Faith.

1. The Grace of *Faith*, whereby the Elect are enabled to beleive to the saving of their souls, is the work of the *Spirit* of *Christ* (*a*) in their hearts; and is ordinarily wrought by the Ministry of the (*b*) Word; by which also, and by the administration of *Baptisme*, and the *Lords Supper*, *Prayer* and other *Means* appointed of *God*, it is increased, (*c*) and strengthned.

 a 2 Cor. 4.13. Eph. 2.8.
 b Rom. 10 14.17.
 c Luk. 17.5. 1 Pet. 2.2. Act. 20.32.

2. By this *Faith*, a Christian believeth to be true, (*) whatsoever is revealed in the *Word*, for the Authority of *God* himself; and also apprehendeth an excellency therein, (*d*) above all other *Writings*; and all things in the *world*: as it bears forth the Glory of *God* in his *Attributes*, the excellency of *Christ* in his Nature and Offices; and the Power and Fullness of the *Holy Spirit* in his Workings, and Operations; and so is enabled to (*e*) cast his Soul upon the truth thus beleived; and also acteth differently, upon that which each particular, passage thereof containeth; yeilding obedience to the (*f*) commands, trembling at the (*g*) threatnings, and embracing the (*h*) promises of *God*, for this life, and that which is to come: But the principal acts of Saving Faith, have immediate relation to *Christ*, accepting, receiving, and resting upon (*i*) him alone, for Justification, Sanctification, and Eternal Life, by vertue of the Covenant of Grace.

 * Act. 24.14.
 d Ps. 19.7,8,9,10. Ps. 119.72.
 e 2 Tim. 1.12.
 f Joh. 15.14.
 g Is. 66.2.
 h Heb. 11.13.
 i Joh. 1.12. Act. 16 31. Gal. 2.20. Act. 15.11.

3. This *Faith* although it be different in degrees, and may be weak, (*k*) or strong; yet it is in the least degree of it, different in the kind, or nature of it (as is all other saving Grace) from the Faith, (*l*) and common grace of temporary beleivers; and therefore though it may be many times assailed, and weakned; yet it gets (*m*) the victory; growing up in many, to the attainment of a full (*n*) assurance through *Christ*, who is both the Author (*o*) and finisher of our *Faith*.

k Heb. 5.13.14. Mat. 6.30 Rom. 4.19 20.

l 2 Pet. 1.1.

m Eph. 6.16. 1 Joh. 5.4,5.

n Heb. 6.11,12. Col. 2.2.

o Heb. 12.2.

~ *Chapter XIV. Of Saving Faith* ~

CHAP. XV.
Of Repentance unto Life and Salvation.

1. **S**uch of the Elect as are converted at riper years, having (*a*) sometimes lived in the state of nature, and therein served divers lusts and pleasures, *God* in their *Effectual Calling* giveth them Repentance unto Life.

    a Tit. 3.2,3,4,5.

2. Whereas there is none that doth good, and sinneth (*b*) not; and the best of men may through the power, and deceitfulness of their corruption dwelling in them, with the prevalency of temptation, fall into great sins, and provocations; God hath in the Covenant of Grace, mercifully provided that Beleivers so sinning, and falling, (*c*) be renewed through Repentance unto Salvation.

    b Eccl. 7.20.
    c Luk. 22.31,32.

3. This saving Repentance is an (*d*) evangelical Grace, whereby a person being by the *Holy Spirit* made sensible of the manifold evils of his sin, doth, by Faith in Christ, humble himself for it, with godly sorrow, detestation of it, and self abhorrency; (*e*) praying for pardon, and strength of grace, with a purpose and endeavour by supplies of the *Spirit*, to (*f*) walk before God unto all well pleasing in all things.

    d Zech. 12.10. Act. 11.18.
    e Ezek. 36.31. 2 Cor. 7.11.
    f Ps. 119 6. Ps. 119.128.

4. As Repentance is to be continued through the whole course of our lives, upon the account of the body of death, and the motions thereof; so it is every mans duty, to repent of his (*g*) particular known sins, particularly.

    g Luk. 19.8. 1 Tim. 1.13.15.

5. Such is the provision which God hath made through Christ in the Covenant of Grace, for the preservation of Believers unto Salvation, that although there is no sin so small, but it deserves (*h*) damnation; yet there is no sin so great, that it shall bring damnation on them that (*i*) repent; which makes the constant preaching of Repentance necessary.

    h Rom. 6.23.

    i Is. 1.16.18. Is. 55.7.

~ *Chapter XV. Of Repentance unto Life and Salvation* ~

CHAP. XVI.
Of Good Works.

1. Good Works are only such as God hath (*a*) commanded in his Holy word; and not such as without the warrant thereof, are devised by men, out of blind zeal, (*b*) or upon any pretence of good intentions.

    a Mic. 6.8. Heb. 13 21.

    b Mat. 15.9. Isa. 29.13.

2. These good works, done in obedience to Gods commandments, are the fruits, and evidences (*c*) of a true, and lively faith; and by them Believers manifest their (*d*) thankfullness, strengthen their (*e*) assurance, edifie their (*f*) brethren, adorn the profession of the Gospel, stop the mouths of the adversaries and glorifie (*g*) God whose workmanship they are, created in Christ Jesus (*h*) thereunto, that having their fruit unto holiness, they may have the end (*i*) eternal life.

    c Jam. 2.18.22.

    d Ps. 116.12,13.

    e 1 Joh. 2 3.5. 2 Pet. 1.5-11.

    f Mat. 5.16.

    g 1 Tim. 6.1. 1 Pet. 2.15. Phil. 1.11

    h Eph. 2.10.

    i Rom. 6.22.

3. Their ability to do good works, is not at all of themselves; but wholly from the *Spirit* (*k*) of Christ; and that they may be enabled thereunto, besides the graces they have already received, there is necessary an (*l*) actual influence of the same *Holy Spirit*, to work in them to will, and to do, of his good pleasure; yet are they not hereupon to grow negligent, as if they were not bound to perform any duty, unless upon a special motion of the Spirit; but they ought to be diligent in (*m*) stirring up the Grace of God that is in them.

    k Joh. 15.4.6.

    l 2 Cor. 3.5. Phil. 2.13.

    m Phil. 2.12. Heb. 6.11 12. Isa. 64.7.

4. They who in their obedience attain to the greatest height which is possible in this life, are so far from being able to superrogate, and to do more then God requires, as that (*n*) they fall short of much which in duty they are bound to do.

    n Job 9.2 3. Gal. 5.17. Luk. 17.10.

5. We cannot by our best works merit pardon of Sin or Eternal Life at the hand of God, by reason of the great disproportion that is between them and the glory to come; and the infinite distance that is between us and God, whom by them we can neither profit, nor satisfie for the debt of our (*o*) former sins; but when we have done all we can, we have done but our duty, and are unprofitable servants; and because as they are good they proceed from his (*p*) Spirit, and as they are wrought by us they are defiled (*q*) and mixed with so much weakness and imperfection that they cannot endure the severity of Gods judgement.

    o Rom. 3.20. Eph. 2.8,9. Rom. 4.6.
    p Gal. 5.22,23.
    q Isa. 64.6. Ps. 143 2.

6. Yet notwithstanding the persons of Believers being accepted through Christ their good works also are accepted in (*r*) him; not as though they were in this life wholly unblameable and unreprovable in Gods sight; but that he looking upon them in his Son is pleased to accept and reward that which is (*s*) sincere although accompanied with many weaknesses and imperfections.

    r Eph. 1.6. 1 Pet. 2.5.
    s Mat. 25.21.23. Heb. 6.10

7. Works done by unregenerate men although for the matter of them they may be things which God commands, and of good use, both to themselves and (*t*) others; yet because they proceed not from a heart purified by (*u*) faith, nor are done in a right manner according to the (*w*) word, nor to a right end the (*x*) glory of God; they are therefore sinful and cannot please God; nor make a man meet to receive grace from (*y*) God; and yet their neglect of them is more sinful and (*z*) displeasing to God.

    t 2 King. 10.30. 1 King. 21.27,29

~ Chapter XVI. Of Good Works ~

u Gen. 4.5. Heb. 11 4.6.
w 1 Cor. 13.1.
x Mat. 6.2.5.
y Amos 5 21,22. Rom. 9.16 Tit. 3.5.
z Job 21.14,15. Mat. 25.41,42,43.

~ *Chapter XVI. Of Good Works* ~

CHAP. XVII.
Of Perseverance of the Saints.

1. Those whom God hath accepted in the beloved, effectually called and Sanctified by his *Spirit*, and given the precious faith of his Elect unto, can neither totally nor finally fall from the state of grace; (*a*) but shall certainly persevere therein to the end and be eternally saved, seeing the gifts and callings of God are without Repentance, (whence he still begets and nourisheth in them Faith, Repentance, Love, Joy, Hope, and all the graces of the Spirit unto immortality) and though many storms and floods arise and beat against them, yet they shall never be able to take them off that foundation and rock which by faith they are fastned upon: notwithstanding through unbelief and the temptations of Satan the sensible sight of the light and love of God, may for a time be clouded, and obscured from (*b*) them, yet he is still the same (*c*) and they shall be sure to be kept by the power of God unto Salvation, where they shall enjoy their purchased possession, they being engraven upon the palm of his hands, and their names having been written in the book of life from all Eternity.

a Joh. 10.28,29. Phi. 1.6. 2 Tim. 2.19. 1 Joh. 2.19.

b Psal. 89.31,32. 1 Cor. 11.32.

c Mal. 3.6.

2. This perseverance of the Saints depends not upon their own free will; but upon the immutability of the decree of (*d*) Election flowing from the free and unchangeable love of God the Father; upon the efficacy of the merit and intercession of Jesus Christ (*e*) and Union with him, the (*f*) oath of God, the abiding of his Spirit & the (*g*) seed of God within them, and the nature of the (*h*) Covenant of Grace from all which ariseth also the certainty and infallibility thereof.

d Rom. 8.30. ch. 9.11.16.

e Rom. 5.9,10. John 14.19.

f Heb. 6.17,18.

g 1 Joh. 3.9.

h Jer. 32.40.

3. And though they may through the temptation of Satan and of the world, the prevalency of corruption remaining in them, and the neglect of means of their preservation fall into grievous (*i*) sins, and for a time continue therein; whereby they incur (*k*) Gods displeasure, and grieve his holy Spirit, come to have their graces and (*l*) comforts impaired have their hearts hardened, and their Consciences wounded, (*m*) hurt, and scandalize others, and bring temporal judgements (*n*) upon themselves: yet they shall renew their (*o*) repentance and be preserved through faith in Christ Jesus to the end.

    i Mat. 26.70,72.74.

    k Is. 64.5.9. Eph. 4.30

    l Psal. 51.10.12.

    m Psa. 32.3,4.

    n 2 Sam. 12.14.

    o Luk. 22.32. & v. 61 62.

~ Chapter XVII. Of Perseverance of the Saints ~

CHAP. XVIII.
Of the Assurance of Grace and Salvation.

1. Although temporary Believers, and other unregenerate men, may vainly deceive themselves with false hopes, and carnal presumptions, of being in the favour of God, and state of salvation, (*a*) which hope of theirs shall perish; yet such as truely believe in the Lord Jesus, and love him in sincerity, endeavouring to walk in all good Conscience before him, may in this life be certainly assured (*b*) that they are in the state of Grace; and may rejoyce in the hope of the glory of God which hope shall never make them (*c*) ashamed.

 a Job 8.13.14. Mat. 7.22 23.
 b 1 Joh. 2.3. ch. 3.14 18,19.21.24. ch. 5.13.
 c Rom. 5.2.5.

2. This certainty is not a bare conjectural, and probable perswasion, grounded upon (*d*) a fallible hope; but an infallible assurance of faith founded on the Blood and Righteousness of Christ (*e*) revealed in the Gospel; and also upon the inward (*f*) evidence of those graces of the Spirit unto which promises are made, and on the testimony of the (*g*) Spirit of adoption, witnessing with our Spirits that we are the children of God; and as a fruit thereof keeping the heart both (*h*) humble and holy.

 d Heb. 6.11.19.
 e Heb. 6.17,18.
 f 2 Pet. 1.4,5,10.11.
 g Rom. 8.15,16.
 h 1 Joh. 3 1,2,3.

3. This infallible assurance doth not so belong to the essence of faith, but that a true Believer, may wait long and conflict with many difficulties before he be (*i*) partaker of it; yet being enabled by the Spirit to know the things which are freely given him of God, he may

without extraordinary revelation in the right use of means (*k*) attain thereunto: and therefore it is the duty of every one, to give all diligence to make their Calling and Election sure, that thereby his heart may be enlarged in peace and joy in the holy Spirit, in love and thankfulness to God, and in strength and chearfulness in the duties of obedience, the proper (*l*) fruits of this Assurance; so far is it (*m*) from inclining men to looseness.

 i Isa. 50.10. Ps. 88. & Psa. 77.1-12.
 k 1 Joh. 4 13. Heb. 6.11 12.
 l Rom. 5.1,2.5. ch. 14,17. Ps. 119.32.
 m Rom. 6.1,2. Tit. 2.11,12.14.

4. True Believers may have the assurance of their Salvation divers ways shaken, diminished, and intermitted; as (*n*) by negligence in preserving of it, by (*o*) falling into som special *Sin*, which woundeth the Conscience, and grieveth the *Spirit*, by some sudden or (*p*) vehement temptation, by Gods withdrawing the (*q*) light of his countenance and suffering even such as fear him to walk in darkness and to have no light; yet are they never destitute of the (*r*) seed of God, and Life (*s*) of Faith, that Love of Christ, and the brethren, that sincerity of Heart, and Conscience of duty, out of which by the operation of the Spirit, this Assurance may in due time be (*t*) revived: and by the which in the mean time they are (*u*) preserved from utter despair.

 n Cant. 5.2,3.6.
 o Ps. 51.8.12.14.
 p Psa. 116.11. Ps. 77.7,8. Ps. 31 22.
 q Ps. 30.7
 r 1 Joh. 3.9.
 s Luk. 22.32.
 t Ps. 42.5.11.
 u Lam. 3.26.27-31.

~ *Chapter XVIII. Of the Assurance of Grace and Salvation* ~

CHAP. XIX.
Of the Law of God.

1. God gave to *Adam* a Law of universal obedience, (*a*) written in his Heart, and a particular precept of not eating the Fruit of the tree of knowledge of good and evil; by which he bound him, and all his posterity to personal entire exact and perpetual (*b*) obedience; promised life upon the fulfilling, and (*c*) threatned death upon the breach of it; and indued him with power and ability to keep it.

    a Gen. 1.27. Eccl. 7.29.
    b Rom. 10 5.
    c Gal. 3.10.12,

2. The same Law that was first written in the heart of man, (*d*) continued to be a perfect rule of Righteousness after the fall; & was delivered by God upon Mount *Sinai*, in (*e*) Ten Commandments and written in two Tables; the four first containing our duty towards God, and the other six our duty to man.

    d Rom. 2.14,15.
    e Deut. 10.4.

3. Besides this Law commonly called moral, God was pleased to give to the people of *Israel* Ceremonial Laws, containing several typical ordinances, partly of worship, (*f*) prefiguring Christ, his graces, actions, sufferings, and benefits; and partly holding forth divers instructions (*g*) of moral duties, all which Ceremonial Laws being appointed only to the time of reformation, are by Jesus Christ the true *Messiah* and only Law-giver who was furnished with power from the Father, for that end, (*h*) abrogated and taken away.

    f Heb. 10.1. Col. 2.17.
    g 1 Cor. 5 7.
    h Col. 2.14,16,17 Eph. 2.14.16.

4. To them also he gave sundry judicial Laws, which expired together with the state of that people, not obliging any now by vertue of that institution; their general (*i*) equity onely, being of moral use.

   i 1 Cor. 9.8,9,10.

5. The moral Law doth for ever bind all, (*k*) as well justified persons as others, to the obedience thereof, and that not only in regard of the matter contained in it, but also in respect of the (*l*) authority of God the Creator; who gave it: Neither doth *Christ* in the Gospel any way dissolve, (*m*) but much strengthen this obligation.

   k Rom. 13 8,9,10. Jam. 2.8.10,11,12
   l Jam. 2 10,11.
   m Mat. 5.17,18,19. Rom. 3.31.

6. Although true *Believers* be not under the Law, as a Covenant of *Works*, (*n*) to be thereby Justified or condemned; yet it is of great use to them as well as to others: in that, as a Rule of *Life*, informing them of the Will of *God*, and their Duty, it directs and binds them, to walk accordingly; (*o*) discovering also the sinfull pollutions of their Natures, Hearts and Lives; so as Examining themselves thereby, they may come to further Conviction of, Humiliation for, and Hatred against Sin; together with a clearer sight of the need they have of *Christ* and the perfection of his Obedience: It is likewise of use to the Regenerate to restrain their Corruptions, in that it forbids Sin; and the Threatnings of it serve to shew what even their Sins deserve; and what afflictions in this Life they may expect for them, although free'd from the Curse and unallayed Rigor thereof. The Promises of it likewise shew them Gods approbation of Obedience, and what blessings they may expect upon the performance thereof, though not as due to them by the Law as a Covenant of Works; so as mans doing Good and refraining from Evil, because the Law incourageth to the one and deterreth from the other, is no Evidence of his being (*p*) under the Law and not under Grace.

   n Rom. 6.14. Gal. 2.16. Rom. 8.1. cha. 10.4.
   o Rom. 3.20. chap. 7.7. & c.
   p Rom. 6.12,13,14. 1 Pet. 3.8.-13.

~ Chapter XIX. Of the Law of God ~

7. Neither are the forementioned uses of the Law (*q*) contrary to the Grace of the Gospel; but do sweetly comply with it; the *Spirit* of *Christ* subduing (*r*) and inabling the Will of man, to do that freely and chearfully, which the will of God revealed in the Law, requireth to be done.

    q Gal. 3.21.

    r Eze. 36.27.

~ *Chapter XIX. Of the Law of God* ~

CHAP. 20.
Of the Gospel, and of the extent of the Grace thereof.

1. The Covenant of Works being broken by Sin, and made unprofitable unto Life; God was pleased to give forth the promise of *Christ*, (*a*) the Seed of the Woman, as the means of calling the Elect, and begetting in them Faith and Repentance; in this Promise, the (*b*) Gospel, as to the substance of it, was revealed, and therein Effectual, for the Conversion and Salvation of Sinners.

    a Gen. 3.15.
    b Rev. 13.8.

2. This Promise of *Christ*, and Salvation by him, is revealed only by (*c*) the Word of God; neither do the Works of Creation, or Providence, with the light of Nature, (*d*) make discovery of *Christ*, or of *Grace* by him; so much as in a general, or obscure way; much less that men destitute of the Revelation of him by the Promise, or Gospel; (*e*) should be enabled thereby, to attain saving Faith, or Repentance.

    c Rom. 1.17.
    d Ro. 10.14,15,17.
    e Pro. 29.18. Isa. 25.7. with ch. 60.2,3.

3. The Revelation of the Gospel unto Sinners, made in divers times, and by sundry parts; with the addition of Promises, and Precepts for the Obedience required therein, as to the Nations, and Persons, to whom it is granted, is meerly of the (*f*) Soveraign Will and good Pleasure of God; not being annexed by vertue of any Promise, to the due improvement of mens natural abilities, by vertue of Common light received, without it; which none ever did (*g*) make, or can so do: And therefore in all Ages the preaching of the Gospel hath been granted unto persons and Nations, as to the extent, or streightning of it, in great variety, according to the Councell of the Will of God.

    f Ps. 147,20. Act. 16.7.
    g Rom. 1.18, &c.

4. Although the Gospel be the only outward means, of revealing *Christ*, and saving Grace; and is, as such, abundantly sufficient thereunto; yet that men who are dead in Trespasses, may be born again, Quickned or Regenerated; there is moreover necessary, an effectual, insuperable (*h*) work of the Holy *Spirit*, upon the whole Soul, for the producing in them a new spiritual Life; without which no other means will effect (*i*) their Conversion unto God.

    h Ps. 110.3. 1 Cor. 2.14. Eph. 1.19 20.

    i Joh. 6.44. 2 Cor. 4.4.6.

~ *Chapter XX. Of the Gospel, and of the extent of the Grace thereof* ~

CHAP. XXI.
Of Christian Liberty and Liberty of Conscience.

1. The Liberty which *Christ* hath purchased for Believers under the Gospel, consists in their freedom from the guilt of Sin, the condemning wrath of God, the Rigour and (*a*) Curse of the Law; and in their being delivered from this present evil (*b*) World, Bondage to (*c*) Satan, and Dominion (*d*) of Sin; from the (*e*) Evil of Afflictions; the Fear, and Sting (*f*) of Death, the Victory of the Grave, and (*g*) Everlasting Damnation; as also in their (*h*) free access to God; and their yielding Obedience unto him not out of a slavish fear, (*i*) but a Child-like love, and willing mind.

All which were common also to Believers under the Law (*k*) for the substance of them; but under the new Testament, the Liberty of Christians is further enlarged in their freedom from the yoke of the Ceremonial Law, to which the *Jewish* Church was subjected; and in greater boldness of access to the Throne of Grace; and in fuller Communications of the (*l*) Free *Spirit* of God, then Believers under the Law did ordinarily partake of.

a Gal. 3.13.
b Gal. 1.4.
c Act. 26.18.
d Rom. 8.3.
e Rom. 8.28.
f 1 Cor. 15.54,55,56.57.
g 2 Thes. 1.10.
h Rom. 8.15.
i Luk. 1.74,75. 1 Joh. 4 18.
k Gal. 3,9:14.
l Joh. 7.38,39. Heb. 10, 19,20,21.

2. God alone is (*m*) Lord of the Conscience, and hath left it free from the Doctrines and Commandments of men, (*n*) which are in any thing

contrary to his Word, or not contained in it. So that to Believe such Doctrines, or obey such Commands out of Conscience, (*o*) is to betray true liberty of Conscience; and the requiring of an (*p*) implicit Faith, and absolute and blind Obedience, is to destroy Liberty of Conscience, and Reason also.

m Jam. 4.12, Rom. 14.4.

n Act. 4.19 & 5.29. 1 Cor. 7.23. Mat. 15.9:

o Col: 2.20 22,23:

p 1 Cor. 3.5: 2 Cor. 1.24.

3. They who upon pretence of Christian Liberty do practice any sin, or cherish any sinfull lust; as they do thereby pervert the main design of the Grace of the Gospel, (*q*) to their own Destruction; so they wholy destroy (*r*) the end of *Christian* Liberty, which is, that being delivered out of the hands of all our Enemies we might serve the Lord without fear in Holiness, and Righteousness before him, all the days of our Life.

q Rom. 6.1,2.

r Gal. 5.13. 2 Pet. 2.18.-21.

~ *Chapter XXI. Of Christian Liberty and Liberty of Conscience* ~

CHAP. XXII.
Of Religious Worship and the Sabbath Day.

1. The light of Nature shews that there is a God, who hath Lordship, and Soveraigntye over all; is just, good, and doth good unto all; and is therefore to be feared, loved, praised, called upon, trusted in, and served, with all the Heart, and all the Soul, (*a*) and with all the Might. But the acceptable way of Worshipping the true God, is (*b*) instituted by himself; and so limited by his own revealed will, that he may not be Worshipped according to the imaginations, and devices of Men, or the suggestions of Satan, under any visible representations, or (*c*) any other way, not prescribed in the Holy Scriptures.

    a Jer. 10.7. Mar. 12.33.
    b Deut. 12 32.
    c Exo 20.4,5,6.

2. *Religious Worship* is to be given to *God* the *Father*, *Son*, and *Holy Spirit*, and to him (*d*) alone; not to *Angels*, *Saints*, or any other (*e*) *Creatures*; and since the fall, not without a (*f*) *Mediator*, nor in the *Mediation* of any other but (*g*) Christ alone.

    d Mat. 4.9,10. Joh 6.23. Mat. 28.19.
    e Rom. 1.25. Col. 2.18. Revel. 19.10.
    f Joh. 14.6.
    g 1 Tim. 2.5.

3. Prayer with thanksgiving, being one special part of natural worship, is by *God* required of (*h*) all men. But that it may be accepted, it is to be made in the (*i*) Name of the Son, by the help (*k*) of the Spirit, according to (*l*) his Will; with understanding, reverence, humility, fervency, faith, love, and perseverance; and when with others, in a (*m*) known tongue.

    h Psal. 95 1-7. Psal. 65.2.
    i Joh. 14.13,14.

k Rom. 8.26.
l 1 Joh. 5.14.
m 1 Cor. 14.16,17.

4. Prayer is to be made for things lawful, and for all sorts of men living, (*n*) or that shall live hereafter; but not (*o*) for the dead, nor for those of whom it may be known that they have sinned (*p*) the sin unto death.

n 1 Tim. 2.1,2. 2 Sam. 7.29.
o 2 Sam. 12.21,22.23.
p 1 Joh. 5.16.

5. The (*q*) reading of the Scriptures, Preaching, and (*r*) hearing the word of God, teaching and admonishing one another in Psalms, Hymns and Spiritual songs, singing with grace in our Hearts to (*s*) the Lord; as also the Administration (*t*) of Baptism, and (*u*) the Lords Supper are all parts of Religious worship of *God*, to be performed in obedience to him, with understanding, faith, reverence, and godly fear; moreover solemn humiliation (*x*) with fastings; and thanksgiving upon (*y*) special occasions, ought to be used in an holy and religious manner.

q 1 Tim. 4.13.
r 2 Tim. 4.2. Luk. 8.18.
s Col. 3.16. Eph. 5.19
t Mat. 28, 19,20.
u 1 Cor. 11 26.
x Esth. 4.16. Joel. 2.12
y Exo. 15.1. &c. Ps. 107.

6. Neither *Prayer*, nor any other part of Religious worship, is now under the Gospel tied unto, or made more acceptable by, any place in which it is (*z*) performed, or towards which it is directed; but God is to be worshipped every where in *Spirit*, and in truth; as in (*a*) private families (*b*) daily, and (*c*) in secret each one by himself, so more solemnly in the publick Assemblies, which are not carelessely, nor wilfuly, to be (*d*) neglected, or forsaken, when God by his word, or providence calleth thereunto.

~ *Chapter XXII. Of Religious Worship and the Sabbath Day* ~

z Joh. 4.21. Mal. 1.11. 1 Tim 2.8.
a Act. 10.2.
b Mat. 6.11. Ps. 55.17.
c Mat. 6.6
d Heb. 10.25. Act. 2.42.

7. As it is of the Law of nature, that in general a proportion of time by Gods appointment, be set a part for the Worship of God; so by his Word in a positive-moral, and perpetual Commandement, binding all men, in all Ages, he hath particularly appointed one day in seven for a (*e*) *Sabbath* to be kept holy unto him, which from the beginning of the World to the Resurrection of Christ, was the last day of the week; and from the resurrection of Christ, was changed into the first day of the week (*f*) which is called the Lords day; and is to be continued to the end of the World, as the *Christian Sabbath*; the observation of the last day of the week being abolished.

    e Exo. 20.8.
    f 1 Cor. 16.1,2. Act. 20.7. Rev. 1.10.

8. The *Sabbath* is then kept holy unto the Lord, when men after a due preparing of their hearts, and ordering their common affairs aforehand, do not only observe an holy (*g*) rest all the day, from their own works, words, and thoughts, about their worldly employment, and recreations, but also are taken up the whole time in the publick and private exercises of his worship, and in the duties (*h*) of necessity and mercy.

    g Isa. 58.13. Neh 13.15-23.
    h Mat. 12.1-13.

CHAP. XXIII.
Of Lawful Oaths and Vows.

1. **A** lawful Oath is a part of religious worship, (*a*) wherein the person swearing in Truth, Righteousness, and Judgement, solemnly calleth God to witness what he sweareth; (*b*) and to judge him according to the Truth or falseness thereof.

    a Exo. 20 7. Deut. 10 20. Jer. 4.2.

    b 2 Cro. 6 22,23.

2. The Name of God only is that by which men ought to swear; and therein it is to be used, with all Holy Fear and reverence, therefore to swear vainly or rashly by that glorious, and dreadful name; or to *swear* at all by any other thing, is sinful and to be (*c*) abhorred; yet as in matter of weight and moment for confirmation of truth, (*d*) and ending all strife, an *Oath* is warranted by the Word of God; so a *lawful Oath* being imposed, (*e*) by lawful Authority, in such matters, ought to be taken.

    c Mat. 5.34.37. Jam. 5.12

    d Heb. 6.16. 2 Cor. 1.23.

    e Neh. 13.25.

3. Whosoever taketh an *Oath* warranted by the Word of God, ought duely to consider the weightiness of so solemn an act; and therein to avouch nothing, but what he knoweth to be the truth; for that by rash, false, and vain *Oaths* the (*f*) Lord is provoked, and for them this Land mournes.

    f Levit. 19.12. Jer. 23.10.

4. An *Oath* is to be taken in the plain, and (*g*) common sense of the words; without equivocation, or mental reservation.

    g Ps. 24.4.

5. A Vow which is not to be made to any *Creature*, but to God alone, (*h*) is to be made and performed with all Religious care, and

faithfulness: But Popish *Monastical Vows*, (*i*) of perpetual single life, professed (*k*) poverty, and regular obedience, are so far from being degrees of higher perfection, that they are superstitious, (*l*) and sinful snares, in which no *Christian* may intangle himself.

h Psal. 76.11. Gen. 28.20,21 22.

i 1 Cor. 7.2.9.

k Eph. 4.28.

l Mat. 19.11.

~ Chapter XXIII. Of Lawful Oaths and Vows ~

CHAP. XXIV.
Of the Civil Magistrate.

1. God the supream Lord, and King of all the World, hath ordained *Civil* (*a*) *Magistrates* to be under him, over the people for his own glory, and the publick good; and to this end hath armed them with the power of the Sword, for defence and encouragement of them that do good, and for the punishment of evil doers.

    a Rom. 13 1,2,3,4.

2. It is lawful for Christians to Accept, and Execute the Office of a *Magistrate* when called thereunto; in the management whereof, as they ought especially to maintain (*b*) Justice, and Peace, according to the wholsome Laws of each Kingdome, and Commonwealth: so for that end they may lawfully now under the New Testament (*c*) wage war upon just and necessary occasions.

    b 2 Sam. 23.3. Ps. 82.3,4.

    c Luk. 3.14.

3. *Civil Magistrates* being set up by God, for the ends aforesaid; subjection in all lawful things commanded by them, ought to be yeilded by us, in the Lord; not only for wrath (*d*) but for Conscience sake; and we ought to make supplications and prayers for Kings, and all that are in Authority, (*e*) that under them we may live a quiet and peaceable life, in all godliness and honesty.

    d Rom. 13.5,6,7. 1 Pet. 2.17.

    e 1 Tim. 2.1,2.

CHAP. XXV.
Of Marriage.

1. **M**arriage is to be between one *Man* and one *Woman*; (*a*) neither is it lawful for any man to have more then one *Wife*, nor for any *Woman* to have more then one *Husband* at the same time.

    a Gen. 2.24. Mal. 2 15. Mat. 19.5,6.

2. Marriage was ordained for the mutual help (*b*) of *Husband* and *Wife*, (*c*) for the increase of Man-kind, with a legitimate issue, and for (*d*) preventing of uncleanness.

    b Gen. 2.18.
    c Gen 1.28.
    d 1 Cor. 7 2,9.

3. It is lawful for (*e*) all sorts of people to *Marry*, who are able with judgment to give their consent; yet it is the duty of *Christians* (*f*) to *marry* in the Lord, and therefore such as profess the true Religion, should not *Marry* with Infidels, (*g*) or Idolaters; neither should such as are godly be unequally yoked, by *marrying* with such as are wicked, in their life, or maintain damnable Heresie.

    e Heb. 13,4. 1 Tim. 4,3.
    f 1 Cor. 7.39.
    g Neh. 13 25,26,27.

4. *Marriage* ought not to be within the degrees of consanguinity, (*h*) or Affinity forbidden in the word; nor can such incestuous *Marriage* ever be made lawful, by any law of *Man* or consent of parties, (*i*) so as those persons may live together as *Man* and *Wife*.

    h Levit. 18.
    i Mar. 6.18. 1 Cor. 5.1.

CHAP. XXVI.
Of the Church.

1. The Catholick or universal Church, which (with respect to the internal work of the Spirit, and truth of grace) may be called invisible, consists of the whole (*a*) number of the Elect, that have been, are, or shall be gathered into one, under Christ the head thereof; and is the spouse, the body, the fulness of him that filleth all in all.

   a Heb. 12.23. Col. 1.18. Eph. 1.10,22.23. & ch. 5.23,27,32.

2. All persons throughout the world, professing the faith of the Gospel, and obedience unto God by Christ, according unto it; not destroying their own profession by any Errors everting the foundation, or unholyness of conversation, (*b*) are and may be called visible Saints; (*c*) and of such ought all particular Congregations to be constituted.

   b 1 Cor. 1 2. Act. 11.26.
   c Rom. 1.7. Eph. 1.20,21,22.

3. The purest Churches under heaven are subject (*d*) to mixture, and error; and som have so degenerated as to become (*e*) no Churches of Christ, but Synagogues of Satan; nevertheless Christ always hath had, and ever shall have a (*f*) Kingdome in this world, to the end thereof, of such as believe in him, and make profession of his Name.

   d 1 Cor. 15. Rev. 2. & ch. 3.
   e Rev. 18.2. 2 Thes. 2.11,12.
   f Mat. 16.18. Ps. 72.17. & Ps. 102.28. Rev. 12.17.

4. The Lord Jesus Christ is the Head of the Church, in whom by the appointment of the Father, (*g*) all power for the calling, institution, order, or Government of the Church, is invested in a supream & soveraigne manner, neither can the Pope of *Rome* in any sense be head thereof, but is (*h*) that Antichrist, that Man of sin, and Son of perdition, that exalteth himself in the Church against Christ, and all that is called God; whom the Lord shall destroy with the brightness of his coming.

   g Col. 1.18. Mat. 28.18,19.20. Eph. 4.11,12.
   h 2 Thes. 2.3-9.

5. In the execution of this power wherewith he is so intrusted, the Lord Jesus calleth out of the World unto himself, through the Ministry of his word, by his Spirit, (*i*) those that are given unto him by his Father; that they may walk before him in all the (*k*) ways of obedience, which he prescribeth to them in his Word. Those thus called he commandeth to walk together in particular societies, or (*l*) Churches, for their mutual edification; and the due performance of that publick worship, which he requireth of them in the World.

    i Joh 10.16. chap. 12,32.
    k Mat. 28.20.
    l Mat. 18.15-20.

6. The Members of these Churches are (*m*) Saints by calling, visibly manifesting and evidencing (in and by their profession and walking) their obedience unto that call of Christ; and do willingly consent to walk together according to the appointment of Christ, giving up themselves, to the Lord & one to another by the will of God, (*n*) in professed subjection to the Ordinances of the Gospel.

    m Rom. 1.7. 1 Cor. 1.2.
    n Act. 2.41,42. ch. 5.13.14. 2 Cor. 9.13.

7. To each of these Churches thus gathered, according to his mind, declared in his word, he hath given all that (*o*) power and authority, which is any way needfull, for their carrying on that order in worship, and discipline, which he hath instituted for them to observe; with commands, and rules, for the due and right exerting, and executing of that power.

    o Mat. 18.17,18. 1 Cor. 5.4,5. with v.13. 2 Cor. 2.6,7,8.

8. A particular Church gathered, and compleatly Organized, according to the mind of Christ, consists of Officers, and Members; And the Officers appointed by *Christ* to be chosen and set apart by the Church (so called and gathered) for the peculiar Administration of Ordinances, and Execution of Power, or Duty, which he intrusts them with, or calls them to, to be continued to the end of the World are (*p*) Bishops or Elders and Deacons.

    p Act. 20:17, with *v.*28. Phil. 1.1.

~ *Chapter XXVI. Of the Church* ~

9. The way appointed by *Christ* for the Calling of any person, fitted, and gifted by the Holy *Spirit*, unto the Office of Bishop, or Elder, in a Church, is, that he be chosen thereunto by the common (*q*) suffrage of the Church it self; and Solemnly set apart by Fasting and Prayer, with imposition of hands of the (*r*) Eldership of the Church, if there be any before Constituted therein; And of a Deacon (*s*) that he be chosen by the like suffrage, and set apart by Prayer, and the like Imposition of hands.

q Act. 14.23: See the original.
r 1 Tim. 4.14.
s Act. 6.3.5.6.

10. The work of Pastors being constantly to attend the Service of *Christ*, in his Churches, in the Ministry of the Word, and Prayer, (*t*) with watching for their Souls, as they that must give an account to him; it is incumbent on the Churches to whom they Minister, not only to give them all due respect, (*u*) but also to communicate to them of all their good things according to their ability, so as they may have a comfortable supply, without being themselves (*x*) entangled in Secular Affairs; and may also be capable of exercising (*y*) Hospitality toward others; and this is required by the (*z*) Law of Nature, and by the Express order of our Lord Jesus, who hath ordained that they that preach the Gospel, should live of the Gospel.

t Act. 6.4. Hcb. 13.17:
u 1 Tim. 5.17,18. Gal. 6.6,7.
x 2 Tim. 2.4.
y 1 Tim. 3.2.
z 1 Cor. 9.6.-14.

11. Although it be incumbent on the Bishops or Pastors of the Churches to be instant in Preaching the Word, by way of Office; yet the work of Preaching the Word, is not so peculiarly confined to them; but that others also (*a*) gifted, and fitted by the Holy *Spirit* for it, and approved, and called by the *Church*, may and ought to perform it.

a Act. 11.19,20,21. 1 Pet. 4.10.11.

12. As all Believers are bound to joyn themselves to particular *Churches*, when and where they have opportunity so to do; So all that

are admitted unto the priviledges of a *Church*, are also (*b*) under the Censures and Government thereof, according to the Rule of *Christ*.

   b 1 Thes. 5.14. 2 Thes 3.6.14,15.

13. No Church-members upon any offence taken by them, having performed their Duty required of them towards the person they are offended at, ought to disturb any *Church* order, or absent themselves from the Assemblies of the *Church*, or Administration of any Ordinances, upon the account of such offence at any of their fellow-members; but to wait upon *Christ*, (*c*) in the further proceeding of the *Church*.

   c Mat. 18.15.16,17. Eph. 4 2,3.

14. As each *Church*, and all the Members of it are bound to (*d*) pray continually, for the good and prosperity of all the *Churches* of *Christ*, in all places; and upon all occasions to further it (every one within the bounds of their places, and callings, in the Exercise of their Gifts and Graces) so the *Churches* (when planted by the providence of God so as they may injoy opportunity and advantage for it) ought to hold (*e*) communion amongst themselves for their peace, increase of love, and mutual edification.

   d Eph. 6.18. Ps. 122.6.
   e Rom. 16.1,2. 3 Joh. 8,9,10.

15. In cases of difficulties or differences, either in point of Doctrine, or Administration; wherein either the Churches in general are concerned, or any one Church in their peace, union, and edification; or any member, or members, of any Church are injured, in or by any proceedings in censures not agreeable to truth, and order: it is according to the mind of Christ, that many Churches holding communion together, do by their messengers meet to consider, (*f*) and give their advice, in or about that matter in difference, to be reported to all the Churches concerned; howbeit these messengers assembled are not entrusted with any Church-power properly so called; or with any jurisdiction over the Churches themselves, to exercise any censures either over any Churches, or Persons: or (*g*) to impose their determination on the Churches, or Officers.

   f Act. 15.2,4,6. & 22,23.25.
   g 2 Cor. 1.24. 1 Joh. 4.1

~ *Chapter XXVI. Of the Church* ~

CHAP. XXVII.
Of the Communion of Saints.

1. **A**ll *Saints* that are united to Jesus Christ their *Head*, by his Spirit, and Faith; although they are not made thereby one person with him, have (*a*) fellowship in his Graces, sufferings, death, resurrection, and glory; and being united to one another in love, they (*b*) have communion in each others gifts, and graces; and are obliged to the performance of such duties, publick and private, in an orderly way, (*c*) as do conduce to their mutual good, both in the inward and outward man.

    a 1 Joh. 1.3. Joh. 1.16. Phil. 3 10 Rom. 6.5 6.
    b Eph. 4.15.16. 1 Cor. 12.7. 1 Cor. 3 21,22,23.
    c 1 Thes. 5.11.14. Rom. 1.12. 1 Joh. 3.17.18. Gal 6.10.

2. *Saints* by profession are bound to maintain an holy fellowship and communion in the worship of God, and in performing such other spiritual services, (*d*) as tend to their mutual edification; as also in relieving each other in (*e*) outward things according to their several abilities, and necessities; which communion according to the rule of the Gospel, though especially to be exercised by them, in the relations wherein they stand, whether in (*f*) families, or (*g*) Churches; yet as God offereth opportunity is to be extended to all the houshold of faith, even all those who in every place call upon the name of the Lord Jesus; nevertheless their communion one with another as *Saints*, doth not take away or (*h*) infringe, the title or propriety, which each man hath in his goods and possessions.

    d Heb. 10 24,25. with ch. 3.12,13.
    e Act. 12.29.30.
    f Eph. 6.4.
    g 1 Cor. 12.14.-27.
    h Act. 5.4 Eph. 4.28

CHAP. XXVIII.
Of Baptism and the Lords Supper.

1. **B**aptism and the Lords Supper are ordinances of positive, and soveraign institution; appointed by the Lord Jesus the only Law-giver, to be continued in his Church (*a*) to the end of the world.

   a Mat. 28 19,20. 1 Cor. 11.26.

2, These holy appointments are to be administred by those only, who are qualified and thereunto called according (*b*) to the commission of Christ.

   b Mat. 28.19. 1 Cor. 4.1.

CHAP. XXIX.
Of Baptism.

1. **B**aptism is an Ordinance of the New Testament, ordained by Jesus Christ, to be unto the party Baptized, a sign of his fellowship with him, in his death, (*c*) and resurrection; of his being engrafted into him; of (*d*) remission of sins; and of his (*e*) giving up unto God through Jesus Christ to live and walk in newness of Life.

    c Rom. 6.3,4,5. Col. 2.12. Gal. 3.27.

    d Mar. 1.4. Act. 26.16.

    e Rom, 6.2,4.

2. Those who do actually professe (*f*) repentance towards *God*, faith in, and obedience, to our Lord Jesus, are the only proper subjects of this ordinance.

    f Mar. 16.16. Act. 8.36,37.

3. The outward element to be used in this ordinance (*g*) is water, wherein the party is to be baptized, in the name of the Father, and of the Son, and of the Holy Spirit.

    g Mat 28.19,20. with Act. 8.38.

4. Immersion, or dipping of the person (*h*) in water, is necessary to the due administration of this ordinance.

    h Mat. 3.16. Joh. 3 23.

CHAP. XXX.
Of the Lords Supper.

1. The Supper of the Lord Jesus, was instituted by him, the same night wherein he was betrayed, to be observed in his Churches unto the end of the world, for the perpetual remembrance, and shewing forth the sacrifice of himself in his death (*a*) confirmation of the faith of believers in all the benefits thereof, their spiritual nourishment, and growth in him, their further ingagement in, and to, all duties which they owe unto him; (*b*) and to be a bond and pledge of their communion with him, and with each other.

    a 1 Cor. 11.23,24.25,26.

    b 1 Cor. 10.16,17.21.

2. In this ordinance Christ is not offered up to his Father, nor any real sacrifice made at all, for remission of sin of the quick or dead; but only a memorial of that (*c*) one offering up of himself, by himself, upon the crosse, once for all; and a spiritual oblation of all (*d*) possible praise unto God for the same; so that the Popish sacrifice of the Mass (as they call it) is most abominable, injurious to Christs own only sacrifice, the alone propitiation for all the sins of the Elect.

    c Heb. 9.25,26.28.

    d 1 Cor. 11.24. Mat. 26.26,27.

3. The Lord Jesus hath in this Ordinance, appointed his Ministers to Pray, and bless the Elements of Bread and Wine, and thereby to set them apart from a common to an holy use, and to take and break the Bread; to take the Cup, (*e*) and (they communicating also themselves) to give both to the Communicants.

    e 1 Cor. 11.23,24,25,26, &c

4. The denyal of the Cup to the people, worshiping the Elements, the lifting them up, or carrying them about for adoration, and reserving them for any pretended religious use, (*f*) are all contrary to the nature of this Ordinance, and to the institution of Christ.

    f Mat 26.26,27,28. Mat. 15.9. Exod. 20.4,5.

5. The outward Elements in this Ordinance, duely set apart to the uses ordained by Christ, have such relation to him crucified, as that truely, although in terms used figuratively, they are sometimes called by the name of the things they represent, to wit the (g) body and Blood of Christ; albeit in substance, and nature, they still remain truly, and only (h) Bread, and Wine, as they were before.

g 1 Cor. 11.27.
h 1 Cor. 11.26. & v.28.

6. That doctrine which maintains a change of the substance of Bread and Wine, into the substance of Christs body and blood (commonly called Transubstantiation) by consecration of a Priest, or by any other way, is repugnant not to Scripture (i) alone, but even to common sense and reason; overthroweth the (k) nature of the ordinance, and hath been and is the cause of manifold superstitions, yea, of gross Idolatries.

i Act. 3.21. Luk. 24.6. & v.39.
k 1 Cor. 11.24,25.

7. Worthy receivers, outwardly partaking of the visible Elements in this Ordinance, do then also inwardly by faith, really and indeed, yet not carnally, and corporally, but spiritually receive, and feed upon Christ crucified (l) & all the benefits of his death: the Body and Blood of *Christ*, being then not corporally, or carnally, but spiritually present to the faith of Believers, in that Ordinance, as the Elements themselves are to their outward senses.

l 1 Cor. 10.16. ch. 11.23-26.

8. All ignorant and ungodly persons, as they are unfit to enjoy communion (m) with *Christ*; so are they unworthy of the Lords Table; and cannot without great sin against him, while they remain such, partake of these holy mysteries, (n) or be admitted thereunto: yea whosoever shall receive unworthily are guilty of the Body and Blood of the Lord, eating and drinking judgement to themselves.

m 2 Cor: 6,14,15.
n 1 Cor. 11.29. Mat. 7.6.

~ *Chapter XXX. Of the Lord's Supper* ~

CHAP. XXXI.
Of the State of Man after Death and of the Resurrection of the Dead.

1. The Bodies of Men after Death return to dust, (*a*) and see corruption; but their Souls (which neither die nor sleep) having an immortal subsistence, immediately (*b*) return to God who gave them: the Souls of the Righteous being then made perfect in holyness, are received into paradise where they are with *Christ*, and behold the face of *God*, in light (*c*) and glory; waiting for the full Redemption of their Bodies; and the souls of the wicked, are cast into hell; where they remain in torment and utter darkness, reserved to (*d*) the judgement of the great day; besides these two places for Souls separated from their bodies, the Scripture acknowledgeth none.

    a Gen. 3.19. Act. 13.36.
    b Eccles. 12.7.
    c Luk. 23.43. 2 Cor. 5.1,6,8. Phil. 1.23 Heb. 12.23.
    d Jud. 6 7. 1 Pet. 3.19. Luk. 16.23,24.

2. At the last day such of the Saints as are found alive shall not sleep but be (*e*) changed; and all the dead shall be raised up with the self same bodies, and (*f*) none other; although with different (*g*) qualities, which shall be united again to their Souls for ever.

    e 1 Cor. 15: 51,52. 1 Thes. 4.17.
    f Job 19.26,27.
    g 1 Cor. 15.42,43.

3. The bodies of the unjust shall by the power of *Christ*, be raised to dishonour; the bodies of the just by his spirit unto honour, (*h*) and be made conformable to his own glorious Body.

    h Act. 24.15. Joh. 5.28,29. Phil. 3.21

CHAP. XXXII.
Of the Last Judgement.

1. God hath appointed a Day wherein he will judge the world in Righteousness, by (*a*) Jesus Christ; to whom all power and judgement is given of the Father; in which Day not only the (*b*) Apostate Angels shall be judged; but likewise all persons that have lived upon the Earth, shall appear before the Tribunal of *Christ*; (*c*) to give an account of their Thoughts, Words, and Deeds, and to receive according to what they have done in the body, whether good or evil.

    a Act. 17.31. Joh. 5.22. 27.

    b 1 Cor. 6 3. Jud. 6.

    c 2 Cor. 5.10. Eccles. 12 14. Mat. 12.36. Rom. 14.10.12. Mat. 25: 32. &c.

2. The end of Gods appointing this Day, is for the manifestation of the glory of his Mercy, in the Eternal Salvation of the Elect; (*d*) and of his Justice in the Eternal damnation of the Reprobate, who are wicked and disobedient; for then shall the Righteous go into Everlasting Life, and receive that fulness of Joy, and Glory, with everlasting reward, in the presence (*e*) of the Lord: but the wicked who know not God, and obey not the Gospel of Jesus Christ, shall be cast into Eternal torments, and (*f*) punished with everlasting destruction, from the presence of the Lord, and from the glory of his power.

    d Rom, 9.22,23.

    e Mat. 25.21. 34. 2 Tim. 4.8.

    f Mat. 25.46. Mar. 9 48. 2 Thes. 1.7,8,9,10.

3. As Christ would have us to be certainly perswaded that there shall be a Day of judgement, both (*g*) to deter all men from sin, and for the greater (*h*) consolation of the godly, in their adversity; so will he have that day unknown to Men, that they may shake off all carnal security, and be always watchful, because they know not at what hour, the (*i*)

Lord will come; and may ever be prepared to say, (*k*) *Come Lord Jesus, Come quickly, Amen.*

   g 2 Cor. 5.10,11.
   h 2 Thes. 1.5,6,7.
   i Mar. 13.35,36,37 Luk. 13.35,36.
   k Rev. 22 20.

~ Chapter XXXII. Of the Last Judgement ~

AN
APPENDIX.

Whosoever reads, and impartially considers what we have in our forgoing confession declared, may readily perceive, That we do not only concenter with all other true Christians on the Word of God (revealed in the Scriptures of truth) as the foundation and rule of our faith and worship. But that we have also industriously endeavoured to manifest, That in the fundamental Articles of Christianity we mind the same things, and have therefore expressed our belief in the same words, that have on the like occasion been spoken by other societies of Christians before us.

This we have done, That those who are desirous to know the principles of Religion which we hold and practise, may take an estimate from our selves (who jointly concur in this work) and may not be misguided, either by undue reports; or by the ignorance or errors of particular persons, who going under the same name with our selves, may give an occasion of scandalizing the truth we profess.

And although we do differ from our brethren who are Paedobaptists; in the subject and administration of Baptisme, and such other circumstances as have a necessary dependence on our observance of that Ordinance, and do frequent our own assemblies for our mutual edification, and discharge of those duties, and services which we owe unto God, and in his fear to each other: yet we would not be from hence misconstrued, as if the discharge of our own consciences herein, did any wayes disoblige or alienate our affections, or conversation from any others that fear the Lord; but that we may and do as we have opportunity participate of the labors of those, whom God hath indued with abilities above our selves, and qualified, and called to the Ministry of the *Word*, earnestly desiring to approve our selves to be such, as follow after peace with holiness, and therefore we alwaies keep that blessed *Irenicum*, or healing *Word* of the Apostle before our eyes; if in any thing ye be otherwise minded, God shall reveal even this unto you; nevertheless whereto we have already attained; let us walk by the same rule, let us mind the same thing, *Phil* 3. *v.* 15, 16.

Let it not therefore be judged of us (because much hath been written on this subject, and yet we continue this our practise different from others) that it is out of obstinacy, but rather as the truth is, that we do herein according to the best of our understandings worship God, out of a pure mind yielding obedience to his precept, in that method which we take to be most agreeable to the Scriptures of truth, and primitive practise.

It would not become us to give any such intimation, as should carry a semblance that what we do in the service of God is with a doubting conscience, or with any such temper of mind that we do thus for the present, with a reservation that we will do otherwise hereafter upon more mature deliberation; nor have we any cause so to do, being fully perswaded, that what we do is agreeable to the will of God. Yet we do heartily propose this, that if any of the Servants of our Lord Jesus shall, in the Spirit of meekness, attempt to convince us of any mistake either in judgement or practise, we shall diligently ponder his arguments; and accompt[1] him our chiefest friend that shall be an instrument to convert us from any error that is in our ways, for we cannot wittingly do any thing against the truth, but all things for the truth.

And therefore we have indeavoured seriously to consider, what hath been already offered for our satisfaction in this point; and are loth to say any more lest we should be esteemed desirous of renewed contests thereabout: yet forasmuch as it may justly be expected that we shew some reason, why we cannot acquiesce in what hath been urged against us; we shall with as much brevity as may consist with plainness, endeavour to satisfie the expectation of those that shall peruse what we now publish in this matter also.

1. As to those Christians who consent with us, *That Repentance from dead works, and Faith towards God, and our Lord Jesus Christ, is required in persons to be Baptized*; and do therefore supply the defect of the (infant being uncapable of making confession of either) by others who do undertake these things for it. Although we do find by Church history that this hath been a very antient practise; yet

---

[1] "Accompt' is an archaic spelling for 'account.'

~ An Appendix ~

considering, that the same Scripture which does caution us against censuring our brother, with whom we shall all stand before the judgment seat of Christ, does also instruct us, *That every one of us shall give an accompt of himself to God,* and *whatsoever is not of Faith is Sin.* Rom. 14:4, 10, 12, 23. Therefore we cannot for our own parts be perswaded in our own minds, to build such a practise as this, upon an unwritten tradition: But do rather choose in all points of Faith and Worship, to have recourse to the holy Scriptures, for the information of our judgment, and regulation of our practise; being well assured that a conscientious attending thereto, is the best way to prevent, and rectifie our defects and errors. 2 *Tim.* 3. 16,17. And if any such case happen to be debated between Christians, which is not plainly determinable by the Scriptures, we think it safest to leave such things undecided until the second coming of our Lord Jesus; as they did in the Church of old, until there should arise a Priest with *Urim* and *Thummim*, that might certainly inform them of the mind of God thereabout, *Ezra* 2. 62, 63.

2. As for those our Christian brethren who do ground their arguments for Infants baptism, upon a presumed faederal Holiness, or Church-Membership, we conceive they are deficient in this, that albeit this Covenant-Holiness and Membership should be as is supposed, in reference unto the Infants of Believers; yet no command for Infant baptism does immediately and directly result from such a quality, or relation.

All instituted Worship receives its sanction from the precept, and is to be thereby governed in all the necessary circumstances thereof.

So it was in the Covenant that God made with *Abraham* and his Seed. The sign whereof was appropriated only to the Male, notwithstanding that the female seed as well as the Male were comprehended in the Covenant and part of the Church of God; neither was this sign to be affixed to any Male Infant till he was eight dayes old, albeit he was within the Covenant from the first moment of his life; nor could the danger of death, or any other supposed necessity, warrant the circumcising of him before the set time, nor was there any cause for it; the commination of being cut off from his people, being only upon the neglect, or contempt of the precept.

~ *An Appendix* ~

Righteous *Lot* was nearly related to *Abraham* in the flesh, and contemporary with him, when this Covenant was made; yet inasmuch as he did not descend from his loynes, nor was of his houshold family (although he was of the same houshold of faith with *Abraham*) yet neither *Lot* himself nor any of his posterity (because of their descent from him) were signed with the signature of this Covenant that was made with *Abraham* and his seed.

This may suffice to shew, that where there was both an expresse Covenant, and a sign thereof (such[2] a Covenant as did separate the persons with whom it was made, and all their off-spring from all the rest of the world, as a people holy unto the Lord, and did constitute them the visible Church of God, (though not comprehensive of all the faithful in the world) yet the sign of this Covenant was not affixed to all the persons that were within this Covenant, nor to any of them till the prefixt season; nor to other faithful servants of God, that were not of descent from *Abraham*. And consequently that it depends purely upon the will of the Law-giver, to determine what shall be the sign of his Covenant, unto whom, at what season, and upon what terms, it shall be affixed.

If our brethren do suppose baptism to be the seal of the Covenant which God makes with every beleiver (of which the Scriptures are altogether silent) it is not our concern to contend with them herein; yet we conceive the seal of that Covenant is the indwelling of the Spirit of Christ in the particular and individual persons in whom he resides, and nothing else, neither do they or we suppose that baptism is in any such manner substituted in the place of circumcision, as to have the same (and no other) latitude, extent, or terms, then circumcision had; for that was suited only for the Male children, baptism is an ordinance suited for every beleiver, whether male, or femal. That extended to all the males that were born in *Abrahams* house, or bought with his money, equally with the males that proceeded from his own loynes; but baptisme is not so far extended in any true Christian Church that we know of, as to be administred to all the poor infidel servants, that the members thereof purchase for their service, and introduce into their families; nor to the children born of them in their house.

---

[2] The original text does not include a final parenthesis mark.

~ An Appendix ~

But we conceive the same parity of reasoning may hold for the ordinance of baptism as for that of circumcision; *Exodus* 12.49. *viz.* one law for the stranger, as for the home born: If any desire to be admitted to all the ordinances, and priviledges of Gods house, the door is open; upon the same terms that any one person was ever admitted to all, or any of those priviledges, that belong to the Christian Church; may all persons of right challenge the like admission.

As for that text of Scripture, Rom. 4. 11. *He received circumcision a seal of the righteousness of the faith which he had yet being uncircumcised*; we conceive if the Apostles scope in that place be duly attended to, it will appear that no argument can be taken from thence to inforce Infant baptism; and forasmuch as we find a full and fair account of those words given by the learned Dr. *Lighfoot* (a man not to be suspected of partiality in this controversie) in his *Hor. Hebrai*, on the I *Cor.* 7. 19. *p.*42, 43. we shall transcribe his words at large, without any comment of our own upon them.

~ *An Appendix* ~

Circumcisio nihil est ratione habita temporis, jam enim evanuerat, adimpleto praecipue ejus fine ob quem fuerat instituta; Istum finem exhibet Apostolus in verbis ist is Rom. 4.11. σφραγίδα τῆς δικαιοσυνης τῆς πίστεως τῆς ἐν ἀκροβυστιᾳ. *At vereor ne a plerisque versionibus non satis aptentur ad finem circumcisionis, & scopum Apostoli, duma b iis interserituraliquid de suo.*[3]

Circumcision is nothing, if we respect the time, for now it was without use, that end of it being especially fulfilled; for which it had been instituted: this end the Apostle declares in these words, *Rom. 4.11 σφραγίδα &c.* But I fear that by most translations they are not sufficiently suited to the end of circumcision, and the scope of the Apostle whilst something of their own is by them inserted.

And after the Doctor hath represented diverse versions of the words agreeing for the most part in sense with that which we have in our Bibles he thus proceeds

Aliae in eundem sensum, ac si circumcision daretur Abrahamo *in sigilum justitiae istius, quam ille habuit, dum adhuc foret praeputitatus; quod non negabimus aliqualiter verum esse, at credimus circumcisionem longe alio praecipue respexisse.*

Other versions are to the same purpose; as if circumcision was given to *Abraham* for a Seal of that Righteousness which he had being yet uncircumcised, which we will not deny to be in some sense true, but we believe that circumcision had chiefly a far different respect.

Liceat mihi verba sic redder. Et signum accepit circumcisionis, sigillum justitiae fidei, quae future in praeputio; *quae future dico,*

Give me leave thus to render the words; *And he received the sign of circumcision, a seal of the Righteousness of Faith, which was to be in the*

---

[3] The "*b*" is in the original.

non quae fuerat. Non quae fuerat Abrahamo *adhuc praeputiato, sed quae future semini ejus praeputiato, id est, gentilibus, fidem olim* Abrahami *imitaturis.*

uncircumcision, Which was to be (I say) not *which had been,* not that which *Abraham* had whilst he was yet uncircumcised; but that which his uncircumcised seed should have, that is the Gentiles, who in time to come should imitate the faith of *Abraham.*

Nunc adverte bene qua occasione institute Abrahamo circumcision, ponens tibi ante oculos historiam ejus, Gen. 17.

Now consider well on what occasion circumcision was instituted unto *Abraham,* setting before thine eyes the history thereof, *Gen.* 17.

Fit primo ei haec promissio, Multarum Gentium eris tu pater (*quonam sensu explicat Apostolus, isto capite*) & *subindex subjungitur duplex sigillum rei corroborandae; immutatioscilicet nominis* Abrami *in* Abrahamum; & *institution circumcisionis: v.4.* Ecce mihi tecum est foedus, eris tu pater multarum gentium. *Quare vocatum est nomen ejus* Abrahamus? *In sigillationem hujus promissionis.* Tu Pater eris multarum gentium. *Et quare institute ei circumcision? In sigillationem ejusdem promissionis.* Tu Pater eris multarem Gentium. *Ita ut hic sit sensus Apostoli, institutioni*

This promise is first made unto him, *Thou shalt be the Father of many Nations* (in what sense the Apostle explaineth in that chapter) and then there is subjoined a double seal for the confirmation of the thing, to wit, the change of the name *Abram* into *Abraham,* and the institution of circumcision. v4. *Behold as for me, my Covenant is with thee, and thou shalt be the Father of many Nations.* Wherefore was his name called *Abraham*? for the sealing of this promise. *Thou shalt be the Father of many Nations.* And wherefore was circumcision instituted to him? For the sealing of the same promise. Thou shalt be the Father of

circumcisionis
congruentissimus; accepit
signum circumcisionis, sigilum
justitiae fidei, quam olim erat
incircumcisio (vel Gentiles)
habitura & adeptura.

many Nations. So that this is
the sense of the Apostle; most
agreeable to the institution of
circumcision; he received the
sign of circumcision, a seal of
the Righteousness of Faith
which in time to come the
uncircumcision (or the
Gentiles) should have and
obtain.

Duplex semen erat Abrahamo;
*natural, Judaeorum; & fidele
gentilium credentium: signatur
natural signo circumcisionis,
primo quidem in sui
distinctionem, ab omnibus aliis
gentibus, dum eae non adhuc
forent semen* Abrahami; *at
praecipue in memoriam
justificationis gentium per
fidem, cum tandem forent ejus
semen. Cessatura ergo merito
erat circumcisio, cum
introducerentur Gentiles ad
fidem, quipped quod tunc
finem suum ultimum as
praecipuum obtinerat, et
perinde* ἡ περίτομη οὐδέν.

Abraham had a twofold seed,
natural, of the Jews; and
faithful, of the believing
Gentiles: his natural seed was
signed with the sign of
circumcision, first indeed for
the distinguishing of them
from all other Nations whilst
they as yet were not the seed of
Abraham, but especially for
the memorial of the
justification of the Gentiles by
faith, when at length they
should become his seed.
Therefore circumcision was of
right to cease, when the
Gentiles were brought in to the
faith, forasmuch as then it had
obtained its last and chief end,
& thenceforth *circumcision is
nothing*.

Thus far he, which we earnestly desire may be seriously weighed, for we plead not his authority, but the evidence of truth in his words.

3. Of whatsoever nature the holiness of the children mentioned, 1 *Cor.* 7. 12. be, yet they who do conclude that all such children (whether Infants or of riper years) have from hence an immediate right to baptism, do as we conceive put more into the conclusion, then will be found in the premisses.

For although we do not determine positively concerning the Apostles scope in the holiness here mentioned, so as to say it is this, or that, and no other thing; Yet it is evident that the Apostle does by it determine not only the lawfulness but the expedience also of a beleivers cohabitation with an unbeliever, in the state of marriage.

And we do think that although the Apostles asserting of the unbelieving yokefellow to be sanctified by the believer, should carry in it somewhat more then is in the bare marriage of two infidels, because although the marriage covenant have a divine sanction so as to make the wedlock of two unbelievers a lawful action, and their conjunction and cohabitation in that respect undefiled, yet there might be no ground to suppose from thence, that both or either of their persons are thereby sanctified; and the Apostle urges the cohabitation of a believer with an infidel in the state of wedlock from this ground that the unbelieving husband is *sanctified* by the believing wife; nevertheless here you have the influence of a believers faith *ascending from an inferior to a superior relation*; from the wife to the husband who is her head, *before it can descend to their off-spring*. And therefore we say, whatever be the nature or extent of the holiness here intended, we conceive it cannot convey to the children an immediate right to baptism; because it would then be of another nature, and of a larger extent, then the root, and original from whence it is derived, for it is clear by the Apostles argument that holiness cannot be derived to the child from the sanctity of one parent only, if either father or mother be (in the sense intended by the Apostle) unholy or unclean, so will the child be also, therefore for the production of an holy seed it is necessary that both the Parents be sanctified; and this the Apostle positively asserts in the first place to be done by the beleiving parent, although the other be an unbeliever; and then consequentially from

~ An Appendix ~

thence argues, the holiness of their children. Hence it follows, that as the children have no other holiness then what they derive from both their Parents; so neither can they have any right by this holiness to any spiritual priviledge but such as both their Parents did also partake of: and therefore if the unbelieving Parent (though sanctified by the believing Parent) have not thereby a right to baptism, neither can we concieve, that there is any such priviledge, derived to the children by their birth-holiness.

Besides if it had been the usual practice in the Apostles dayes for the father or mother that did beleive, to bring all their children with them to be baptised; then the holiness of the beleiving *Corinthians* children, would not at all have been in question when this Epistle was written; but might have been argued from their passing under that ordinance, which represented their new birth, although they had derived no holiness from their Parents, by their first birth; and would have layen as an exception against the Apostles inference, *else were your Children unclean*, &c. But of the sanctification of all the children of every beleiver by this ordinance, or any other way, then what is beforementioned, the Scripture is altogether silent.

This may also be added; that if this birth holiness do qualifie all the children of every believer, for the ordinance of baptism; why not for all other ordinances? for the Lords Supper as was practiced for a long time together? for if recourse be had to what the Scriptures speak generally of this subject; it will be found, that the same qualities which do intitle any person to baptism, do so also for the participation of all the Ordinances, and priviledges of the house of God, that are common to all believers.

Whosoever can and does interrogate his good Conscience towards God when he is baptised (as every one must do that makes it to himself a sign of Salvation) is capable of doing the same thing, in every other act of worship that he performs.

4. The arguments and inferences that are usually brought for, or against Infant baptism from those few instances which the Scriptures afford us of whole families being baptised; are only conjectural; and therefore cannot of themselves, be conclusive on either hand: yet in regard most that treat on this subject for Infant baptism, do (as they conceive) improve these instances to the advantage of their argument:

~ An Appendix ~

we think it meet (in like manner as in the cases before mentioned so in this) to shew the invalidity of such inferences.

Cornelius worshipped God with all his house, the *Jaylor*, and *Crispus* the chief ruler of the Synagogue, *believed God with each of their houses*. *The houshold of* Stephanus *addicted themselves to the Ministry of the Saints*: so that thus far *Worshipping*, and *Believing* runs parallel with *Baptism*. And if *Lydia*, had been a married person, when she believed, it is probable her husband would also have been named by the Apostle, as in like cases, inasmuch as he would have been not only a part, but the head of that baptised houshold.

Who can assign any probable reason, why the Apostle should make mention of four or five housholds being baptised and no more? or why he does so often vary in the method of his salutations, *Rom.* 1. 6. sometimes mentioning only particular persons of great note, other times such, and the Church in their house? the Saints that were with them; and them belonging to *Narcissus*, who were in the Lord; thus saluting either whole families, or part of families, or only particular persons in families, considered as they were in the Lord, for if it had been an usual practise to baptize all children, with their parents; there were then many thousands of the Jews which believed, and a great number of the Gentiles, in most of the principle Cities in the World, and among so many thousands, it is more then probable there would have been some thousands of housholds baptised; why then should the Apostle in this respect signalize one family of the Jews and three or four of the Gentiles, as particular instances in a case that was common? whoever supposes that we do willfully debar our children, from the benefit of any promise, or priviledge, that of right belongs to the children of believing parents; they do entertain over severe thoughts of us: to be without natural affections is one of the characters of the worst of persons; in the worst of times. Wee do freely confesse our selves guilty before the Lord, in that we have not with more circumspection and diligence train'd up those that relate to us in the fear of the Lord; and do humbly and earnestly pray, that our omissions herein may be remitted, and that they may not redound to the prejudice of our selves, or any of ours: but with respect to that duty that is incumbent on us, we acknowledge our selves obliged by the precepts of God, to bring up our children in the nurture and admonition of the

~ An Appendix ~

Lord, to teach them his fear, both by instruction and example; and should we set light by this precept, it would demonstrate that we are more vile then the unnatural Heathen, that like not to retain God in their knowledge, our baptism might then be justly accompted, as no baptism to us.

There are many special promises that do incourage us as well as precepts, that do oblige us to the close pursuit of our duty herein: that God whom we serve, being jealous of his Worship, threatens the visiting of the Fathers transgression upon the children to the third and fourth generation of them that hate him: yet does more abundantly extend his mercy, even to thousands (respecting the offspring and succeding generations) of them that love him, and keep his commands.

When our Lord rebuked his disciples for prohibiting the access of little children that were brought to him, that he might pray over them, lay his hands upon them, and blesse them, does declare, *that of such is the Kingdom of God*. And the Apostle *Peter* in answer to their enquiry, that desired to know what they must do to be saved, does not only instruct them in the necessary duty of repentance and baptism; but does also thereto encourage them, by that promise which had reference both to them, and their children; if our Lord Jesus in the forementioned place, do not respect the qualities of children (as elsewhere) as to their meekness, humility, and sincerity, and the like; but intend also that those very persons and such like, appertain to the Kingdom of God, and if the Apostle *Peter* in mentioning the aforesaid promise, do respect not only the present and succeeding generations of those Jews, that heard him, (in which sense the same phrase doth occurre in Scripture) but also the immediate off-spring of his auditors; whether the promise relate to the gift of the Holy Spirit, or of eternal life, or any grace, or priviledge tending to the obtaining thereof; it is neither our concerne nor our interest to confine the mercies, and promises of God, to a more narrow, or lesse compasse then he is pleased gratiously to offer and intend them; nor to have a light esteem of them; but are obliged in duty to God, and affection to our children; to plead earnestly with God and use our utmost endeavours that both our selves, and our off-spring may be partakers of his Mercies and gracious Promises: yet we cannot from either of these texts collect a

~ An Appendix ~

sufficient warrant for us to baptize our children before they are instructed in the principles of the Christian Religion.

For as to the instance in little children, it seems by the disciples forbidding them, that they were brought upon some other account, not so frequent as Baptism must be supposed to have been, if from the beginning believers children had been admitted thereto: and no account is given whether their parents were baptised believers or not; and as to the instance of the Apostle; if the following words and practice, may be taken as an interpretation of the scope of that promise we cannot conceive it does refer to infant baptism, because the text does presently subjoyn; *Then they that gladly received the word were baptised.*

That there were some believing children of believing parents in the Apostles dayes is evident from the Scriptures, even such as were then in ther fathers family, and under their parents tuition, and education; to whom the Apostle in several of his Epistles to the Churches, giveth commands to obey their parents in the Lord; and does allure their tender years to hearken to this precept, by reminding them that it is the first command with promise.

And it is recorded by him for the praise of *Timothy*, and encouragement of parents betimes to instaruct, and children early to attend to godly instruction, that ἀπὸ βρέφος from a child, he had known the holy Scriptures.

The Apostle *John* rejoyced greatly when he found of the children of the Elect Lady walking in the truth; and the children of her Elect Sister joyn with the Apostle in his salutation.

But that this was not generally so, that all the children of believers were accounted for believers (as they would have been if they had been all baptised) may be collected from the character which the Apostle gives of persons fit to be chosen to Eldership in the Church which was not common to all believers; among others this is expressely one, *viz. If there be any having believing, or faithful children*, not accused of Riot or unruly; and we may from the Apostles writings on the same subject collect the reason of this qualification, *viz.* That in case the person designed for this office to teach and rule in the house of God, had children capable of it; there might be first a proof of his ability, industry, and successe in this work in his own

~ An Appendix ~

family; and private capacity, before he was ordained to the exercise of this authority in the Church, in a publick capacity, as a Bishop in the house of God.

These things we have mentioned as having a direct reference unto the controversie between our brethren and us; other things that are more abstruse and prolix, which are frequently introduced into this controversie, but do not necessarily concern it, we have purposely avoided; that the distance between us and our brethren may not be by us made more wide; for it is our duty, and concern so far as is possible for us (retaining a good conscience towards God) to seek a more entire agreement and reconciliation with them.

We are not insensible that as to the order of Gods house, and entire communion therein there are some things wherein we (as well as others) are not at a full accord among our selves, as for instance; the known principle, and state of the consciences of diverse of us, that have agreed in this Confession is such; that we cannot hold Church-communion, with any other then Baptized-believers, and Churches constituted of such; yet some others of us have a greater liberty and freedom in our spirits that way; and therefore we have purposely omitted the mention of things of that nature, that we might concurre, in giving this evidence of our agreement, both among our selves, and with other good Christians, in those important articles of the Christian Religion, mainly insisted on by us: and this notwithstanding we all esteem it our chief concern, both among our selves, and all others that in every place call upon the name of the Lord Jesus Christ our Lord, both theirs and ours, and love him in sincerity, to endeavour to keep the unity of the Spirit, in the bond of peace; and in order thereunto, to exercise all lowliness and meekness, with long-suffering, forbearing one another in love.

And we are perswaded if the same method were introduced into frequent practice between us and our Christian friends who agree with us in all the fundamental articles of the Christian faith (though they do not so in the subject and administration of baptism) it would soon beget a better understanding, and brotherly affection between us.

In the beginning of the Christian Church, when the doctrine of the baptism of *Christ* was not universally understood, yet those that knew

~ An Appendix ~

only the baptism of *John*, were the Disciples of the Lord Jesus; and *Apollos* an eminent Minister of the Gospel of Jesus.

In the beginning of the reformation of the Christian Church, and recovery from that *Egyptian* darkness wherein our forefathers for many generations were held in bondage; upon recourse had to the Scriptures of truth, different apprehensions were conceived, which are to this time continued, concerning the practise of this Ordinance.

Let not our zeal herein be misinterpreted: that God whom we serve is jealous of his worship. By his gracious providence the Law thereof, is continued amongst us; and we are forewarned by what hapned in the Church of the Jews, that it is necessary for every generation, and that frequently in every generation to consult the divine oracle, compare our worship with the rule, and take heed to what doctrines we receive and practise.

If the ten commands exhibited in the popish Idolatrous service books had been received as the entire law of God, because they agree in number with his ten commands, and also in the substance of nine of them; the second Commandment forbidding Idolatry had been utterly lost.

If *Ezra* and *Nehemiah* had not made a diligent search into the particular parts of Gods law, and his worship; the Feast of Tabernacles (which for many centuries of years, had not been duly observed, according to the institution, though it was retained in the general notion) would not have been kept in due order.

So may it be now as to many things relating to the service of God, which do retain the names proper to them in their first institution, but yet through inadvertency (where there is no sinister design) may vary in their circumstances, from their first institution. And if by means of any antient defection, or of that general corruption of the service of God, and interruption of his true worship, and persecution of his servants by the Antichristian Bishop of *Rome*, for many generations; those who do consult the Word of God, cannot yet arrive at a full and mutual satisfaction among themselves, what was the practise of the primitive Christian Church, in some points relating to the *Worship* of God: yet inasmuch as these things are not of the essence of Christianity, but that we agree in the fundamental doctrines thereof, we

~ An Appendix ~

do apprehend, there is sufficient ground to lay aside all bitterness and prejudice, and in the spirit of love and meekness to imbrace and own each other therein; leaving each other at liberty to perform such other services, (wherein we cannot concur) apart unto God, according to the best of our understanding.

FINIS.

~ *An Appendix* ~

9

A Brief Instruction in the Principles of Christian Religion

Introduction

Our final document is the Baptist adaptation of the much-loved Westminster *Shorter Catechism*. Commissioned by the 1693 General Assembly, and after an apparent delay again requested by the 1694 Bristol Assembly, it was published as agreed. The earliest known extant version bears the date 1695 and claims to be the Fifth edition; by 1703 it was in its tenth edition. This almost certainly refers to the number of times it was printed.

Frequently identified with Benjamin Keach, it is more likely to have been edited first by William Collins of London's Petty France church. Certainly he was specifically requested to do this work, and there is no documentary evidence to assume otherwise. If in fact he had been co-editor of the Confession, it would make sense to ask him to edit the Catechism as well. The attribution of the Catechism to Benjamin Keach perhaps arises from later versions, possibly supplemented by him.

Although the first five or six questions seem unfamiliar to those who know well the Westminster *Shorter Catechism*, the majority of the text follows it verbatim. This was the specific intention of those who called for the writing of this Catechism, since the older document was already used by families throughout the Particular Baptist churches. At the end of the Catechism proper, a note is added which expresses the appreciation these churches had for the broader Reformed theology of the Westminster Assembly and Savoy Synod, acknowledging that the publication of this Catechism intentionally demonstrates the shared theological commitments of these congregations.

A
Brief Instruction
in the
PRINCIPLES
of
Christian Religion:

Agreeable to the Confession of Faith, *put forth by the* ELDERS *and* BRETHREN *of many Congregations of Christians, (baptized upon Profession of their Faith) in* London *and the Country; owning the Doctrine of* Personal Election, *and* Final Perseverance.

Deut. 6.6,7. *And these Words which I command thee this Day, shall be in thine Heart. And thou shalt teach them diligently unto thy Children, and shalt talk of them when thou sittest in thine House,* &c.

The Fifth Edition.

London, Printed in the Year 1695.

A *Brief* Instruction *in the* Principles *of Christian Religion,* &c.

Question 1.

*W*ho is the First and Chiefest being?
Answer. God is the First and Chiefest Being *a. a*[1] Isa. 44:6 & 48.12.

Q. 2. *Ought every One to believe there is a God?*
A. Every One ought to believe there is a God *b*; and it is their great Sin and Folly who do not *c. b* Heb. 11.6. *c* Psal. 14.1.

Q. 3. *How may we know there is a God?*
A. The Light of Nature in man, and the Works of God plainly declare that there is a God *d*; but His Word and Spirit only, do it fully and effectually, for the Salvation of Sinners *e. d* Rom. 1.19,20. Psal. 19.1,2;3. Acts 17.24. *e* 1 Cor. 2.10. 2 Tim. 3.15,16.

Q. 4. *What is the Word of God?*
A. The Holy Scriptures of the Old and New Testament, are the Word of God, and the only certain Rule of Faith and Obedience *c. c*[2] 2 Tim. 3.16. Ephes. 2.20.

Q. 5. *May all Men make use of the Scriptures?*
A. All Men are not only permitted, but commanded and exhorted, to read, hear, and understand the Holy Scriptures *d. d* John 5.39. Deut. 6.8. Rev. 1.3. Acts 8.30.

Q. 6. *What things are chiefly contained in the Holy Scripture?*
A. The Holy Scriptures chiefly contain what Man ought to believe concerning God, and what Duty God requireth of Man *e. e* 2 Tim. 1.13. & 3.15,16.

---

[1] In the original, the references are placed in the margin.
[2] *Sic.*

Q. 7. *What is God?*
A. God is a Spirit *f*, Infinite *g*, Eternal *h*, and Unchangeable *i*, in his Being *k*, Wisdom *l*, Power *m*, Holiness *n*, Justice, Goodness and Truth *o*. *f* John 4.24. *g* Job 11.7,8,9. *h* Psal. 90.2. *i* Jam. 1.17. *k* Exod. 3.14. *l* Psal. 147.5. *m* Rev. 4.8. *n* Rev. 15.4. *o* Exod. 34.6,7.

Q. 8. *Are there more Gods than One?*
A. There is but one only, the Living and True God *p*. *p* Deut. 6.4. Jer. 10.10.

Q. 9. *How many Persons are there in the Godhead?*
A. There are Three Persons in the Godhead, the Father, the Son, and the Holy Spirit; and these Three are one God, the same in Essence, equal in Power and Glory *q*. *q* 1 John 5.7. Mat. 28.19.

Q. 10. *What are the decrees of God?*
A. The Decrees of God are his Eternal Purpose, according to the Counsel of his Will, whereby for his own Glory, He has foreordained whatsoever comes to pass *r*. *r* Eph. 1.4, 11. Rom. 9.22,23.

Q. 11. *How does God execute His Decrees?*
A. God executeth his Decrees in the Works of Creation and Providence.[3]

Q. 12. *What is the Work of Creation?*
A. The Work of Creation is God's making all Things of Nothing, by the Word of his Power, in the space of six Days, and all very Good *s*. *s* Gen. 1. *throughout.* Heb. 11.3.

Q. 13. *How did God create Man?*
A. God created Man, Male and Female, after his own Image, in Knowledge, Righteousness, and Holiness, with Dominion over the Creatures *t*. *t* Gen. 1.26, 27; 28. Col. 3.10. Eph. 4.24.

Q. 14. *What are God's Works of Providence?*

---

[3] No Scripture proofs are attached to Question 11. The *Shorter Catechism* also lacks Scripture proofs for this question.

~ A Brief Instruction in the Principles of Christian Religion ~

A. God's Works of Providence are his most Holy *u*, Wise *w*, and Powerful preserving *x*, and Governing all his Creatures, and all their Actions *y*. *u* Psal. 145.17. *w* Psal. 104.24. Isa. 28.29. *x* Heb. 1.3. *y* Psal. 103.19. Mat. 10.29,30,31.

Q. 15. *What special Act of Providence did God exercise towards man in the estate wherein he was created?*
A. When God had created man, he entered into a Covenant of Life with him, upon Condition of perfect Obedience, forbidding him to eat of the Tree of the Knowledg of Good and Evil, upon Pain of Death *z*. *z* Gal. 3.12. Gen. 2.17.

Q. 16. *Did our first Parents continue in the Estate wherein they were created?*
A. Our first Parents, being left to the freedom of their own Will, fell from the Estate wherein they were created, by sinning against God *a*. *a* Gen. 3.6,7,8,13. Eccles. 7.29.

Q. 17. *What is Sin?*
A. Sin is any want of Conformity unto, or Transgression of, the law of God *b*. *b* 1 Joh. 3.4.

Q. 18. *What was the Sin whereby our first Parents fell from the Estate wherein they were created?*
A. The sin whereby our first Parents fell from the Estate wherein they were created, was their eating the forbidden Fruit *c*. *c* Gen. 3.6,12.

Q. 19. *Did all Mankind fall in Adam's first Transgression?*
A. The Covenant being made with *Adam*, not only for himself, but for his Posterity, all Mankind descending from him by ordinary Generation, sinned in him, and fell with him in his first Transgression *d*. *d* Gen. 2.16,17. Rom. 5.12. 1 Cor. 15.21,22.

Q. 20. *Into what Estate did the Fall bring Mankind?*
A. The fall brought Mankind into an Estate of Sin and Misery *e*. *e* Rom. 5.12.

Q. 21. *Wherein consists the sinfulness of that Estate whereunto man fell?*
A. The sinfulness of that Estate whereunto Man fell, consists in the Guilt of *Adam's* first Sin, the want of Original Righteousness, and the Corruption of his whole Nature, which is commonly called *original sin*, together with all actual Transgressions which proceed from it *f*. *f* Rom. 5.12, *to the end*. Eph. 2.1,2,3. Jam. 1.14,15. Mat. 15.19.

Q. 22. *What is the Misery of that Estate whereunto Man fell?*
A. All Mankind by their Fall lost Communion with God *g*, are under his Wrath and Curse *h*, and so made liable to all Miseries in this Life, to Death it self, and to the Pains of Hell for ever *i*. *g* Gen. 3.8,10,24. *h* Eph. 2.2,3. Gal. 3.10. *i* Lam. 3.39. Rom. 6.23. Mat. 25.41,46.

Q. 23. *Did God leave all Mankind to perish in the Estate of Sin and Misery?*
A. God, having out of His mere good pleasure, from all Eternity, elected some to Everlasting Life *k*, did enter into a Covenant of Grace, to deliver them out of the Estate of Sin and Misery, and to bring them into an Estate of Salvation, by a Redeemer *l*. *k* Eph. 1.4,5. *l* Rom. 3.20,21,22. Gal. 3.21,22.

Q. 24. *Who is the Redeemer of God's Elect?*
A. The only Redeemer of God's Elect is the Lord Jesus Christ *m*, who being the Eternal Son of God, became Man *n*, and so was, and continues to be God and Man, in two distinct Natures, and one person, for ever *o*. *m* 1 Tim. 2.5;6. *n* John 1.14. Gal 4.4. *o* Rom. 9.5. Luke 1.35. Col. 2.9. Heb. 7.24,25.

Q 25. *How did Christ, being the Son of God, become Man?*
A. Christ the Son of God became Man by taking to himself a true Body *p*, and a reasonable Soul *q*; being conceived by the Power of the Holy Spirit in the Womb of the Virgin *Mary* and born of her *r*, yet without Sin *s*. *p* Heb. 2.14;16, & 10.5. *q* Mat. 26.38. *r* Luke 1.27,31,34,35;42. Gal. 4.4. *s* Heb. 4.15. & 7.26.

Q. 26. *What offices doth Christ execute as our Redeemer?*
A. Christ as our Redeemer executeth the Offices of a Prophet, of a Priest, and of a King, both in his Estate of Humiliation and Exaltation *t*. *t* Acts 3.22. Heb. 12.25. *with* 2 Cor. 13.3. Heb. 5.5,6;7. & 7.25. Psal. 2.6. Isa. 9.6,7. Mat. 21.5. Ps. 2.8,9,10,11.

Q. 27. *How doth Christ execute the Office of a Prophet?*
A. Christ executeth the Office of a Prophet, in revealing to us, by his Word and Spirit, the Will of God for our Salvation *u*. *u* John 1.18. 1 Pet. 1.10,11,12 John 15.15. & 20.31.

Q. 28. *How doth Christ execute the Office of a Priest?*
A. Christ executeth the Office of a Priest, in his once offering up of himself a Sacrifice to satisfy Divine Justice *w*, and reconcile us to God *x*, and in making continual Intercession for us *y*. *w* Heb. 9.14,28 *x* Heb. 2.17, *y* Heb. 7.24,25.

Q. 29. *How doth Christ execute the Office of a King?*
A. Christ executeth the Office of a King, in subduing us to himself *z*, in ruling *a*, and defending us *b*, and in restraining and conquering all his and our Enemies *c*. *z* Acts 15.14,15,16. *a* Isa. 33.22. *b* Isa. 32.1,2. *c* 1 Cor. 15.25. Psal. 110. *throughout.*

Q. 30. *Wherein did Christ's Humiliation consist?*
A. Christ's humiliation consisted in His being born, and that in a low Condition *d*, made under the Law *e*, undergoing the Miseries of this Life *f*, the Wrath of God *g*, and the cursed Death of the Cross *h*, in being buried *i*, and continuing under the Power of Death for a time *k*. Mat. 12.40.[4] *d* Luke 2.7. *e* Gal. 4.4. *f* Heb. 12.2,3. Isa. 53. 2,3. *g* Luke 22.44. Mat. 27.40. *h* Phil. 2.8. *i* 1 Cor. 15.4. *k* Act. 2.24,25,26,27,31.

Q. 31. *Wherein consisteth Christ's Exaltation?*
A. Christ's Exaltation consisteth in His rising again from the Dead on the third Day *l*, in ascending up into Heaven *m*, in sitting at the right Hand of God the Father *n*, and in coming to judg the World at the last

---

[4] This Scripture reference is placed immediately after the end of the sentence in the original.

Day *o*. *l* 1 Cor. 15.4. *m* Mark 16.19. *n* Ephes. 1.20. *o* Acts 1.11. & 17.31.

Q. 32. *How are we made Partakers of the Redemption purchased by Christ?*
A. We are made Partakers of the Redemption purchased by Christ, by the effectual Application of it to us *p* by His Holy Spirit *q*. *p* John 1.11,12. *q* Tit. 3.5,6.

Q. 33. *How doth the Spirit apply to us the Redemption purchased by Christ?*
A. The Spirit applieth to us the Redemption purchased by Christ, by working Faith in us *r*, and thereby uniting us to Christ, in our effectual Calling *s*. *r* Eph.1.13,14. John 6.37,39. Ephes. 2:8. *s* Ephes. 3.17. 1 Cor. 1.9.

Q. 34. *What is effectual calling?*
A. Effectual Calling, is the Work of God's Spirit *t*, whereby, convincing us of our Sin and Misery *u*, enlightening our Minds in the Knowledg of Christ *w*, and renewing our Wills *x*, he doth perswade and enable us to embrace Jesus Christ freely offered to us in the Gospel *y*. *t* 2 Tim. 1.9. 2 Thes. 2.13,14. *u* Acts 2.37. *w* Acts 26.18. *x* Ezek. 36.26,27. *y* Joh. 6.44,45. Phil. 2.12.

Q. 35. *What benefits do they that are effectually called, partake of in this Life?*
A. They that are effectually called, do in this Life partake of Justification *z*, Adoption *a*, Sanctification, and the several Benefits which in this Life do either accompany or flow from them *b*. *z* Rom. 8.30. *a* Ephes. 1.5. *b* 1 Cor. 1.30.

Q. 36. *What is Justification?*
A. Justification is an Act of God's free grace, wherein he pardoneth all our Sins *c*, and accepteth us as Righteous in his sight *d*, only for the Righteousness of Christ imputed to us *e*, and received by Faith alone *f*. Rom. 3.24;25 & 4.6,7,8. *d* 2 Cor. 5.19,21. *e* Rom. 5.17,18,19. *f* Gal. 2.16. Phil. 3.9.

Q. 37. *What is Adoption?*
A. Adoption is an Act of God's free Grace *g*, whereby we are received into the Number, and have a Right to all the Privileges of the Sons of God *h*. *g* 1 John 3.1. *h* John 1.12. Rom. 8:14.

Q. 38. *What is Sanctification?*
A. Sanctification is the Work of God's free Grace *i* whereby we are renewed in the whole Man after the Image of God *k*, and are enabled more and more to die unto Sin, and live unto Righteousness *l*. *i* 2 Thess. 2.13. *k* Eph. 4.23,24. *l* Rom. 6:4,6.

Q. 39. *What are the Benefits which in this Life do accompany or flow from Justification, Adoption, and Sanctification?*
A. The Benefits which in this Life do accompany or flow from Justification, Adoption, and Sanctification, are Assurance of God's Love, Peace of Conscience *m*, Joy in the Holy Spirit *n*, Increase of Grace *o*, and Perseverance therein to the End *p*. *m* Rom. 5.1,2,5. *n* Rom. 14.17. *o* Prov. 4:18. *p* 1 John 5.13. 1 Pet. 1.5.

Q. 40. *What Benefits do Believers receive from Christ at their Death?*
A. The Souls of Believers are at their Death made perfect in Holiness *q*, and do immediately pass into Glory *r*: And their Bodies being still united to Christ's, do rest in their Graves *t*, till the Resurrection *u*. *q* Heb. 12.23. *r* 2 Cor. 5.1,6,8. Phil. 1.23. Luke 23.43. *s* 1 Thess. 4.14. *t* Isa. 57.2. *u* Job 19.26,27.

Q. 41. *What Benefits do Believers receive from Christ at the Resurrection?*
A. At the Resurrection Believers being raised up in Glory *w*, shall be openly acknowledged, and acquitted in the Day of Judgment *x*, and made perfectly blessed, both in Soul and Body, in the full enjoyment of God *y*, to all Eternity *z*. *w* 1 Cor. 15.43. *x* Mat. 25.23. Mat. 10.32. *y* 1 John 3.2. 1 Cor. 13.12. *z* 1 Thess. 4.17,18.

Q. 42. *But what shall be done to the Wicked at their Death?*
A. The Souls of the Wicked shall at their Death be cast into the Torments of Hell, and their Bodies lie in their Graves till the

Resurrection and Judgment of the Great Day.*[5] *Luke 16.23,24. Acts 1.25. Jude *v*.7. 1 Pet. 3.19. Psal. 49.14.

Q. 43. *What shall be done to the Wicked at the Day of Judgment?*
A. At the Day of Judgment, the Bodies of the Wicked being raised out of their Graves, shall be sentenced, together with their Souls, to unspeakable Torments with the Devil and his Angels for ever†. † Joh. 5.28,29. Mat. 25.41,46. 2 Thess. 1.8,9.

Q. 44. *What is the Duty which God requireth of Man?*
A. The Duty which God requireth of Man, is obedience to His Revealed Will *a*. *a* Mich. 6.8. 1 Sam. 15.22.

Q. 45. *What did God at first reveal to Man for the Rule of his Obedience?*
A. The Rule which God at first revealed to Man for his Obedience was the Moral Law *b*. *b* Rom. 2.14,15. & 10.5.

Q. 46. *Where is the Moral Law summarily comprehended?*
A. The Moral Law is summarily comprehended in the Ten Commandments *c*. *c* Deut. 10.4. Mat. 19.17.

Q. 47. *What is the Sum of the Ten Commandments?*
A. The Sum of the Ten Commandments is, to love the Lord our God, with all our Heart, with all our Soul, with all our Strength, and with all our Mind; and our Neighbour as our Selves *d*. *d* Mat. 22.37,38,39,40.

Q. 48. *What is the Preface to the Ten Commandments?*
A. The Preface to the Ten Commandments, is in these words, [*I am the Lord thy God, which have brought thee out of the Land of Egypt, out of the House of Bondage*] *e*. *e* Exod. 20.2.

---

[5] In the original, the Scripture references for the answers to questions 42 and 43 are attached with the symbols noted. There are no questions parallel to these in the Westminster *Shorter Catechism*. Because of the unusual use of these symbols, they may have been added after the first edition of this Catechism was published, so that the consecutive use of letters to designate Scripture references would not have to be revised in all succeeding questions.

~ A Brief Instruction in the Principles of Christian Religion ~

Q. 49. *What doth the Preface to the Ten Commandments teach us?*
A. The Preface to the Ten Commandments teacheth us, that because God is the LORD, and our God, and Redeemer, therefore we are bound to keep all his Commandments *f. f* Luk. 1.74,75. 1 Pet. 1.15,16,17,18,19.

Q. 50. *Which is the first Commandment?*
A. The first Commandment is, [*Thou shalt have no other Gods before me*] *g. g* Exod 20.3.

Q. 51. *What is required in the first Commandment?*
A. The first Commandment requireth us to know and acknowledg God to be the only true God, and our God *h*, and to worship and glorify him accordingly *i. h* 1 Chron. 28.9. Deut. 26.17. *i* Mat. 4.10. Psal. 29.2.

Q. 52. *What is forbidden in the first Commandment?*
A. The first commandment forbiddeth the denying *k*, or not worshipping and glorifying the true God, as God *l*, and our God *m*; and the giving that Worship and Glory to any other, which is due unto him alone *n. k* Ps. 14.1. *l* Rom. 1.21. *m* Psal. 81.10,11. *n* Rom. 1.25,26.

Q. 53. *What are we specially taught by these words*, [before me] *in the first Commandment?*
A. These words [*before me*] in the first Commandment, teach us, that God who seeth all things, takes notice of, and is much displeased with the Sin of having any other God *o. o* Ezek. 8.5, *to the end.*

Q. 54. *Which is the second Commandment?*
A. The second Commandment is, [*Thou shalt not make unto thee any graven Image, or any Likeness of any thing that is in Heaven above, or that is in the Earth beneath, or that is in the Water under the Earth; thou shalt not bow down thy self to them, nor serve them: For I the LORD thy God am a jealous God, visiting the Iniquity of the Fathers upon the Children, unto the Third and Fourth Generation of them that hate me; and shewing Mercy unto Thousands of them that love me and keep my Commandments*] *p. p* Exod. 20.4,5,6.

Q. 55. *What is required in the second Commandment?*
A. The second Commandment requireth the receiving, observing, and keeping pure and entire all such religious Worship and Ordinances, as God hath appointed in his Word *q. q* Deut. 32.46. Mat. 28.20. Acts 2.42.

Q. 56. *What is forbidden in the second Commandment?*
A. The second Commandment forbiddeth the worshipping of God by Images *r*, or any other Way not appointed in his Word *s. r* Deut. 4.15,16;17,18,19. Exod. 32.5,8.

Q. 57. *What are the Reasons annexed to the second Commandment?*
A. The Reasons annexed to the second Commandment are, God's Soveraignty over us *t*, his Propriety in us *u*, and the Zeal he has for his own Worship *w. t* Psal. 95.2,3,6. *u* Psal. 45.11. *w* Exod. 34.13,14.

Q. 58. *Which is the third Commandment?*
A. The third commandment is, [*Thou shalt not take the name of the Lord thy God in vain: for the Lord will not hold him guiltless that taketh his name in vain*] *x. x* Exod. 20.7.

Q. 59. *What is required in the third Commandment?*
A. The third Commandment requireth the Holy and Reverent Use of God's Names *y*, Titles *z*, Attributes *a*, Ordinances *b*, Word *c*, and Works *d. y* Mat. 6.9. Deut. 28.58. *z* Psal. 68.4. *a* Rev. 15.3,4. *b* Mal. 1.11,14. *c* Psal. 138.1,2. *d* Job 36.24.

Q. 60. *What is forbidden in the third Commandment?*
A. The third Commandment forbiddeth all profaning and abusing of any thing whereby God makes Himself known *e. e* Mal. 1.6,7;12. & 2.2. & 3.14.

Q. 61. *What is the Reason annexed to the third Commandment?*
A. The Reason annexed to the third Commandment, is, that however the breakers of this Commandment may escape Punishment from Men, yet the Lord our God will not suffer them to escape his Righteous Judgment *f. f* 1 Sam. 2.12, 17, 22, 24, 29. 1 Sam. 3.13. Deut. 28.58,59.

~ *A Brief Instruction in the Principles of Christian Religion* ~

Q. 62. *Which is the fourth Commandment?*
A. The fourth Commandment is, [*Remember the Sabbath Day to keep it holy: Six Days shalt thou labour, and do all thy work; but the Seventh Day is the Sabbath of the LORD thy God,* in it *thou shalt not do any Work, thou, nor thy Son, nor thy Daughter, thy Man-servant, nor thy Maid-servant, nor thy Cattel, nor thy Stranger that is within thy Gates: For in six Days the LORD made Heaven and Earth, the Sea, and all that in them is, and rested the seventh Day; wherefore the LORD blessed the Sabbath Day and hallowed it*] g. g Exod. 20.8,9,10,11.

Q. 63. *What is required in the fourth Commandment?*
A. The fourth Commandment requireth the keeping Holy to God one whole Day in Seven to be a Sabbath to himself *i. i* Exod. 20.8,9,10,11. Deut. 5.12, 13, 14.

Q. 64. *Which Day of the seven hath God appointed to be the Weekly Sabbath?*
A. Before the Resurrection of Christ, God appointed the Seventh Day of the Week to be the Weekly Sabbath *k*; and the First Day of the Week ever since, to continue to the End of the World, which is the Christian Sabbath *l. k* Exod. 20.8,9,10,11. Deut. 5.12,12,14. *l* Psal. 118.24. Mat. 28.1. Mar. 2.27,28. & 16.2. Luk. 24. 1,30, *to* 36. Joh. 20.1,19,20,21,26. Acts 1.3. & 2.1,2. & 20.7. 1 Cor. 16.1,2. Rev. 1.10.

Q. 65. *How is the Sabbath to be sanctified?*
A. The Sabbath is to sanctified by a holy Resting all that Day *m*, even from such worldly Employments and Recreations as are lawful on other Days *n*; and spending the whole Time in the Publick and Private Exercises of God's Worship *o*, except so much as is to be taken up in the Works of Necessity and Mercy *p. m* Exod. 20.8,10. *n* Exod. 16.25,26,27,28. Nehem. 13.15,16,17,18,19,21,22. *o* Luke 4.16. Acts 20.7. Psal. 92. *title.* Isa. 66.23. *p* Mat. 12.1, *to* 13.

Q. 66. *What is forbidden in the fourth Commandment?*
A. The fourth Commandment forbiddeth the Omission or careless Performance of the Duties required *q*, and the profaning the Day by

Idleness *r*, or doing that which is in it self sinful *s*, or by unnecessary Thoughts, Words, or Works, about Worldly Employments or Recreations *t*. *q* Ezek. 22.26. Amos 8.5. Mal. 1.13. *r* Acts 20.7,9. *s* Ezek. 23.38. *t* Jer. 17.24,25,26,27. Isa. 58.13.

Q. 67. *What are the Reasons annexed to the fourth Commandment?*
A. The Reasons annexed to the fourth Commandment, are God's allowing us six Days of the Week for our own lawful Employments *u*, his challenging a special Propriety in a Seventh, his own Example, and his blessing the Sabbath Day *w*. *u* Exod. 20.9. *w* Exod. 20.11.

Q. 68. *Which is the fifth Commandment?*
A. The fifth commandment is, *[Honor thy Father and thy Mother; that thy Days may be long upon the Land which the LORD thy God giveth thee]* *x*. *x* Exod. 20.12.

Q. 69. *What is required in the fifth Commandment?*
A. The fifth Commandment requireth the preserving the Honour, and performing the Duties belonging to every one in their several Places and Relations, as Superiours *w*,[6] Inferiours *x*, or Equals *y*. *w* Eph. 5.21. *x* 1 Pet. 2.17. *y* Rom. 12.10.

Q. 70. *What is forbidden in the fifth Commandment?*
A. The fifth Commandment forbideth the neglecting of, or doing any thing against the Honour and Duty which belongeth to every one in their several Places and Relations *z*. *z* Mat. 15.4,5,6. Ezek. 34.2,3,4. Rom. 13.8.

Q. 71. *What is the Reason annexed to the fifth Commandment?*
A. The Reason annexed to the fifth Commandment, is a Promise of long Life and Prosperity (as far as it shall serve God's glory and their own Good), to all such as keep this Commandment *a*. *a* Deut. 5.16. Ephes. 6.2,3.

Q. 72. *What is the sixth Commandment?*
A. The sixth Commandment is, *[Thou shalt not kill]* *b*. *b* Exod. 20.13.

---

[6] *Sic.*

Q. 73. *What is required in the sixth Commandment?*
A. The sixth Commandment requireth all lawful Endeavours to preserve our own Life *c*, and the Life of others *d. c* Eph. 5.28,29. *d* 1 King. 18.4.

Q. 74. *What is forbidden in the sixth Commandment?*
A. The sixth commandment absolutely forbiddeth the taking away of our own Life; or the Life of our Neighbour unjustly, or whatsoever tendeth thereunto *e. e* Acts 16.28. Gen. 9.6.

Q. 75. *Which is the seventh Commandment?*
A. The seventh Commandment is, [*Thou shalt not commit Adultery*] *f.* *f* Exod. 20.14.

Q. 76. *What is required in the seventh Commandment?*
A. The seventh Commandment requireth the Preservation of our own, and our Neighbour's Chastity, in Heart, Speech, and Behaviour *g. g* 1 Cor. 7.2;3,4,5,34,36. Col. 4.6. 1 Pet. 3.2.

Q. 77. *What is forbidden in the seventh Commandment?*
A. The seventh Commandment forbideth all unchast Thoughts, Words, and Actions *h. h* Matt. 15.19. & 5.28. Eph. 5.3,4.

Q. 78. *Which is the eighth Commandment?*
A. The eighth Commandment is, [*Thou shalt not steal*] *i. i* Exod. 20.15.

Q. 79. *What is required in the eighth Commandment?*
A. The eighth Commandment requireth the lawful procuring, and furthering the Wealth and outward Estate of our selves and others *k. k* Gen. 30.30. 1 Tim. 5.8. Levit. 25.35. Deut. 22.1,2,3,4,5. Exod. 23.4,5. Gen. 47.14,20.

Q. 80. *What is forbidden in the eighth Commandment?*
A. The eighth Commandment forbideth whatsoever doth, or may, unjustly hinder our own, or our Neighbour's Wealth or outward Estate *l. l* Prov. 21.17. & 23.20,21. & 28.19. Eph. 4.28.

Q. 81. *Which is the ninth Commandment?*
A. The ninth Commandment is, [*Thou shalt not bear false Witness against thy Neighbour*] *m. m* Exod. 20.16.

Q. 82. *What is required in the ninth Commandment?*
A. The ninth Commandment requireth the maintaining and promoting of Truth between Man and Man *n*, and of our own and our Neighbour's good Name *o*, especially in Witness bearing *p. n* Zech. 8.16. *o* 3 Joh. *v.* 12. *p* Prov. 14.5,25.

Q. 83. *What is forbidden in the ninth Commandment?*
A. The ninth commandment forbiddeth whatsoever is prejudicial to Truth, or injurious to our own or our Neighbour's good Name *q. q* 1 Sam. 17.28. Levit. 19.16. Ps. 15.3.

Q. 84. *Which is the tenth Commandment?*
A. The tenth Commandment is, [*Thou shalt not covet thy Neighbour's House, thou shalt not covet thy Neighbour's Wife, nor his Man-servant, nor his Maid-servant, nor his Ox, nor his Ass, nor anything that is thy Neighbour's*] *r. r* Exod. 20.17.

Q. 85. *What is required in the tenth Commandment?*
A. The tenth Commandment requireth full Contentment with our own Condition *s*, with a right and charitable frame of Spirit toward our neighbour, and all that is his *t. s* Heb. 13.5. 1 Tim. 6.6. *t* Job 31.29. Rom. 12.15. 1 Tim. 1.5. 1 Cor. 13.4-7.

Q. 86. *What is forbidden in the tenth Commandment?*
A. The tenth Commandment forbiddeth all Discontentment with our own Estate *u;* envying or grieving at the Good of our Neighbour *w*, and all inordinate Motions and Affections to anything that is his *x*. 1 King. 21.4. Esth. 5.13. 1 Cor. 10.10. *w* Gal. 5.26. Jam. 3.14,16. *x* Rom. 7.7,8. & 13.9. Deut. 5.21.

Q. 87. *Is any man able perfectly to keep the Commandments of God?*
A. No mere Man since the Fall, is able in this Life, perfectly to keep the Commandments of God *y*, but daily break them in Thought, Word,

and Deed *z*. *y* Eccles. 7.20. 1 John 1.8;10. Gal. 5.17. *z* Gen. 6.5. & 8.21. Rom. 3.9, *to* 21. Jam. 3.2; *to* 13.

Q. 88. *Are all transgressions of the Law equally heinous?*
A. Some Sins in themselves, and by reason of several Aggravations, are more heinous in the sight of God than others *a*. *a* Ezek. 8.6,13,15. 1 John 5.16. Psal. 78.17,32,56.

Q. 89. *What doth every Sin deserve?*
A. Every Sin deserveth God's Wrath and Curse, both in this Life, and in that which is to come *b*. *b* Ephes.5.6. Gal. 3.10. Lam. 3.39. Mat. 25.41. Rom. 6.23.

Q. 90. *What doth God require of us, that we may escape his Wrath and Curse, due to us for Sin?*
A. To escape the Wrath and Curse of God due to us for Sin, God requireth of us Faith in Jesus Christ, Repentance unto Life *c*, with the diligent use of all the outward Means, whereby Christ communicateth to us the Benefits of Redemption *d*. *c* Acts 20.21. *d* Prov. 2.1, *to* 6. 8.33, *to the end.* Isa. 55.2,3.

Q. 91. *What is Faith in Jesus Christ?*
A. Faith in Jesus Christ is a saving Grace *e*, whereby we receive, and rest upon him alone for Salvation, as he is offered to us in the Gospel *f*. *e* Heb. 10.39. *f* John 1.12 Isa. 26.3,4. Phil. 3.9. Gal. 2.16.

Q. 92. *What is Repentance unto Life?*
A. Repentance unto Life is a saving Grace *g*, whereby a Sinner, out of a true Sense of his Sin *h*, and Apprehension of the Mercy of God in Christ *i*, doth, with grief and hatred of his Sin, turn from it unto God *k*, with full Purpose of, and Endeavor after, new Obedience *l*. *g* Acts 11.28. *h* Acts 2.37,38. *i* Joel 2.12. Jer. 3.22. *k* Jer. 31.18,19. Ezek. 36.31. *l* 2 Cor. 7.11. Isa. 1.16,17.

Q. 93. *What are the outward Means, whereby Christ communicateth to us the Benefits of redemption?*
A. The outward and ordinary Means, whereby Christ communicateth

to us the Benefits of Redemption, are his Ordinances, especially the Word, Baptism, the Lord's Supper, and Prayer; all which Means are made effectual to the Elect for Salvation *m. m* Mat. 28.19,20. Acts 2.42,46,47.

Q. 94 *How is the Word made effectual to Salvation?*
A. The Spirit of God maketh the Reading, but especially the Preaching of the Word, an effectual Means of convincing and converting Sinners; and of building them up in Holiness and Comfort through Faith unto Salvation *n. n* Nehem. 8.8. 1 Cor. 14.24,25. Acts 26.18. Psal. 19.8. Acts 20.32. Rom. 15.4. 1 Tim. 3.15,16,17. Rom. 10.13,14,15,16,17. & 1.16.

Q. 95. *How is the Word to be read and heard, that it may become effectual to Salvation?*
A. That the Word may become effectual to Salvation, we must attend thereunto with Diligence *o*, Preparation *p*, and Prayer *q*; receive it with Faith and Love *r*, lay it up in our Hearts *s*, and practice it in our Lives *t. o* Prov. 8.34. *p* 1 Peter 2.1,2. *q* Psal. 119.18. *r* Heb. 4.2. 2 Thess. 2.10. Psal. 119.11. *t* Luke 8.15. James 1.25.

Q. 96. *How do Baptism and the Lord's Supper become effectual Means of Salvation?*
A. Baptism and the Lord's Supper become effectual Means of Salvation, not for any Virtue in them, or in him that doth administer them, but only by the Blessing of Christ *u*, and the working of the Spirit in those that by Faith receive them *w. u* 1 Pet. 3.21. Mat. 3.11. 1 Cor. 3.6,7. *w* 1 Cor. 12.13.

Q. 97. *What is Baptism?*
A. Baptism is an Ordinance of the New Testament instituted by Jesus Christ *x*, to be unto the Party baptized, a Sign of his Fellowship with him, in his Death, Burial, and Resurrection; of his being ingrafted into him *y*, of Remission of Sins *z*, and of his giving up himself unto God thro Jesus Christ, to live and walk in newness of life∗.[7] *x* Mat. 28.19. *y*

---

[7] *Sic.*

Rom. 6.3,4,5. Col. 2.12. Gal. 3.27. *z* Mark 1.4. Acts 2.38. & 22.16. *
Rom. 6.3,4.

Q. 98. *To whom is Baptism to be administered?*
A. Baptism is to be administered to all those, who actually profess
Repentance toward God, Faith in, and Obedience to our Lord Jesus
Christ; and to none other *a*. *a* Matt. 3.6. &28.29. Acts 2.37,38. &
8.36,37,38.

Q. 99. *Are the Infants of such as are Professing Believers to be
baptized?*
A. The Infants of such as are professing Believers are not to be
baptized; because there is neither Command, or Example in the Holy
Scriptures, or certain Consequence from them to baptize such.[8]

Q. 100. *How is Baptism rightly administered?*
A. Baptism is rightly administered, by Immersion, or *dipping* the
whole Body of the Party in Water, in the Name of the Father, and of
the Son, and of the Holy Spirit, according to Christ's Institution, and
the Practice of the Apostles *c*; and not by sprinkling or pouring of
Water, or dipping some Part of the Body, after the Tradition of Men. *c*
Matt. 3.16. John 3.23. Mat. 28.19,20. Acts 8.38. & 10.48. Rom. 6.4.
Col. 2.12.

Q. 101. *What is the Duty of such who are rightly baptized?*
A. It is the Duty of such who are rightly baptized, to give up
themselves to some particular and orderly Church of Jesus Christ, that
they may walk in all the Commandments and Ordinances of the Lord
blameless *d*. *d* Acts 2.41,42. & 5.13,14. & 9.26. 1 Pet. 2.5. Luke 1.6.

Q. 102. *What is the Lord's Supper?*
A. The Lord's Supper is an Ordinance of the New Testament instituted
by Jesus Christ; wherein by giving and receiving Bread and Wine,
according to his Appointment, his Death is shewed forth; and the

---

[8] No Scripture proofs are attached to Question 99.

~ A Brief Instruction in the Principles of Christian Religion ~

worthy Receivers are, not after a Corporal and Carnal manner, but by Faith, made partakers of his Body and Blood, with all his benefits, to their spiritual Nourishment, and growth in Grace *e*. *e* Mat. 26.26,27,28. 1 Cor. 11.23,24,25,26. & 10.16.

Q. 103. *Who are the proper Subjects of this Ordinance?*
A. They who have been baptized upon a personal Profession of their Faith in Jesus Christ, and Repentance from dead Works∗.[9] ∗Act. 2.41,42.

Q. 104. *What is required to the worthy receiving of the Lord's Supper?*
A. It is required of them that would partake of the Lord's Supper, that they examine themselves, of their Knowledg to discern the Lord's Body *f*, of their Faith to feed upon him *g*, of their Repentance *h*, Love *i*, and new Obedience *k*, lest coming unworthily, they eat and drink Judgment to themselves *l*. *f* 1 Cor. 11.28,29. *g* 2 Cor. 13.5. *h* 1 Cor. 11.31. *i* 1 Cor. 10. 16,17. *k* 1 Cor. 5.7,8. *l* 1 Cor. 11.28,29.

Q. 105. *What is Prayer?*
A. Prayer is an offering up of our Desires to God *m*, by the Assistance of the Holy Spirit *n*, for things agreeable to his will *o*, in the Name of Christ *p* believing *q*; with Confession of our Sins *r*, and thankful Acknowledgment of his Mercies *s*. *m* Psal. 62.8. *n* Rom. 6.26.[10] *o* 1 John 5.14. *p* John 16.23. *q* Mat. 21.22. James 1.6. *r* Psal. 32.5,6. Dan. 9.4. *s* Phil. 4.6.

---

[9] The Scripture reference to this question is attached with this symbol. Its presence may indicate that the Fifth edition of this Catechism has been edited, with this question and answer added to earlier editions. The strict view of communicating at the Lord's Table taught here does not reflect the universal practice of the churches present at the General Assemblies. Without question, the Broadmead, Bristol, church was an open membership church, and there are reasons to believe that others may have been also.
[10] This is evidently a typographical error in the original. It should most likely read Rom. 8.26.

~ A Brief Instruction in the Principles of Christian Religion ~

Q. 106. *What Rule has God given for our Direction in Prayer?*
A. The whole Word of God is of use to direct us in Prayer*; but the special Rule of Direction is that Prayer, which Christ taught his Disciples, commonly called, *the Lord's Prayer†.* * 1 Joh. 5.14. † Mat. 6.9,10,11,12,13. *with* Luk. 11.2,3,4.

Q. 107. *What doth the Preface of the Lord's Prayer teach us?*
A. The Preface of the Lord's Prayer, which is, [*Our Father which art in Heaven* t,] teacheth us to draw near to God with all holy Reverence and Confidence, as Children to a Father, able and ready to help us *u;* and that we should pray with and for others *w. t* Mat. 6.9. *u* Rom. 8.15. Luke 11.13. *w* Acts 12.5. 1 Tim. 2.1,2.

Q. 108. *What do we pray for in the first Petition?*
A. In the first Petition, which is, [*Hallowed be thy name x,*] we pray, that God would enable us and others, to glorify him in all that, whereby he maketh himself known *y;* and that he would dispose all things to his own Glory *z. x* Mat. 6.9. *y* Psal. 67.2,3. *z* Psal. 83. *throughout.*

Q. 109. *What do we pray for in the second Petition?*
A. In the second Petition, which is, [*Thy kingdom come a,*] we pray that Satan's Kingdom may be destroyed *b,* and that the Kingdom of Grace may be advanced *c,* ourselves and others brought into it and kept in it *d,* and that the Kingdom of Glory may be hastened *e. a* Mat. 6.10. *b* Psal. 68.1,18. *c* Rev. 12.10,11. *d* 2 Thess. 3.1. Rom. 10.1. John 17.19,20. *e* Rev. 22.20.

Q. 110. *What do we pray for in the third Petition?*
A. In the third Petition, which is, [*Thy Will be done in Earth, as it is in Heaven f,*] we pray, that God by his Grace would make us able and willing to know, obey, and submit to his Will in all things *g,* as the Angels do in Heaven *h. f* Mat. 6.10. *g* Psal. 67 *throughout.* Psal. 119.36. Mat. 26.39. 2 Sam. 15.25. Joh. 1.21. *h* Psal. 103.20,21.

Q. 111. *What do we pray for in the fourth Petition?*
A. In the fourth Petition, which is, [*Give us this Day our daily Bread i,*] we pray, that of God's free Gift, we may receive a competent Portion of the good Things of this Life, and enjoy his Blessing with them *k*. *i* Mat. 6.11. *k* Prov. 30.8,9. Gen. 28.20. 1 Tim. 4.4,5.

Q. 112. *What do we pray for in the fifth Petition?*

A. In the fifth Petition, which is, [*And forgive us our Debts as we forgive our Debtors* l,] we pray that God for Christ's sake would freely pardon all our Sins *m*, which we are the rather encouraged to ask, because by his Grace we are enabled from the Heart to forgive others *n*. *l* Mat. 6.12. *m* Psal. 51.1,2,7,9. Dan. 9.17,18,19. *n* Luke 11.4. Mat. 18.35.

Q. 113. *What do we pray for in the sixth Petition?*
A. In the sixth Petition, which is, [*And lead us not into Temptation, but deliver us from Evil* o,] we pray that God would either keep us from being tempted to Sin *p*, or support and deliver us when we are tempted *q*. *o* Mat. 6.13. *p* Mat. 26.41. *q* 2 Cor. 12.8.

Q. 114. *What doth the Conclusion of the Lord's Prayer Teach?*
A. The Conclusion of the Lord's Prayer, which is, [*For thine is the Kingdom, and the Power, and the Glory, for ever, Amen* ɪ,] teacheth us to take our Encouragement in Prayer from God only *s*, and in our Prayers to praise him, ascribing Kingdom, Power and Glory to him *t*, and in testimony to our Desire, and Assurance to be heard, we say, *Amen* u. *r* Mat. 6.13. *s* Dan. 9.4,7,8,9,16,17,18,19. *t* 1 Chron. 29.10,11,12,13. *u* Rev. 22.20,21.

An Advertisement *to the* *READER.*[11]

Having a desire to shew our near Agreement with many other Christians, of whom we have great Esteem; we some Years since put forth a Confession of our Faith, almost in all Points the same with the *Assembly*, and *Savoy*, which was subscribed by the Elders and Messengers of many Churches baptized on profession of their Faith; and do now put forth a short Account of *Christian Principles*, for the Instruction of our Families, in most things agreeing with the *Shorter Catechism* of the *Assembly*. And this we were the rather induced to, because we have commonly made use of that *Catechism* in our Families: And the Difference being not much, it will be more easily committed to Memory.

---

[11] This advertisement was found at the end of the 1695 edition. A cursory comparison will demonstrate how closely this work is related to the Westminster *Shorter Catechism*.

~ A Brief Instruction in the Principles of Christian Religion ~

Other RBAP Titles[1]

An Orthodox Catechism, edited by Michael A. G. Haykin and G. Stephen Weaver, Jr. Foreword by James M. Renihan. Recommended by Tom Ascol, Nathan A. Finn, Crawford Gribben, and Tom Nettles.

Better than the Beginning: Creation in Biblical Perspective, Richard C. Barcellos. Recommended by Joel R. Beeke, David P. Murray, and Samuel E. Waldron.

By Common Confession: Essays in Honor of James M. Renihan, edited by Ronald S. Baines, Richard C. Barcellos, and James P. Butler

Confessing the Impassible God: The Biblical, Classical, & Confessional Doctrine of Divine Impassibility, edited by Ronald S. Baines, Richard C. Barcellos, James P. Butler, James M. Renihan, and Stefan T. Lindblad. Foreword by Paul Helm. Recommended by James E. Dolezal, J. V. Fesko, Ryan M. McGraw, David VanDrunen, Jeffrey C. Waddington, and Fred Sanders.

Covenant Theology From Adam to Christ, Nehemiah Coxe and John Owen, edited by Ronald D. Miller, James M. Renihan, and Francisco Orozco. Recommended by Tom Ascol, Michael A. G. Haykin, and Robert W. Oliver.

God without Passions: A Primer, Samuel Renihan. Recommended by Paul Helm, Dennis E. Johnson, Fred A. Malone, D. Scott Meadows, and Joe Thorn.

---

[1] For a full listing of all RBAP books, go to www.rbap.net.

God without Passions: A Reader, edited by Samuel Renihan. Foreword by Carl R. Trueman. Recommended by James E. Dolezal, Paul Helm, Michael Horton, David VanDrunen, and Sam Waldron.

Journal of the Institute of Reformed Baptist Studies

MacArthur's Millennial Manifesto, Samuel E. Waldron. Recommended by James M. Renihan, Kim Riddlebarger, and Cornelis P. Venema.

Recovering a Covenantal Heritage: Essays in Baptist Covenant Theology, edited by Richard C. Barcellos. Recommended by Voddie Baucham, Leonardo De Chirico, Nathan A. Finn, Crawford Gribben, Conrad Mbewe, Tom Nettles, and Robert W. Oliver.

www.ingramcontent.com/pod-product-compliance
Lightning Source LLC
Chambersburg PA
CBHW062149080426
42734CB00010B/1616